Once Upon a Tomb

Once Upon a Tomb

✝

Stories
from
Canadian
Graveyards

NANCY MILLAR

FIFTH
HOUSE
PUBLISHERS

Front cover photograph by John de Visser/Masterfile
Back cover photograph by Rob Millar
Cover design by Brian Smith/Articulate Eye

The publisher gratefully acknowledges the support received from
The Canada Council and the Department of Canadian Heritage.

Printed in Canada by Best Book Manufacturers
97 98 99 00 01 / 5 4 3 2 1

Editor's note: Spelling and grammatical errors in the epitaphs were left
as they appeared on the gravemarkers. The order of words was changed
in some cases.

CANADIAN CATALOGUING IN PUBLICATION DATA

Millar, Nancy

Once upon a tomb

Includes index
ISBN 1-895618-87-8

1. Epitaphs – Canada. 2. Cemeteries – Canada.
3. Sepulchral monuments – Canada. 4. Canada – History.
I. Title.

PN6291.M54 1997   929'.5'0971   C96-920176-1

FIFTH HOUSE LTD.
#9 – 6125 – 11th Street SE
Calgary AB Canada T2H 2L6

Contents

Acknowledgements

✝

I would like to acknowledge the assistance of The Canada Council. It, above all, made it possible for me to explore the graveyards of this enormous country.

I could not have travelled this vast land with such impunity if I had not had my friend Judy Swan at my side. She kept us on course and on time.

John Adams and other members of the Old Cemeteries Society in Victoria, BC, reassured me that graveyard exploration was a sensible and indeed necessary thing to do. It was the push I needed to begin this project.

As I travelled west to east and south to north, I encountered many helpful people: those who gave me directions, who looked up information, who cheerfully said, "Come with me. I'll show you where that is." There were others who dried our wet socks, warned us of the wildlife, and performed kindnesses too numerous to mention. Thank you all.

Thanks also to author, historian, and friend James Gray, who supported me in more ways than one.

And, finally, to my family far and near and dear, thank you, always.

Introduction

✝

I Brake for Graveyards

I NEVER REALIZED THAT THERE WAS HISTORY TOO,
CLOSE AT HAND, BESIDE MY VERY OWN HOME.
I DID NOT REALIZE THAT THE OLD GRAVE
THAT STOOD AMONG THE BRAMBLES
AT THE FOOT OF OUR FARM
WAS HISTORY.

Thank you, Stephen Leacock.

You see, people think I'm plumb nuts when they hear that I'm interested in graveyards and the stories they tell. There's history out there, I explain earnestly, and I try to look as normal as possible. But I'm still regarded as a bit of an odd duck, which is why it's so nice to have a respected author like Stephen Leacock on my side. I need all the help I can get.

Graveyards *do* contain history, and that's why I like them. They speak to me. The little white lamb on the round marble marker tells me that a baby died once upon an awful time when hospitals were few and far between and medicine scarce. The lonely homemade wooden cross beside a northern river tells me about a trapper, a goldseeker, a river voyageur, who died in transit. Rest in peace where you fall. The worn slate marker covered

A child's grave in the Spirit River Mission cemetery, AB.

with words of praise and piety speaks of a bygone time when we said things like, "Departed this life in the firm belief of a blessed hereafter."

Sometimes, when I'm lucky, gravemarkers give me specific information such as this line from a grave in the Three Hills, Alberta, cemetery: "The Last Survivor of General Custer." Stopped me in my tracks, that one did, because the books tell us there were no survivors of the famous battle of Little Bighorn in Montana, and even if there were, what was one of them doing in an Alberta graveyard?

You'll have to read the Alberta chapter to see how that story ends. But in the course of tracking down that one small hint, I uncovered a tale of immigration, war, wandering, homesteading, a house by the side of the road—in other words, a microcosm of how the West was won.

That's what graveyards are—microcosms of our communities. You can pick out the richer members of the community; they have the tall markers, the ones with lots of words. You can find the babies by their ever-present lambs and doves. You can find the dutiful daughters and the virtuous wives; their gravemarkers say so. You can find the first settlers, the last missionaries, the sons who went to war, and the fathers who didn't come home. It's all out there for us to read.

Of course there are always blank pages in graveyards, but after a while you learn to see beyond them. Next to the lamb or the dove is a woman who died at the same time as her baby. It seldom says she died in childbirth, but you know. Sometimes there are empty spaces in the middle of an otherwise full graveyard. That's likely where the victims of some awful disease were buried in so much haste and fear that records weren't kept and markers weren't provided. Or maybe it's the potter's field where those who had neither friends nor money were laid to rest. Sometimes there are one

A touching monument to a baby in the cemetery at Cardston, AB.

or two graves off in a corner, separated from the others. You can guess they were suicides. Sometimes there are sections within a grave-yard—Orthodox crosses in one corner, Latin crosses in another, no crosses in yet another. This is a graveyard where religious differences mattered, where denomina-tions insisted on lines being drawn.

See what I mean? It's all so interesting, not creepy or morbid at all. In fact, what I am doing in the graveyards is what I'm supposed to do there. I am remembering. Why else do we put up monuments to mark our loved ones, if not to remember them? As it says on Henry Hardisty's grave in the Edmonton, Alberta, cemetery:

REMEMBER ME AS YOU PASS BY
SO AS YOU ARE, SO ONCE WAS I
SO AS I AM, SO SOON YOU'LL BE
PREPARE FOR DEATH AND ETERNITY.

It's an old epitaph that appears in a variety of forms, and while I'm not so keen on the last line, I do like the first one. When I stop before a gravemarker and read names and dates, see symbols and flowers, hear birds and windsong, I think about the people buried there. I remember them as I pass by. And whether that's like a butterfly stirring its wings in Japan and thereby changing something in the forests of Canada, I don't know, but I do it anyhow. I am compelled to remember and to reconstruct some of the story.

Thus, this book looks at Canadian history from the back end, from the graveyard instead of the cradle. Instead of saying, "Mary Jones was born in 1800 and this is what she did," I say, "Mary Jones has a really interesting gravemarker. This is what it says and here's why."

I suppose I am overexplaining myself, but I have found that people are somewhat unnerved by the combination of history and graveyards. Don't be. I am a cheerful historian, even if I start from the other end.

And why, you ask, did I start on this doleful exercise if I'm such a cheerful person?

A whole lot of reasons. I had always wanted to write about our history but couldn't exactly find a new way of doing it. I hated to retell what others had already told well. But one day a museum friend said, "Have you seen the grave in Henry Kemtrup's field?"

No, I hadn't, and when I did, it made all the difference.

The story according to Henry is this: A young couple came to a hardscrabble farm in central Alberta in the 1920s. They had nothing. It was too late in the year to plant a garden or a crop, so the husband proposed that he go to a nearby brick plant and work for a few months, thereby getting enough money to buy food and supplies. He'd be home before winter, before the baby was due.

So that's what happened. He went into Innisfail, some twenty-five

Poignant gravemarkers such as those on the past three pages, erected in memory of those who left too soon, are found in cemeteries across Canada.

kilometres away, and stayed there until he had his hard-earned cash. Then one late fall day, with cash in hand and supplies on his back, he started walking home. How he happened to meet up with a bad guy on a remote road in the middle of nowhere is hard to understand, but he did. The stranger robbed him and killed him, then left the body alongside the road in an area still known as Deadman's Lake.

He wasn't discovered until spring when the snow melted. The police finally identified him, found out that he had a wife in the bush somewhere, and went out to notify her. But when they found her, she was dead too. She had died in childbirth, and her twin babies were dead alongside her. She had died alone, except for her babies. They had died alone, except for their mother. It is the most heart-rending, terrible story. Yet it is a part of our history. Terrible things happened. The good old days were often bad.

Neighbours helped the police bury the woman and her children near the house. They didn't know her name so they simply covered the grave with rocks and left it there. When Henry bought the land in the 1940s, he cleared most of it but left the pile of rocks intact. He just couldn't bring himself to disturb it. "Every spring when we come to this field, I think of them all alone like that," he told me. "Must have been terrible."

At various times, he and others in the community tried to find out more about the young couple, but the brick plant had burned down—no more records there. The young couple had not applied for title to the land—no records there. Police records had been lost or destroyed. There was just nothing left of the story except the pile of rocks and the man who respected it all those years, ploughing around it in the spring, harvesting around it in the fall.

The two things—the terrible, sad story and the respect of the old farmer—made that pile of rocks absolutely rivetting. I couldn't get it out of my mind so I told its story at a family dinner. My niece Jennifer was thirteen at the time, thoroughly bored with anything that resembled history. History was for old aunts, not young, cool kids. But she listened to my story with amazement and then asked, "Why didn't she walk to some neighbours?"

"Maybe she didn't know her neighbours," I said. "Maybe there wasn't a road."

"Why didn't she call her mom?"

Don't ask me how a thirteen-year-old could get through seven years of school without knowing that phones were not often found in rural Alberta in the 1920s, but again I said, "Maybe her mother wasn't even in Canada. Maybe she didn't speak English."

"Why didn't she go with her husband?"

"Maybe she had a cow to look after. Maybe they couldn't afford to pay for two people to have room and board in town. There are lots of reasons," I said. But Jennifer wasn't satisfied. Something should have been done.

Later that summer, my sister and I were in northern Alberta to pay a visit to my parents' original homestead house. It's surrounded by bush and caraganas now, the roof is falling in, and the cellar has collapsed. It's neither pretty nor clean, but we wanted the kids to see it. *We* wanted to see it, for that matter. Anyway, Jennifer wasn't exactly thrilled with the whole idea. When we finally beat back the bush and got near the old house, she suddenly came to and said, "Aunt Nancy, where was the road and where did Grandma have her babies?"

It was then I realized she had made the transfer from the pile-of-rocks story to the story of her own grandmother. She was, in other words, asking historical questions. Maybe, I thought, I'm on to something.

Then I went to Canmore, and I was hooked. Again, Jennifer provided the push.

Canmore is a small mountain town just outside Banff National Park. The graveyard looks pretty standard at first glance—neat rows of markers, grass mowed, weeds controlled, petunias here and there, hoodoos on the hillside overlooking the graveyard. In fact, the hoodoos are the best part . . . until you discover the old graveyard at the back. It was the town's

Whitewashed by sun and snow, small picket fences surround many graves in the old Canmore cemetery.

original graveyard, but records got lost and eventually the town had to shut it down. They just didn't know who was buried where, so they fenced it off and left it to its own devices. The result is a magic garden, a wonderful tangle of trees and weeds and grass and saskatoon bushes and wild roses. And hidden here and there among all this exuberant growth are little wooden picket fences and small hidden marble markers and iron fences that look like bedsteads looking for a bed, and wooden crosses so bleached by the weather that you'd swear a paintbrush had done the work.

It takes your breath away; it is such a fantastic combination of light and dark, wild and tame, old and new.

I couldn't resist it, of course, and that's when I found Nelio. His little white marble cross inside one of the picket boxes read:

NELIO,
SON OF SEROFINO AND EMMA VOLA
BORN AUG. 22, 1910
DIED NOV. 2, 1910

Nothing too unusual there, unfortunately. A baby who lived two months and then died. It happened all the time in those bad old days. But as I leaned over the fence to push the wild rose bush out of the way, the better to read the date, I found a new bouquet of plastic flowers attached to the base of Nelio's grave. It hadn't just blown in from some other grave. It was wired onto the base of the cross.

It was goose bump time. Who came to this child's grave some eighty years later and put flowers on him? Who still remembered him? Did he have brothers and sisters? What happened to Serofino and Emma?

And the essential question, the one that Jennifer asked as soon as she heard the story, "Why did he die?"

Why, indeed?

I never did find the ending to Nelio's story. The local museum couldn't find any record of the family; oldtimers couldn't remember the name. But I can guess, reading between the lines of Canmore history.

Canmore was a mining town. Lots of Italian immigrants came to the area to work in the mines. When the mines closed, they moved on. Canmore was also a lumbering town, which is why there are so many picket fences in the graveyard. The pickets were cheap and available, and a fence kept the graves safe from animals.

In its early days, Canmore also had a problem with typhoid fever. Outhouses were built too close to water supplies; typhoid resulted. That's

Though it was eighty years since little Nelio died, someone remembered him with new flowers.

probably not what happened to Nelio, however. More likely, he died because there were no hospitals nearby, no doctors or antibiotics or special formulas. To be a baby was to be an endangered species in those years. Parents almost expected that some of their children would be lost along the way. How could they bear it?

That and more, I asked, as I stood in front of that tiny white cross. It said so little. It said so much.

It was then that I decided to work backwards, to see what I could see, and I would begin with what I knew—Alberta.

For the next three summers, I explored graveyards. And when I was done exploring, I wrote *Remember Me As You Pass By*. At first, I feared I wouldn't have enough for a book in that Albertans are aggravatingly silent in their graveyards—the old cowboy dictum of strong and silent, I fear. Mostly names and dates for us. No bragging. Thank goodness there were some exceptions, and then I began to get very good at reading between the lines. It was the best possible preparation for doing the rest of Canada because the rest of the country is much better at tomb talk. I didn't have to look very hard to find words and stories in the graveyards of central and eastern Canada. They were right there, begging to be noticed.

I noticed. I drove across the country—west to east—in the summer of 1994 and learned more history than I ever knew existed. Oh, I knew we had history, but so much? So interesting? Time and time again, I'd stand in front of a gravemarker and say, "I didn't know that." Or I'd check with the local museum, I'd read a book to fill in the spaces, and I'd say again, "I didn't know that."

Let me tell you—we are an interesting bunch. We are not boring. Our history is not boring. Go read some tombstones; you'll see what I mean.

For a while, I thought I should call this book "I Brake for Graveyards." That's what it says on my bumper sticker, but those words don't say enough. Yes, I brake for graveyards, but I also learn from them, get lost in them, laugh and cry in them, get wet feet in them, meet the friendliest people, find stories in them. Especially stories.

So the name became *Once Upon a Tomb: Stories from Canadian Graveyards.*

Come with me, then, on a different kind of transcontinental trip. Come visit graveyards with me.

British Columbia

✝

Where the Grass Is Greener

AS I SET OUT ON MY TRANSCANADA TRAVELS,
I FELT LIKE AN EXPLORER OF OLD – DAVID THOMPSON
OR ALEXANDER MACKENZIE MAYBE. AFTER ALL,
I WAS HEADING WEST OVER THE MOUNTAINS
INTO UNKNOWN TERRITORY, THERE TO BRING BACK
REPORTS OF THE NATIVES AND THEIR SOCIOCULTURAL
PRACTICES RE GRAVEYARDS.

Mind you, I looked more like the Most Boring Woman on Earth, safely behind the wheel of a modern minivan, safely headed down the best roads in the world, equipped with credit cards and apples—just in case British Columbia didn't have any. But I *felt* like an explorer. It was exciting to be heading out to see what I could find in Canadian graveyards, to read our stories from the back end.

BC wasn't exactly unknown territory either. We who live in Alberta go there all the time. It's close, it's different, it's green. Especially in April, it's green, and that's when I started out.

It's such an inadequate word—green. How could the same word be applied to the blush green on trees just beginning to bud on the other side of the mountains, the dark confident green in the Okanagan, the mean green at the top of the Coquihalla, the sexy green on Vancouver streets, the modest sweet green in Victoria? All quite different and yet all green. Can't deny it.

Other provinces, I was soon to discover, are also green, but they don't have the quantity that BC has. This place is one big green.

Not that the residents notice any more. I twittered away to a service station attendant in Hope one afternoon. So beautiful, so fresh, so unlike Alberta at this time of the year, blah, blah, blah. "You want your oil checked?" he said.

So I got on with things.

The graveyards of BC are, by and large, green. They are also pink, purple, white, yellow, and variegated. Things grow in and around them without nearly the coaxing that goes on in other parts of the country.

The graveyards of BC are also fairly informative. The oldest ones were established when it was still the style to put words on gravemarkers, which means that some of the history is out there, some of the stories are there, among the green ruins. I had to look for them, however. Canadian graveyards do not make it easy for the explorer.

The Best Graveyard in BC

Before I am told never to darken the doorway of, say, Victoria again, let me explain. The best graveyard in BC is Barkerville because it's so easy to read, it's so original, and it's hauntingly lovely with all the picket fences and tree roots growing everywhere. It's even funny in places. What's more, if gold had not lured thousands of innocents to BC, Victoria wouldn't be the splendid capital that it is now. Nor would Vancouver be what it is, etc., etc. The province would have been green but not gold. Get it?

For the benefit of those who've never been to Barkerville, I should explain how to get there. What you do is you drive straight up the middle of BC. When you can't possibly stand the idea of another mile, you turn right and keep on driving. One of the historical markers along the way explains that Edgar Dewdney's first job in Canada was the construction of a road into the Cariboo, said road to be at least four feet (1.2 m) wide.

Imagine making your way through BC's spectacular mountain passes on a one-metre road. No thank you, but that's exactly what those crazy gold seekers did.

The lure of gold lingers on if I'm to believe the excitement of four boys in Barkerville the day I was there. "We found some," they said, dancing

The unique Barkerville cemetery, with its picket fences, unruly tree roots, and bits of humour, is the last resting place of many hopeful goldseekers.

around me with some water sloshing in a pan. "We found gold. See. Take our picture." Then they tore off to find more.

That must have been the reaction, magnified many times, of the thousands of men and women who came to the Barkerville area after Billy Barker discovered gold there in 1862. Never mind that there were no roads, no bridges, no beds and breakfasts along the way. They just hitched up their pants and moved north. Some got rich, some didn't, and some died:

IN MEMORY OF ANDREW HANSON NATIVE OF SWEDEN
DIED IN THE R.C. HOSPITAL ON THE 10TH OF OCT. 1883
FROM THE EFFECT OF A FALL IN A SHAFT
BY WHICH HE BROKE HIS BACK
AND DIED AFTERWARD WITHIN SIX HOURS.

Others prospered and ended up with much more cheerful information on their gravemarkers:

IN MEMORY OF CHARTRES BREW
BORN AT CORSFIN, COUNTY CLARE, IRELAND,
31 DECEMBER 1815
DIED AT RICHFIELD 31 MAY 1870
GOLD COMMISSIONER AND COUNTY COURT JUDGE

A MAN IMPERTURBABLE IN COURAGE AND TEMPER
ENDOWED WITH A GREAT & VARIED
ADMINISTRATIVE CAPACITY A MOST READY WIT
A MOST PURE INTEGRITY
AND A MOST HUMANE HEART.

His epitaph does him proud, but it could also have mentioned that he served in the Spanish Legion, the Irish Constabulary, and the Crimean War, and when there were no more wars to be fought on European soils, he came to northern BC and kept the peace there. Isn't life interesting!

Everyone in Barkerville came from somewhere else—England, Russia, Syracuse in the US, Glengarry County in Ontario are just a few of the places mentioned on the gravemarkers—but John Fraser, son of the famous explorer, Simon Fraser, at least knew something about the country. His father had explored and named parts of it, after all. That didn't help John, however, who killed himself in 1865 at the age of thirty-two. Apparently, he was not able to find either gold or love, and the combination did him in. There's a sign near his grave that explains all of this.

Another sign tells the story of J.B. Malamon, who made a name for himself as a violinist in the Paris Opera but then moved to Barkerville and took up carpentry. Why he would do such a thing we are not told, but apparently he kept his sense of humour to the end. On his death bed in 1879, he made a bet with another patient as to who would die first. Near dawn, Malamon spoke up and said, "You win, I lose, I die now." And he did.

Just how he paid up is not explained.

Women and children paid

Chartres Brew, a civil servant, has more words than most on his tombstone in the Barkerville cemetery.

John Fraser found neither love nor money in the Cariboo gold rush.

their dues on the goldfields as well. A beautiful marble marker remembers Margaret Jane Blair, aged twenty-one, and her daughter, aged ten days. "O Cruel Death," the epitaph begins.

Speaking of cruel deaths, Billy Barker, who first discovered the riches in the Cariboo rivers, died a pauper and was buried in a cemetery in Victoria. His grave wasn't even marked until a few years ago, when the Barkerville Restoration Committee had a plaque installed over his last resting place. He, like many others, found gold but couldn't keep it.

That was the story of John "Cariboo" Cameron, who's also buried in the Barkerville cemetery. Mind you, when he was buried there in 1888, it was called the Cameronton cemetery, the town of Cameronton having been named for him. He found gold, got tremendously rich, founded a town close to Barkerville, established a cemetery between the two centres, and then lost everything except the cemetery. None of this appears on his gravemarker.

The town of Barkerville is a historic site now, houses and businesses ranged neatly up and down a main street, good coffee and cinnamon buns available for sale in a tea shop. It's great, but it can't beat the graveyard for telling it like it was.

The Other Best Graveyard in BC

Ross Bay cemetery in Victoria is a splendid graveyard, full of important names and interesting monuments and good stories, but more than that, it's got the OCS on its side. We should all be so lucky.

The Old Cemeteries Society is, simply, a remarkable band of people who take an interest in old cemeteries. There's a constitution and all those pesky things you have to have for an organization, but the rules don't seem to rule. The graveyards do.

Ross Bay was the first cemetery adopted by the OCS, and it shows. Many of the old markers have been spruced up, gates and fences are straight and proud, markers mark the unmarked, little kids play hide-and-seek among the trees just as if the graveyard were a park—which, in fact, it was intended to be. Back in the mid 1800s, graveyards were established away from city centres, in the surrounding countryside, partly because graveyards were pretty awful in those days—often smelly, damp, and neglected; a source, it was feared, of foul "miasmas" that would lead to disease. Better to remove the nasty business and create "rural cemeteries," which was what Ross Bay was at the beginning—a cemetery on farmland east of Victoria. With its winding roadways, formal flowerbeds, and sombre trees (the yew was a favourite for graveyards), it was intended to be a solemn place that would encourage contemplation and high moral behaviour.

But even as the graveyard planners urged high moral behaviour on others, they went right ahead and assigned the area nearest the sea, the least desirable spot, to "Aborigines and Mongolians not attached to any of the established churches." Only after a terrible storm that left coffins littered on Victoria beaches did the city finally build a seawall to prevent the graves from literally washing away to sea.

By the 1970s, Ross Bay cemetery was in trouble again, this time from benign neglect. It was so much a part of the city scene that it was almost invisible, which meant that vandals began to enjoy it more than ordinary folk. That's when the OCS took shape here. A few people agreed to patrol the graveyard Hallowe'en night—not to arrest people or anything. They didn't have the authority to do that. They'd just talk to people about the graveyard and whom it held. Can you imagine? Stopping a gang of young people in the middle of a dark night and telling them stories? Took guts, I'd say, but it worked. Without a lot of fanfare, they began to get things done in the graveyard, and the rest is history.

They still patrol on Hallowe'en, incidentally. Vandalism has been drastically reduced. And every Sunday, and all weekend in the tourist season, members lead tours through Ross Bay or one of the other island cemeteries. I know, I know, BC doesn't get snow, which is why we couldn't do the same thing in other parts of Canada, but what a remarkable revolution. To turn local graveyards into tourist destinations.

Needless to say, I love going to Victoria.

Now, who and what is in Ross Bay? Well, to begin with, most of the big names from BC's early history are there.

James Douglas (1803-1877) is there. A plaque at the base of his marker says:

FOUNDED VICTORIA AS A FORT 1843
GOVERNOR OF THE CROWN COLONY
OF VANCOUVER ISLAND 1851-64.
GOVERNOR OF THE CROWN COLONY
OF BRITISH COLUMBIA 1858-64
KNIGHTED BY QUEEN VICTORIA 1863

Not too far from Douglas is Edgar Dewdney (1835-1916). There's a path running right past him—about a metre wide—that should remind him of the terrifying job he had when he arrived in BC. After overseeing construction of the impossible Dewdney Trail into the Cariboo, he went into provincial and federal politics in a major way, eventually serving as lieutenant governor of the Northwest Territories and then British Columbia.

Robert Dunsmuir (1825-1889) is in Ross Bay also, buried beneath a surprisingly modest gravemarker. One expects a bit more flash after seeing Craigdarroch Castle, the mansion Dunsmuir built after he made tons of money in coal mining and other business ventures in BC. His marker says only, "HE SLEEPETH."

The modest grey marker for the Hon. John Robson (1824-1892) might also reveal a bit more. His stone does admit he was premier of BC, and it mentions that he died in London, England. It says nothing, however, about the cause of his death: he got blood poisoning after he closed a London cab door on his finger.

Sir Matthew Baillie Begbie (1819-1894) is buried there beneath a plain grey granite cross, mounted on a fairly substantial three-tiered base. It was supposed to be a plain wooden cross mounted without any fuss at all, or so Begbie had instructed. But his relatives decided he deserved a little more ceremony. After all, he was known far and wide as "the hanging judge," a reputation that brought him great fame. Historians tell us that he didn't hang any more criminals than other judges did; it just seemed that way. Besides, he was dealing with desperate people desperately seeking gold in isolated corners of a huge country. There were temptations everywhere.

And speaking of gold, Billy Barker, he who started the Cariboo gold rush, is in Ross Bay. The marker finally erected by the Barkerville Restoration Committee over his last resting place says:

A NATIVE OF CORNWALL, ENGLAND, "BILLY BARKER"
CAME TO BRITISH COLUMBIA IN 1858.
IN AUGUST 1862, HE MADE THE FIRST DISCOVERY
OF GOLD BELOW THE CANYON OF WILLIAMS CREEK.
THE RUSH THAT ENSUED CREATED BARKERVILLE,
GOLD METROPOLIS OF CARIBOO.
HE DIED IN POVERTY IN VICTORIA, JULY 11, 1894.

And my favourite—Bill Smith (1825-1897)—is also buried in Ross Bay. This is what his gravemarker says:

WILLIAM ALEXANDER SMITH
BY ACT OF THE CALIFORNIA LEGISLATURE
CHANGED HIS NAME TO AMOR DE COSMOS
LOVER OF THE UNIVERSE.
HE FOUNDED THE COLONIST DEC. 11, 1858.
HE WAS 2ND PREMIER OF BRITISH COLUMBIA
DEC. 23, 1872 -FEB. 11, 1874.
HE WAS MEMBER OF PARLIAMENT FOR VICTORIA 1872-1882.
WELL AND NOBLY DID HE GIVE HIS ALL
FOR A UNITED BRITISH COLUMBIA
A UNITED CANADA.

Smith changed his name to Amor de Cosmos because, as he said, "the name tells what I love most . . . order, beauty, the world, the universe." Good for him, except that there are other more cynical opinions as to why Bill Smith changed his name. Running from the law is one, crazy as a bedbug is another.

Whatever his reasons, he made life interesting for Victoria, first as a newspaper editor who criticized the ruling elite—mostly Governor James Douglas—and then as a politician who made waves wherever he could. For a couple of years, he was both premier of BC and a federal MP. No wonder he went crazy.

John Dean (1850-1943) was of a different opinion about the world. Not for him mushy sentiments about "lover of the universe." His gravemarker in Ross Bay tells us:

IT IS A ROTTEN WORLD.
ARTFUL POLITICIANS ARE ITS BANE.
ITS SAVING GRACE IS THE ARTLESSNESS OF THE YOUNG
AND THE WONDERS OF THE SKY.

Dean had lines 1, 3, and 4 inscribed upon a tombstone and erected in Ross Bay years before he died. Somewhere along the way he adjusted it to include line 2. Maybe he felt he needed to point the finger a bit more specifically since he ran for mayor of Victoria in 1928 and 1929 and lost both times. Other politicians had done him in, he felt, and the world should know about them.

But what about the women, you ask? Where are they in this Who's Who of Ross Bay cemetery? They are, as ever, modest to a fault, silent to the end.

The very first person buried there was a woman, Mary Laetitia Pearse, who died Christmas Day, 1872, aged thirty-two years. Her inscription is fairly lengthy, but it doesn't give much away other than that she was a good Christian:

> FAIR IN FORM, FAIRER IN MIND,
> SHE DISPLAYED DURING A LONG AND SEVERE ILLNESS
> GREAT CHRISTIAN PATIENCE AND RESIGNATION
> SHOWING TO ALL BY HER FAITH
> THAT DEATH HAD LOST ITS STING
> AND THE GRAVE ITS VICTORY.

Amelia Douglas (1812-1890), wife of the first governor, is also there, marked only by her name and dates. Not a word about the time she saved her husband's life when she talked some members of the Stuart Lake band into releasing him from capture. Amelia, whose mother was Cree, was sixteen then. For the next few decades, she had babies, thirteen in all, of whom only five survived. Her gravemarker doesn't mention any of that.

Jane Saunders (1843-1897) is there, but again her gravemarker is silent on the interesting stuff. There's no mention that she was one of the "bundles of crinoline" who came on the bride ship *Tynemouth* in 1862.

The Cameron name appears in Ross Bay cemetery also, but there's no specific mention of Agnes Deans Cameron, another powerful woman. She was the first female high school principal in Victoria, but when her students did so well on a provincial art exam that it was suspected they had drawn with a ruler rather than by freehand, she was sacked. She protested, ran for the school board, and won. But she didn't get her job back. So she changed jobs, went north, and became a world-famous author and lecturer.

When she died in Victoria in 1912, she had the biggest funeral the city had ever seen with a cortege that went on for blocks. Sweet revenge, if ever there was such a thing, but none of that appears in the graveyard.

There *is* a slight hint on a black marble bench that marks Maria Grant (1854-1937) that she too may have been a woman to pay attention to. On the

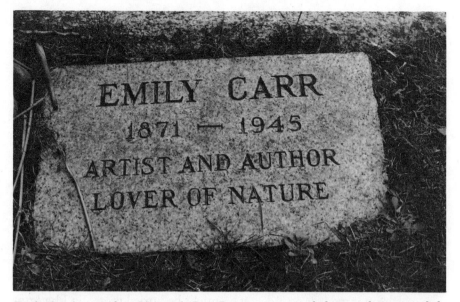

Emily Carr's epitaph in Victoria's Ross Bay cemetery merely hints at her accomplishments.

edge of the bench are the words, writ large: WOMAN'S SUFFRAGIST. Apparently, Maria petitioned the legislature for woman's suffrage for so many years that it was almost an annual event, one that the male members joked about and ignored. When it finally happened, Maria was not invited to the special ceremonies held in the legislature. It figures. Mind you, Maria had other things on her plate—membership in most every politically active group in town plus, oh yes, nine children.

As for artist Emily Carr, about the most famous woman on the west coast, she gets a long story made short:

> EMILY CARR, 1871-1945
> ARTIST AND AUTHOR
> LOVER OF NATURE

The Surprising Graveyard

The Fraser cemetery in New Westminster is full of surprises.

For instance, Capt. William Irving, a paragon of virtue if I'm to believe his obituary, is buried near Gassy Jack Deighton, who was no paragon at all, if I'm to believe *his* obituary. An interesting man, I gather, but no paragon. Irving ran steamboats on the Fraser and became a very wealthy and influential man in New Westminster; Gassy Jack also ran steamboats and a hotel now and then, but he'd never go down in history for good behaviour. Mind you, to give credit where credit is due, he did build one of his hotels on the piece of Burrard Inlet that is now the centre of Vancouver, otherwise known as Gastown. The place had potential, he thought.

His gravemarker says:

> HERE LIES JOHN "GASSY JACK" DEIGHTON 1830-1875
> SAILOR, PROSPECTOR, STEAMBOATMAN
> PIONEER HOTELMAN AT NEW WESTMINSTER AND GRANVILLE.

Capt. Irving's marker in the same section of the cemetery is substantial but silent.

In the Church of England section of the Fraser cemetery—for entirely logical reasons—is a Church of England minister, the well-known Father Pat Irwin. The reason I count his grave as a surprise is that I had found a memorial stone with his name on it outside a little church in Windermere. The words on it made it sound as if he might be buried there. So I had not expected to come across him here.

> HENRY IRWIN (FATHER PAT) MISSION PRIEST 1885-1902
> SON OF REV. HENRY IRWIN OF NEWTOWN, MT. KENNEDY, IRE.
> DIED JAN. 13, 1902 AGED 42 YEARS
> FRANCES STEWART WIFE OF HENRY IRWIN 1858-1890
> INFANT SON DIED NOV. 17, 1890

Father Pat soldiered for God and the Anglican Church all over southern BC, lighting for a time in Donald—long enough to build a church; and then in New Westminster—long enough to get married, only to lose his young wife the same year in childbirth. He hung on for a while, but he never regained his zeal, and on a trip to Ireland, he left the train for some unknown reason near Montréal and started walking. When he was finally picked up, he was suffering from exposure and died soon after in a Montréal hospital.

His little church in Donald had better luck, although some people might say it was a very unChristianlike ending for a church. The CPR moved the town of Donald, lock, stock, and barrel, to Revelstoke, but before they could get the church on skids, it disappeared. Lock, stock, and barrel.

Eventually, someone discovered that it was alive and well and standing proudly on new foundations in Windermere. How come? Nobody knew (except one guy in Windermere and he wasn't talking). Letters were written to Windermere. Nobody answered. Church, civic, and government officials all demanded its return. Nothing moved. So the church got to stay where it was. It's still there. The sign out front says, "St. Peter's Anglican Church, The Stolen Church."

The Trapp story wouldn't be such a surprise to me today; I've been to so many graveyards now and seen so many memorials to men who "made the final sacrifice." But on that spring day in New Westminster with every tree in the place popping buds and every blade of grass standing at attention, I couldn't believe my eyes. Three sons, young as spring, died in war: Stanley Trapp, killed in France, December 10, 1916; George Trapp, killed in France, November 12, 1917; Donovan Trapp, killed in France, July 19, 1918.

> THEY ARE NUMBERED AMONG THOSE
> WHO AT THE CALL OF KING AND COUNTRY
> LEFT ALL THAT WAS DEAR TO THEM,
> ENDURED HARDSHIP, FACED DANGER,
> AND FINALLY PASSED OUT OF THE SIGHT OF MEN
> BY THE PATH OF DUTY AND SELF SACRIFICE
> GIVING UP THEIR OWN LIVES
> THAT OTHERS MIGHT LIVE IN FREEDOM.

The only surviving son, I found out later, was the eldest. He also went off to war but got typhoid fever and had to come home. Lucky him, I thought. But after I read about the Trapp brothers, I realized he probably didn't feel lucky. They all wanted to go, especially after Stanley was killed, and they all picked the flying service, which was about as dangerous as any assignment could be.

The "I Can't Believe I Drove All This Way" Graveyard

John Adams of the OCS told me that the Hazelton cemetery in northern BC was a must. The tombstones look like marble totem poles, he said. It's incredibly interesting. You mustn't miss it.

So I did. Miss it, that is. How I managed to be so stupid haunts me still, but there you are. All I know is I have to go back.

To get to Hazelton, you get back onto that road that goes straight up the middle of BC. You do not stop at 100 Mile House to look at the world's biggest cross-country skis. After turning west at Prince George, you do not stop in Houston to look at the world's largest fly rod. You don't need to—you can see them from the highway. They are the world's biggest, after all. Eventually, you will see a sign that says Hazelton, and you will find a tourist information place. They're everywhere in BC, thank goodness.

The two young women in this one were very helpful. When I asked about the graveyard, they pointed out the window and said, "It's over there. You can't miss it."

I should have known. Every time someone tells me I can't miss it, I usually do. Anyway, I drove in the general direction of their wave and found a graveyard up on a hill overlooking a wide, beautiful valley. A lovely setting but no outstanding gravemarkers. Several had animals carved into the surface of pedestal markers—a deer for Jenny Tsich, died 1904; a muskrat or some similar four-footed animal "in memory of Old Sam who died 1933"; a bird for Chief Lasfeal Smogemk, died 1908. But nothing that could be described as a totem pole.

Back I went to the tourist information place.

"Is there another graveyard?" I asked. "There has to be another."

"Did you go over the bridge?" they asked.

Well, yes, I'd been over sort of a bridge.

"Then, that's it," they said.

So I went to the graveyard again and looked some more. Still no marble totem poles. Once again, with feeling, to the tourist information place.

They were beginning to feel sorry for me so they dragged out the story of John J. Caux, a.k.a. Cataline. Spanish-born Cataline came to northern BC in search of gold, of course, but stayed on to become the best-known pack train driver in the north. Everybody wanted Cataline to bring in their supplies, their families, themselves. Cataline stopped for nothing— not storms, rain, fires, insects, wilderness.

He was a bit of a character. Before every expedition, he'd buy himself a new white shirt, put it on, and leave it on for the whole trip. No such sissy stuff as wash-

"Old Sam's" gravemarker and others in the Hazelton cemetery have animals carved on the headstones.

ing it or himself enroute, which may explain why he got into the habit of rubbing a shot of whisky into his hair whenever he had the chance.

It was a good story, and I thanked the young tourist directors for it. But where is he buried? I asked. I have to start from a gravemarker.

Uh, oh. They leafed through more stuff and finally told me with regret that as far as they could tell from their records, he was buried in the Old Hazelton cemetery, the one that I had just been to. What's more, he was unmarked. They were awfully sorry but . . .

To make a long story short, and a long drive longer, it turned out that there are four settlements at Hazelton. There's Hazelton, New Hazelton, South Hazelton, and Ksan Indian Village. I should have been in the Ksan Indian Village. That's where the remarkable gravemarkers are, and that's where I'm going as soon as I can make my van head that way again.

When missionaries came along to that part of BC in the mid 1850s, they taught the Tsimshian people that they should bury their loved ones in the manner to which Christians had become accustomed. The Indians obliged except that they added a few original touches. For instance, if they wanted family crests and tribal symbols on a gravemarker, they'd draw a picture or send along a roughly carved pattern in wood to the monument makers in the south. There the stone masons would copy the designs as best they could and send the monuments back to the northern Indians.

Which is why many of the tombstones look like marble totem poles. And that's what John Adams was talking about.

I've seen pictures of some of them since, and they are by far the most original marble gravemarkers in Canada. For the most part, immigrants to Canada brought graveyard art and tradition with them from other countries. We didn't exactly make it our own. We just kept on using the same old designs. Only the Tsimshians managed to make an old art so uniquely their own.

Their spirit houses showed similar originality. Built of wood, some were complete little houses with doors and glass windows, some were fences with elaborate corner posts and complicated lattice designs; some were a combination of the two. But here we go again. I didn't see them, not for lack of directions this time but because most of them have disappeared, victims of weather, time, and vandalism.

A spirit house is a tough concept to explain. I'm not sure I can do justice to it because every time I asked for an explanation, I got a different answer. The one thing I know for sure is it's a wooden, sometimes metal, structure built over a grave. It shelters the spirits of the deceased until they are ready to join the ancestors, indicates status and community regard, holds possessions for the next world, and keeps away animals. One young woman in a northern Native community told me this is just an old-fashioned custom that nobody bothers with any more. So take your pick, although I must admit I'm persuaded by the more poetic reasons.

I eventually found spirit houses in other parts of northern BC, Alberta, and the Yukon. None were as elaborate as those built by the Tsimshians, but all of them had an ambience about them that made the name "spirit house" seem appropriate.

While the Tsimshians on the mainland of northwestern BC were blending their graveyard traditions with Christian customs, the Haida of the Queen Charlotte Islands were losing their graveyard monuments. Their mortuary practices were so original, so fascinating to outside museums and anthropologists when they came across them in the late 1800s that most of the mortuary artifacts were carried off to museums and private collections. Which is why I got to see Haida mortuary boxes and memorial poles in downtown Victoria behind the glass walls of the museum.

Some of these "totem poles" have a small box near the top of the carved pole. That's a mortuary box, or casket. A prominent member of the community, a chief perhaps, would warrant having his bones placed at the top of the totem pole. Both the pole and the box would be carved and painted with symbols depicting the deceased and beliefs about life and death. No two mortuary poles were the same.

Sometimes a family member died elsewhere—at sea or far from home— in which case a memorial pole would be erected. No mortuary box, because the body wasn't there.

The traditions were incredibly rich and meaningful, and when you see the pictures of the villages in the 1800s, when explorers with cameras first reached them, you have to marvel at the forest of poles in front of each village. Some were simply totem poles, if ever you could call a totem pole simple. But others were mortuary and memorial poles, which, unlike the Tsimshian marble totem poles, were not combined with any other tradition. They were, are, Canada's most original, all-Canadian grave monuments.

What a Difference a Word Makes

In the Yale cemetery one sunny afternoon, I had a cup of tea with an older man who was there to visit his wife. "She died two years ago," he explained, "so I bring my tea in a thermos every now and then and tell her all the news."

I was absolutely smitten with such affection, but there was more that lovely afternoon. As we visited, two young women walked into the cemetery—modern, strong young women wearing heavy-duty boots and matching expressions. They read the inscriptions matter-of-factly until they got to the gravemarker for Daisy Sumner, 1877-1883:

> SHE FALTERED BY THE WAYSIDE
> AND THE ANGELS TOOK HER HOME.

"Oh," said one strong young woman.
"Oh dear," said the other. "What could have happened?"
"She was so young, only six. Imagine."
"She faltered."
"Yes."
And they stood there a long time before moving on.

In the graveyard beside St. Stephen's Anglican Church in Saanichton, north of Victoria, is a lovely message with just the right words. It's in memory of Marjorie Edith Shaw, 1912-1985:

> IF I COULD DO ONE THING ALONE
> A VERSE OR PRAYER OF LASTING WORTH,
> I'D SEEK ST. STEPHEN'S GENTLE SLOPE
> AND CARVE THERE THE WORDS,
> "I LOVE YOU."

In the same graveyard is a marker that says, instead of the word "death":

> I HEARD THE OWL CALL MY NAME.

In the Windermere cemetery is about the most succinct explanation of death that I've found in a long time:

> JOE YOUNG RANCHER
> BORN GLENGARRY 1839
> KILLED 1920
> HORSES RAN AWAY

And speaking of succinct, I wish I knew the story behind this inscription for Nellie Chapman in the Vernon cemetery, but here it is anyway, all six words of it:

> SHE LOVED, WAS LOVED, AND DIED

Ghost Graveyards

One misty moisty morning, I drove north of Victoria to Cumberland and found there the old Japanese graveyard. I'll never forget it. Under dripping

This brief message of life and death is in the Vernon cemetery.

evergreen trees were worn gravemarkers arranged in a circle on a concrete pad. They looked like old people huddling under the trees, trying to stay together but still be invisible against the green forest behind them.

If the true mark of great art is a fusion of form and function, then these sad little gravemarkers circling their wagons against the rest of the world are great art.

In 1913, mine owners brought Japanese labourers to the Cumberland area to replace striking workers; how to be unpopular right from the beginning. Labour troubles were eventually settled, however, and the Japanese continued to live and work in the area. They also died there, so a graveyard was established—a graveyard with neat rows and upright markers, much like any other graveyard.

Then came the bombing of Pearl Harbor in 1941. Everything changed for the Japanese, particularly the ones who lived on the west coast and who, it was feared, might help Japan from within Canada. Thus were most of the Japanese on the west coast, including those who were Canadian citizens, moved arbitrarily to the BC interior and the prairies. The government seized their lands and property; overnight they became noncitizens.

The little graveyard in Cumberland was left to moulder in the rain. Eventually, vandals attacked it. When the community finally got around to righting things in the 1960s, records were lost, locations couldn't be verified, so the markers were arranged as they are now—in a circle. A terrible, silent reminder of what war does to us.

Worn Japanese gravemarkers huddle together in the rainforest near Cumberland.

Harling Point Chinese cemetery, established in 1903 in Victoria, is another graveyard that could tell us a few things if it chose. A windblown piece of grassland on the Strait of Juan de Fuca, it looks for all the world like a piece of land that Victoria forgot. No condos, no rollerbladers zipping by on paved paths, no rhododendrons blooming their blooming heads off. Just wild grass with an odd pair of columns in the centre of it. Get a little closer, however, and you can see several upright gravemarkers hidden in the grass, and here and there, big flat granite markers with Chinese words on them.

The first Chinese to arrive in Canada may have come for jobs and opportunities, like every newcomer, but they had no intention of remaining in Canada after their death. According to ancient beliefs, the soul of the Chinese could not be at rest until their bones were buried with the ancestors. Then and only then could the soul begin to enjoy eternity.

How to manage this ancient tradition in their new home presented some problems, to say the least, which is why the Chinese community in Victoria bought the land out on Harling Point. There they buried their fellow Chinese. There they disinterred the bodies after a suitable length of time and sent them back home. They had to wait until there were enough bones to make a boatload so eventually a holding shed, known as a bone house, was built on the cemetery land.

Neighbours weren't always too keen on having a bone house in their midst, and they didn't hesitate to say so. In fact, the citizens of Victoria were often quite awful to the Chinese in their community. In the records of the Ross Bay cemetery, the first Chinese burials were listed as "Chinaman #1" and "Chinaman #2." Mind you, Victoria was not alone in this contempt for Chinese. When I talked to the sweet old man in the Yale cemetery, he recalled his father telling him that the Chinese who were killed on road-building or railway gangs were often dumped off a cliff somewhere.

Some lives were cheaper then.

The Harling Point cemetery survived all the neighbouring nastiness until the world changed in more ways than one. Bones could not be shipped back to China during World War II, the bone house got full, the graveyard got full, on top of which a lot of second- and third-generation Chinese decided that Canada was home. They and their descendants would be buried here.

So the bones were sorted—don't ask me how—and buried on December 15, 1961, in thirteen mass graves according to home county and family. Chinese from all over Canada came to a special funeral service, and that was pretty well the end of Harling Point as an active graveyard. It's still a lovely passive one, however, and Chinese Canadians continue to come to burn ceremonial papers on the altars in the brick chimneys, and leave food offerings in honour of their ancestors.

Working Men Unite

Just because BC is breathtakingly beautiful, soft as a baby's bum, doesn't mean it hasn't had its share of troubles. Take the words on a distinctive gravemarker in the Cumberland community cemetery:

GINGER GOODWIN
SHOT JULY 26 1918
A WORKERS FRIEND

The word "shot" is written in bold red letters, and the symbol of the hammer and sickle above the words is red also. A sure sign that Ginger Goodwin's story has something to do with communist ideals and labour unrest.

In the 1920s and 1930s, Canada had quite an active Communist Party. The label was pinned on most anyone who dared to stand up for workers' rights in the mining, lumbering, and construction camps early in this century. At any rate, Goodwin did just that—he incited fellow workers to

Ginger Goodwin, buried in Cumberland cemetery, became a martyr of the working class.

strike at a mining camp in Trail, and for his trouble, he promptly received a draft notice. Until then, he had been classified as "unfit for military service," but suddenly, in spite of continuing medical problems, he was reclassified as "fit." Goodwin decided to defy the order. It seemed too coincidental that he'd be sent packing to war just after he'd organized a strike. So he hid out in the bush around Cumberland instead.

He didn't last long. The police chased him down and shot him, which is how Ginger Goodwin became a martyr of the working class with words on his gravemarker that are carefully repainted in red every year.

The Prince George cemetery has more of the same—different era, same problems, same red ink:

TO THE MEMORY OF A PROLETARIAN
COM. S. BERLINIC DIED 27 FEBRUARY, 1933
A VICTIM OF RELIEF CAMPS
THIS MONUMENT HAS BEEN ERECTED
BY HIS COMRADES
AS A WARNING MAY 3, 1933

It seems hard to believe now but during the Dirty Thirties, relief camps were set up for single, homeless, unemployed men. If you had no work, you had to report to these camps and do whatever was assigned—road work, construction, etc. In return, you got room and board and five dollars a

The man beneath this unusual marker in the Prince George graveyard fell victim to the hard times of the Great Depression.

month. The trouble was that the five dollars soon dipped to less than half that amount, and working conditions were usually awful. No wonder communist organizers, also known as "red agitators" by their detractors, were welcomed into the camps.

Berlinic was, by all accounts, a "red agitator." He belonged to the Communist Party and marched and hollered with the best of them whenever an opportunity presented itself. Unfortunately for him, one of the best opportunities for a show of strength and anger occurred at his own funeral—one of the biggest Prince George had seen to that time. Men came from camps all around, and somehow out of their measly salaries, they put together enough money for the gravemarker that tells their story to this day.

I never found out how Berlinic died, although judging by the number of times dysentery is mentioned in connection with the camps, I would have to guess disease aggravated by a poor diet. Also aggravated by anger and disappointment, what do you bet? Life wasn't supposed to turn out this way, even for the proletariat.

In Nelson's graveyard is a gravemarker with quite another view of communism. It belongs to John Koliberda, 1902-1986:

> BROTHER! SISTER! I BEG YOU.
> READ THIS TRAGIC EPISODE OF MY LIFE.
> IT MAY PREVENT YOU FROM THE DELUSION INTO WHICH I FELL
> DUE TO NAIVETY OF MY YOUTHFUL YEARS

WHEN I WAS FASCINATED BY THE IDEA OF COMMUNISM.
HOWEVER, SOON I REALIZED MY ERROR
WHEN I SAW DECEIT, VIOLENCE, OPPRESSION, TERROR . . .
THE RED BUTCHERS TOOK THE LIVES
OF MY FATHER, BROTHER AND MOTHER.
BROTHERS AND SISTERS!
LIVING AMONG YOU IN CANADA
I WAS DELIGHTED TO ENJOY THE RIGHTS
OF FREEDOM AND DEMOCRACY

He continues to praise "hospitable Canada" on the sign above his grave, and it's kind of nice. A reminder that we have a lot going for us in this country.

Will That Be Golf or Graves?

Watch out for flying golf balls when you visit the Veterans cemetery in Esquimalt, the only graveyard I've found so far that is smack dab in the middle of a golf course. Not beside it or near it but *in* it.

The combination seems to work just fine. Both are green, quiet, and peaceful, but it wasn't always so. Esquimalt being a naval base and Victoria being a seaport meant there were lots of sailors around, lots of rowdiness, and more watery accidents than usual:

SACRED TO THE MEMORY OF JOSEPH JEFFS
ORD^Y. SEAMAN H.M.S. GANGES
WHO WAS KILLED BY FALLING
FROM THE MIZEN TOP OCT. 23, 1859
DEEPLY REGRETTED BY HIS SHIPMATES
AGED 18 YEARS.

RIP THOMAS P. BENNETT
STOKER WHO WAS FATALLY SCALDED
THROUGH THE BURSTING OF A
STEAM PIPE ON BOARD H.M.S. IMPERIEUSE
JAN. 16, 1899 AGED 25.

These are not the kind of stories we find in prairie graveyards, although there is one story in the Esquimalt cemetery that connects directly to the prairies:

THOMAS DRUDY, AGED 24 A.B. OF H.M.S. CAROLINE
WHO WAS ACCIDENTLY KILLED WHILE FIRING A SALUTE
ON BOARD OCT. 3, 1888

The Veterans graveyard in Esquimalt reflects BC's naval history.

Col. Frederick Middleton was in town, getting the usual military welcome. He had commanded the Canadian forces that defeated Louis Riel and his troops in the 1885 North-West Rebellion. All went well with the thirteen-gun salute until the ninth charge jammed in the breech of the cannon and blew up. Thomas Drudy was killed instantly, and Middleton had to make do with an eight-gun salute.

The most impressive marker in the naval cemetery belongs to Frederick Seymour, Esq:

GOVERNOR AND COMMANDER IN CHIEF OF BRITISH COLUMBIA,
WHO DIED AT SEA, ON BOARD H.M.S. SPARROWHAWK,
WHILE IN THE DISCHARGE OF AN IMPORTANT OFFICIAL DUTY,
ON 10TH OF JUNE, 1869.

The "important official duty" was the negotiation of a treaty with the Tsimshians in northern BC, but there are hints in history that "the drink" may have had something to do with Seymour's demise. In fact, during the tour I took through the cemetery, I heard a lot about "the drink," and we're not talking water here. Could it be that "the drink" is another fact of maritime service? I've never found it mentioned on a gravemarker, however.

The Son Was Not So Lucky

When you drive over the Kicking Horse Pass and River in the Rocky Mountains, give a thought to Sir James Hector. He was a member of the Palliser Expedition sent out from England to explore the potential of western Canada. One day, while crossing a river, he got such a vicious kick from his horse that his companions gave him up for dead. By the time he revived, members of his party were already digging a grave for him. Naturally, Hector named the river the Kicking Horse.

Years later, he returned to western Canada with his son, a sort of sentimental journey during which he intended to revisit the site of his near demise. However, before that could happen, his son Douglas was stricken with appendicitis and died in the Revelstoke hospital. He's buried there under the words:

DOUGLAS HECTOR
OF WELLINGTON, NEW ZEALAND.
DIED AUGUST 15, 1903
AGED 26 YEARS

The Biggest Epitaph in Canada

I knew that Peter Verigin was a big hero to most of his Doukhobor followers, but I didn't know how big until I turned away from his gravesite and saw his epitaph on the bare rocks towering behind the site. These words are written in Russian and English with white paint on grey rock:

THIS BLESSED ROCKY BLUFF CASTS ITS MOURNFUL SAD LOOK
ON A GRAVE SUFFERINGLY MOURNFUL. HOLY.
TO CONVEY PEOPLE TRUTH OF A STORY:
HERE FLOWED ONCE IN DOUKHOBOR TEARS
A COFFIN WITH BODY OF A LEADER STRONG. MIGHTY
WITH MOURNFUL PRAYER OF SPIRITUAL WRESTLERS.
INTO THE BOWELS OF EARTH GRIEVOUSLY LOWERED,
HIS SPIRIT—ARISE FOR MEMORY EVERLASTING
IN MANY LOVING HEARTS.
HE BEQUEATHED TO US IN HOLY COVENANT
"TOIL AND PEACEFUL LIFE" WITH CHRIST.

The rocks must be ten metres tall. The epitaph would cover an average billboard, but there's more.

The grave site is a veritable fortress located on a rocky ledge above the Kootenay River near Brilliant and surrounded by a high chain-link fence topped by three strands of barbed wire. The gate is locked unless the caretaker is there—not only does this grave have the biggest epitaph, it's also the most carefully guarded.

Inside the fence is a tiny, perfect park—flower beds and carefully trimmed bushes—and at the back of the park is a long, low, white concrete

Canada's largest "tombstone" looms over the grave of Peter Verigin near Brilliant.

platform. No tombstone on the platform, however, and I couldn't get close enough to see if there was a plaque or sign to explain things. That's when I turned around to leave and saw the incredible epitaph stretched across the rocks.

Later I found out from a researcher at the Doukhobor museum in Brilliant that Verigin is indeed buried there, but there's no tombstone. Someone blew up the original, an elaborate Italian marble monument with columns and an above-ground sarcophagus, soon after it was installed. That's when Verigin's followers placed his body beneath the concrete bunker and blasted fences into the rock. That's when the place became a fortress.

That was explosion #2 for Verigin. He was killed in 1924 by a bomb as he travelled by train from one problem area to another, trying to keep the peace between his Doukhobor followers and Canadian authorities, trying to keep the peace among the Doukhobors themselves. It is thought that the breakaway sect, the Sons of Freedom, might have had something to do with both explosions, but nothing was ever proven. He was only sixty-five.

Graves That Stand Alone

I don't know if Charles Morgan Blessing had gold jingling in his pockets as he walked along the lonesome road near Barkerville one spring day in

1866, but for one reason or another, he was shot and robbed. Amazingly, police somehow found the perpetrator, James Barry, in the never-ending bush in the north country, and he went to trial before Judge Matthew Begbie. Although there are those who claim that Begbie's reputation as "the hanging judge" was not deserved, this time it was. He sentenced Barry to hang.

In the meantime, the miners and merchants of Barkerville buried Blessing near the scene of the crime and erected a wooden headboard over his grave. The headboard is still there, now enclosed within a white picket fence, alongside the Barkerville highway:

IN MEMORY OF C.M. BLESSING
A NATIVE OF OHIO AGED 30 YEARS
WAS MURDERED NEAR THIS SPOT
MAY 31, 1866

Fort St. James began as a fur-trading post, but it has ended up the nicest small town in the world. At least, that's the way it appeared to me the evening I drove in. The sun was setting over Stuart Lake, making the water gleam with gold. It was absolutely stunning, but it must happen all the time in Fort St. James. Nobody was even looking at the beauty around them. Instead, little kids were riding their bikes down the middle of the roads, moms were chatting over back fences, teenage boys and girls were teasing one another at the neighbourhood gas station. It was a scene from the 1950s when the world was kinder, smaller, and little kids could ride their bikes wherever they wanted.

The graveyard next to Our Lady of Good Hope was equally lovely. Lots of white white crosses against green green grass with a golden lake behind them. Several gravemarkers were written in the language of the Carrier Indians from that area, and one of them featured a face barely scratched onto the surface, looking for all the world like a ghost peering through the rock. It was most unusual, not at all like the death heads or cherub faces carved into some of the older stones in eastern Canada. It marks Chief Maise Tayor, who died in 1904.

Also in Fort St. James is Russ Baker, 1910-1958, buried beside that incredible lake, under a propeller mounted on a cairn of rocks:

IN MEMORY OF ONE OF CANADA'S
OUTSTANDING AVIATION PIONEERS.
HIS FAITH IN THE FUTURE OF AVIATION KNEW NO BOUNDS.
HE PIONEERED THE TRACKLESS REALMS OF SPACE,

ONE OF THE NOBLE BREED OF MEN
WHO BROUGHT COURAGE AND GLORY
TO THE NEW AGE OF FLIGHT.

The inscription pretty well tells the tale, leaving out only that Russ Baker founded Pacific Western Airlines, which eventually became part of Canadian Airlines. With airplanes so much a part of his life, it was fitting that he be flown to his last resting place in a DC-3 and that his mourners would follow in another—the first funeral cortege composed of DC-3s.

The final lines on his cairn are particularly moving. They were written by a PWA employee and chosen by Baker's wife, Madge:

I WOULD HAVE LENT THEE WINGS, DEAR HEART
EVEN THOUGH IT PUT US WORLDS APART
BUT WILD THE WINGS AND WILD THE HEART
THAT COULD US IN DEATH NOW PART.

Speaking of isolated graves, we wouldn't even know where Father Charles Marie Pandosy is buried if a BC archaeological professor hadn't gotten curious.

Father Pandosy was one of those incredibly dedicated churchmen who came to this New World to bring God and "the prayer" to those already living here. The fact that the Natives weren't particularly keen on either, that they already had a spiritual life, didn't change the dedication of those early missionaries. They soldiered on in spite of everything.

The Okanagan area was almost a piece of cake for Father Pandosy. He didn't have to worry about the Indian wars that had so plagued his first mission in the US, and he didn't have to be hungry any more—the land in the Okanagan was rich and grew whatever he planted in it. So his gardens thrived right along with his mission.

When he died in 1891, his parishioners buried him near the mission, but the exact location of his grave was lost in the shuffle when the mission lands were sold years later. It wasn't until 1983, almost one hundred years after Pandosy's death, that archaeologists found his grave in a garden patch across the road from the old mission site. It's still a garden patch—which seems rather fitting for a man who introduced gardening to the Okanagan— but one corner has been returned to grass, thanks to the Rampone family of Kelowna, who now own the land. On a big rock in the middle of the grassy patch is a plaque that says:

TO THE MEMORY OF CHARLES MARIE PANDOSY, OMI
PIERRE RICHARD, OMI, FLORIMOND GENDRE, OMI

AND THE MANY NATIVE PEOPLE
WHOSE ANCESTORS LIVED FOR CENTURIES
IN THIS VALLEY
AND THE PIONEER FAMILIES,
FOUNDERS OF THE COMMUNITY
AT ANSE AU SABLE, NOW KELOWNA

People Who Stand Alone

That's the image I have of Terry Fox, a solitary figure hip-hopping down some stretch of endless highway in Canada, on his way to raising awareness about cancer and money for research. By the time he ended his marathon in Thunder Bay, Ontario, he belonged to all of Canada, but he was born in BC and buried in BC, in the Port Coquitlam cemetery:

TERRENCE STANLEY FOX
JULY 28, 1958–JUNE 28, 1981
HE MADE HIS TOO SHORT LIFE
INTO A MARATHON OF COURAGE AND HOPE.
"SOMEWHERE THE HURTING MUST STOP." -TERRY

By Land, Not by Sea

Before planes, trains, and cars, people had enormous difficulty getting to BC. Pandosy, for example, sailed from France in February of 1847. Two months later, he landed in New York. From then on, it was horse and buggy, so that it was another six months before he finally reached his destination in northwestern Washington. Others came via the Panama Canal, which meant they were on ships for months.

When you're in Winnipeg, however, there's not much water between you and BC so it's got to be an overland trip. Thus the 160 men, women, and children who left Fort Garry in 1862 bound for the bounties of BC became known as the Overlanders.

They made it, but what a trip. Catherine Schubert had a baby about three hours after she got to Kamloops. I would have had a fit, but these pioneers were sturdier stuff. Mother and baby were fine.

In front of Enderby's United Church is a memorial to Alexander Leslie Fortune, 1831-1915, one of the famous Overlanders:

A MEMBER OF THE CARIBOO OVERLAND PARTY OF 1862
THE FIRST SETTLER IN THE NORTH OKANAGAN 1866
THE FIRST ELDER OF THE PRESBYTERIAN CHURCH IN THE VALLEY.
A FRIEND OF ALL CLASSES AND CREEDS, INDIAN AND WHITE

A GRACIOUS GENTLEMAN.
INTERRED IN LANSDOWNE CEMETERY.

Cornelius O'Keefe also arrived in the Okanagan by land. When he saw the countryside and the grass it would grow, he decided to stay on the land. The heck with gold. A good decision, as it turned out, since his stopping place and ranch turned out to be a gold mine of another sort.

When O'Keefe went back to Ontario to get himself a wife after fifteen years in the West, he got two for the price of one, one for himself and one for his partner, Thomas Greenhow. That wasn't exactly the plan, but that's how it worked out. Elizabeth Coughlan came west with her newly married friend Mary Anne, and fell in love with the man next door.

They were married by a certain Father Pandosy.

By Sea, Not by Land

In the St. Mark's Anglican Church cemetery at Ganges on Saltspring Island is a gravemarker that tells the sad tale of the *Princess Sophia*:

SACRED TO THE MEMORY
OF JEREMIAH CHIVERS SHAW
MASTER MARINER WHO WAS LOST
IN THE SINKING OF THE SS PRINCESS SOPHIA
IN THE LYNN CANAL, ALASKA, ON OCT. 25. 1918
BORN IN GLASGOW, SCOTLAND, 1875

It was such a terrible accident. The ship ran aground on a reef in a storm and hung there for three days, but rescue vessels couldn't get to it–the storm was too severe. Three hundred and sixty-four passengers and crew perished.

There are hints of other watery misfortunes in BC graveyards, naturally so since BC shares a lot of space with water. In Ross Bay alone are three such references: Dr. T.B. Baillie "was lost 62 miles off Cape Flattery, Nov. 12, 1880," Captain Magnus Thompson died at Carmanah "through the wreck of the ship *Janet Cowan* Dec. 31, 1895," and Patrick Burke "perished in the wreck of the SS *Islander* near Juneau in one of his brave acts on Aug. 15, 1901."

What a tantalizing hint—"in one of his brave acts." What other brave acts were there, I wonder? I haven't found out yet, but I'd like to.

Also in Ross Bay are several references to the Point Ellice Bridge disaster, Victoria Day, 1896. I found out later that on that terrible day the Point Ellice Bridge collapsed without warning. A streetcar on the bridge plunged into the water beneath, and some fifty-five men, women, and children were killed. That they were on their way to celebrations of the day made the whole thing seem even more tragic.

Ashes to Ashes

Pauline Johnson was a poet. Therefore, her ashes should have been scattered over Siwash Rock near Stanley Park. It would have been the poetic thing to do and, in fact, most Canadians think that's exactly what happened.

But no, when Pauline Johnson died in 1913, her body was cremated, that much is true, but her ashes were buried in Stanley Park, not thrown away at all. Along with the ashes were buried two of her books: *Legends of Vancouver* and *Flint and Feather*.

Together, the books and the ashes lie beneath a boulder close to the large official monument beside the road through Stanley Park. There are signs. You can't miss it.

Butchart Gardens on Vancouver Island came about because Robert Butchart was in the cement business, which meant he needed gravel, which meant he left behind unsightly quarries. One day his wife said she'd had enough, and she began to plant things in the quarry nearest her house. The rest is history.

With the most beautiful garden in her back yard, one would expect flowers at a funeral, right? Wrong. When Robert Butchart died in 1943, his widow directed that there be one small spray of flowers on his casket, no more, and no elaborate grave site either. His ashes were scattered on the waters of the Saanich Inlet below the famous gardens.

Ditto when she died. She directed that every detail of her funeral should be exactly the same as her husband's, and so it was.

Roderick Haig-Brown got flowers, sort of. The well-known writer, angler, and conservationist lived for many years on an acreage called Above Tide, near Campbell River. After his death in October 1976, his wife scattered his ashes in a copse of trees near their home, within sight of a daffodil garden that he had prepared for the next spring.

J.S. Woodsworth, the founder of the Co-operative Commonwealth Federation (CCF), died in 1942 at age sixty-seven. Like the well-organized politician he was, he had arranged every detail of his funeral in advance including the instruction that his body was to be cremated and then scattered over the waters of the Gulf of Georgia. His wife carried out his last wish, casting the ashes onto the water, and then added her own touch. From a shamrock plant that he had given her years before, she took a few leaves and threw them into the ocean alongside the ashes.

The Night the Turtle Roared

When I saw the name Leitch in the Cranbrook cemetery, I wondered why it rang a bell. There were six of them buried there, including Alexander and his wife, Rosemary, along with four young sons: John, Allan, Athol, and Wilfred. It was when I registered the date of their deaths—all died April 29, 1903—that I realized I had found the family of Frankie Slide.

When Turtle Mountain came crashing down on the Crowsnest Pass town of Frank on the Alberta side of the border, it destroyed almost everything in its path—houses, roads, stores, people. It even covered up the Frank cemetery so there's a cemetery underneath the cemetery formed by that terrible pile of rocks. But here and there were unaccountable escapes, like a baby found unharmed, apparently thrown from her bed by the wind that preceded the actual avalanche and lying safely beyond the wreckage. That was the theory anyway; the baby was too young to tell her own story.

The media loved the tale—a child miraculously spared and apparently unclaimed. That's when she got the name Frankie Slide. But, in fact, she wasn't unknown at all. She was Marion Leitch, youngest of the Leitch family, and her two older sisters, who had also survived, were quite able to identify her. It was still a good story, however, and remains a part of the folklore of the Frank Slide.

In Remembrance of Four Little Girls

The four Hoffstrom girls were asleep as their dad Otto drove onto the ferry to cross the Peace River. They'd had a long day at the Dawson Creek Stampede, and they were tuckered out. No need to get out of the car. They'd been across this stretch of the river many times.

But this time, something went terribly wrong, and the car plunged into the fast-flowing river. Otto escaped but try as he might, he couldn't get his girls out. The doors wouldn't open; the current was too strong. Lillian, Florence, Olga, and Agnes drowned.

How any parent could deal with such a tragedy, I don't know, but Otto chose to build a church in memory of his girls. He was a builder, he had already built two churches in northern BC, and he just happened to have a sawmill. It all fit, and within six weeks, he and neighbours and friends had completed the Church of the Good Shepherd in Taylor.

It's still in use, more than sixty years after the terrible accident that inspired it.

The Last Word

Lead with your strong suit, I say. This is the inscription on the gravemarker in the Windermere cemetery of Mary Evelyn Grieve Powles, who died December 19, 1923:

> I HAVE THE BODY OF BUT A WEAK
> AND FEEBLE WOMAN,
> BUT I HAVE THE HEART OF A KING.

Alberta

✝

Where Seldom Is Heard
a Praiseworthy Word

WHEN I WAS A KID GROWING UP IN ALBERTA'S
PEACE RIVER COUNTRY, I DAYDREAMED THAT I WOULD
LIVE ALL OVER THE WORLD WHEN I GREW UP.
JUST LET ME OUT OF HERE, I'D SAY TO MYSELF,
AND I'LL BE A MISSIONARY IN AFRICA MAYBE
OR A BRAIN SURGEON IN LONDON OR AN ACTRESS
ON BROADWAY. THE WORLD WILL BE MY OYSTER.
JUST GIVE ME ROOM!

Well, what can I say? It didn't work out that way, and many years later I'm still in Alberta, which is why I can speak of Albertans with some authority. I am one, I'm surrounded by them, I even gave birth to three of them. I know this bunch.

That being the case, believe me when I say we are the most aggravating people in the graveyard. Strong and silent to the end. It's the cowboy in us, I guess, that and the fact that we're young. We didn't start formal graveyards until the late 1800s, and by then we had neither the time nor the money to get fancy out there. Nor the inclination, for that matter. Somehow, Alberta started silent in its graveyards and has more or less stayed that way.

Our most popular epitaph, for example, is the totally safe, totally boring, "Ever Loved, Ever Remembered." Where is the passion? I would grouse over and over again when I found those words. Where is the drama?

I knew the answer, of course. The drama, the passion, is there, but we don't let it show. We are Albertan. We don't carry on. However, there were times in my research when, after driving what seemed like thousands of kilometres of straight roads to nowhere, I would gladly have traded a strong silent Albertan for a noisy, sentimental, boastful citizen of somewhere else. Please, I would say as I approached a strange cemetery, please tell me something.

Now and then, it would. This is what I found on the gravemarker of Hulbert (Hullie) Henry Orser, 1897-1981, in the Earlville Rutherford cemetery near Ponoka:

HE FEARED GOD, DID NOTHING MEAN
SHOT STRAIGHT AND STAYED CLEAN.

That, to me, is the quintessential Alberta sentiment. No-nonsense, a tip of the hat to God and cleanliness, a kind word for guns and kindness. What more could you want?

Eventually I managed to find, here and there, now and then, enough historical hints to fill this chapter and then some. Alberta's reticence proved to be good training ground for the rest of my graveyard travels because exploring graveyards is not just a matter of reading the words. It's a matter of feeling them. In Calgary's Union cemetery, one day, I found a small insignificant marker in memory of "Dear Old Fred, Killed in Action, Vimy Ridge, April 9, 1917, Aged 21 Years."

No last name on the marker, no indication of who might have known Fred as "Dear Old Fred." Not a mother, surely, or a girlfriend. Maybe companions? But why weren't they at the war too? And why wasn't this marker among the Legion markers in the veterans sections?

I still had Fred on the mind when I read about the battle at Vimy Ridge. It was a terrible thing—thousands died before it was over, but Fred died the first day. Fred didn't even know if they'd won or not. Fred died before it was even named. I couldn't get him out of my mind, still can't, even though I was given very little to work with.

That emotional involvement, I learned from Alberta graveyards, is the key to exploring when words are few and far between.

Before the Missionaries

Before the white man came to tell the Indians how to live and die, they did both in a variety of ways. Every tribe, every season, every place required a different set of behaviours, so if a member of the community died, for example, he or she might be buried underground—unless it was winter. He or she might be left under a pile of rocks or tree branches—unless there were no trees or rocks. They might be left in a tipi filled with artifacts to speed their entry into the next world—unless they weren't of sufficient status to get this kind of treatment, and so on. There were no hard and fast rules that covered every occasion so I can't say that such and such happened without fail. What I learned is that tree burials or platform burials often took place in southern Alberta even though "burial" isn't quite the right word since it connotes being put underground. Indians who put their dead on hillsides or ledges or platforms did so specifically to avoid being underground. They believed that the spirit of the deceased had to be as close as possible and as free as possible to join the ancestors above. Thus the word "burial" in this context means disposition.

When Mrs. Eli Hodder wrote about Coalbanks—which later became Lethbridge—she recorded that she looked out of her window the first morning she was there expecting to see the river valley. Instead, she was rivetted by the sight of four platforms built in the trees nearby, a body carefully wrapped and left on each one. That was in 1883, not that many years ago as history is measured.

And the most famous tree burial of all, the one for the Blood chieftain Seen From Afar, remained in the valley near the Oldman River in Lethbridge until 1902 when finally a flood carried it away. He died in the smallpox epidemic of 1869.

There's one tree grave left in Alberta, ironically in northern Alberta where the custom was not particularly prevalent. Years ago, a child died and was enclosed in a hollowed-out log that was then placed in the branches of a small poplar near the community of Indian Cabins. Over the years, the poplar grew, so the tiny bundle is now near the top of a very tall poplar, where it is, I hope, high enough and remote enough to remain.

Speaking of children, there's a lovely story in the Rosebud local history book about the cottonwood trees in that area. When an Indian baby died, according to this story, its body would be left in the branches of a big cottonwood. In the spring when the seed pods formed on the tree and flew through the air like so much fluff, it was thought to be the spirit of the child winging its way to another life.

A Clash of Traditions

When I found Chief Crowfoot's grave, I kept wondering why there wasn't more. After all, he was just about the most famous and respected of all Indian leaders in western Canada. Surely his grave site should be marked with some grandeur, signs at the very least, but it's just a modest little metal gravemarker enclosed by an iron grille fence on the southern tip of the Cluny graveyard. The inscription says:

CHIEF CROWFOOT

DIED APRIL 26, 1890

FATHER OF OUR PEOPLE

Poor Crowfoot. He died when life for Indians was a little bit Christian, a little bit traditional, and a whole lot confusing. He was right on the cusp between old and new, and that tension coloured everything that happened around his death. For one thing, he is supposed to have made a wonderful deathbed speech. It's quoted everywhere, but there's no solid proof that he actually said the words credited to him. Still, I figure, what does it matter? They are lovely, they sound like him, and history can afford to be generous. This is what he is supposed to have said:

> A little while and I will be gone from among you, whither I cannot tell. From nowhere we come, into nowhere we go. What is life? It is a flash of firefly in the night. It is a breath of a buffalo in the wintertime. It is as the little shadow that runs across the grass and loses itself in the sunset.

And, he might have added, it is the fluff that flies from a cottonwood tree in the spring breezes.

Early in April 1890, Crowfoot moved his lodge to a protected spot in the lee of a hillside near Blackfoot Crossing. He knew his time was near in spite of all the work the medicine men did to drive away the evil spirits, in spite of the efforts of Dr. George, who wanted the medicine men to hush up for a while so that Crowfoot could sleep. Nothing helped. He slipped into a coma and then into death, at which point his wives began a traditional death wail, and the camp announcer ran through the area saying, "He is no more. No one like him will fill his place."

When it came time for the funeral, Father Leon Doucet took charge and conducted a full Catholic burial service, claiming Crowfoot had been baptized in the Catholic faith and would have wanted it that way. J.W. Tims, an Anglican minister who had also served among the Indians of southern

Chief Crowfoot's modest grave near Cluny overlooks historic Blackfoot Crossing.

Alberta, wasn't so sure about that. "He died as he had lived in the faith of his father," Tims claimed, pointing out that Crowfoot's favourite horse had been shot upon his death so that the chief might ride it in the spirit world. Didn't sound like standard Christian practice to Tims.

At the graveyard, Doucet and the Indian agent wanted the casket to be buried in the Christian tradition, completely covered with earth, but the Blackfoot people wanted it to remain above ground so that his spirit would be free to enter the spirit world. How to break such a cultural impasse? Compromise, of course. The casket was buried half in and half out of the ground, and a small log house built over it for shelter. And that's how it stayed until the cemetery was cleaned up years later and the casket reburied completely.

When you stand on the hill that holds Crowfoot, you can look south and see Blackfoot Crossing where the historic Treaty #7 was signed in 1877. It's still empty of people and houses. Use your imagination and it could be 1877. Turn around, however, and the grave looks down upon a town, a major highway, and fields as far as the eye can see. It's not 1877 by any stretch of the imagination in that direction.

In other words, Crowfoot is still on the cusp.

After the Missionaries Came the Graveyards

Don't get me wrong—the missionaries didn't cause people to die; they did, however, bring along Christian practices concerning death and burial, and that meant graveyards. In fact, some of the very first graveyards appeared because they needed them for their own families.

Rev. George McDougall came to western Canada in 1862 to establish the Methodist church among the Indians. He believed, as did most Christians in those days, that it was the responsibility of civilized Christians to bring both their religion and their civilization to those who had neither. Such a goal seems arrogant by today's standards, but McDougall was not at all arrogant. He was a humble servant of the Lord—that's how he would have expressed it—and as such he established the Victoria Mission east of Edmonton on the North Saskatchewan River to serve the Indians of the area. With a church and school, a farm and grist mill, it was to be a model operation, providing food for both soul and body.

The trouble was the mission didn't have a hospital, and more to the point, they didn't have the smallpox vaccine. When a terrible smallpox epidemic swept across the west from 1869 to 1870, thousands of Indians and Metis died—some say as many as half of the total population. And in the McDougall household, first eleven-year-old Flora "entered into rest," then Georgiana, nineteen years old, and a year later Abigail, wife of John McDougall, George's son.

Their graves remain, all alone beside the river at the old mission south of Smoky Lake, the only clue to their deaths being the dates: 1870 and 1871.

From there, the McDougalls moved to Edmonton and then to Morley, each time establishing another church and ministry among the Natives of the area. He was a remarkable man, and I sometimes think he must have had a lot of fun. He was kind of king of the west—most of the Native people liked and trusted him, certainly the Canadian government appreciated him because he'd wade in where angels and eastern politicians feared to tread, so he had access to everyone and everywhere. The western skies and mountains were his, all his—except when Father Lacombe claimed his share. But there was plenty to go around.

It all came to an abrupt end one wintry day when McDougall didn't return to base camp during a buffalo-hunting expedition. After two weeks of searching, they found his body. He had died of an apparent heart attack at the age of fifty-four.

He's not buried with his girls on the river bank. He's on a hillside instead, within sight of the Rocky Mountains, across the road from the McDougall United Church near Morley:

THE DECEASED WAS FOR 16 YEARS CHAIRMAN
OF THE WESLEYAN MISSIONS IN THE NORTHWEST.
HE LOST HIS WAY ON THE PRAIRIE ABOUT 40 MILES

EAST OF THIS PLACE ON JAN. 24, 1876.
HIS BODY WAS FOUND
ON THE 5TH OF THE FOLLOWING MONTH
AND INTERRED HERE BY HIS SORROWING FAMILY
WHO HAVE ERECTED THIS TRIBUTE IN HIS MEMORY.

Most Unusual Burial Request

Father Albert Lacombe had his hand and his heart in just about everything that happened in western Canada for over sixty years. But you would never know it from the no-nonsense words over his last resting place in a crypt at the Roman Catholic Church in St. Albert:

PERE LACOMBE, OMI
BORN IN QUEBEC IN 1827
CAME TO THE WEST IN 1849
DIED IN 1916, RIP

Actually, that should read last resting *places*. Father Lacombe divided himself up at death, which is why he gets my nod for most unusual burial arrangements. When he died in Calgary in 1916, he asked that his body be returned to St. Albert, where he had started his missionary work in the west, but that his heart remain in Blackfoot country. I took that to mean that his heart would have returned long ago—dust to dust, etc.—to some sun-parched hill in southern Alberta. How very appropriate, I thought.

But no, his heart never made it onto the prairie. It stayed, instead, for the next seventy-six years in a sealed container in a locked room under the care of the Sisters of Charity of Providence. It wasn't until 1992 that it was finally buried in the regular manner in a cemetery behind the Father Lacombe Nursing Home in Calgary beneath a small stone that says:

HERE RESTS HIS HEART

Seems a bit anticlimactic for such an important heart. Still, I saw the heart before it went underground and talked to the nuns who cared for it the last few years, so I can understand why they did what they did.

It's hard to look after a heart, as it turns out. Sister Helen, who showed it to me, had so many worries: that I as a journalist might scoff at it and her, that the container might one day spring a leak, that vandals might do it harm, that they—the nuns—weren't doing enough to honour the blessed Father, and so on. At one point, she showed me Father Lacombe's sock darner and I very nearly blurted out, "Did poor old Father Lacombe have to darn his own socks in between saving souls and railways?" But it was exactly the sort of thing Sister Helen dreaded—any levity about the man and his heart. So I bit my tongue and tried to understand such devotion.

From the moment he arrived in western Canada, the young priest picked up his clerical robes and got to work spreading the word of God; establishing schools, farms, and social services for the needy; mediating disputes between the Indians, the railway, and the settlers; raising money for good causes; ministering to the sick and dying. During the awful smallpox epidemic, he went wherever he was called, with no thought for his own health, although I did read that he sometimes held a camphor-filled quill between his teeth, whether as a preventive measure or a way of screening out the terrible smells, I don't know. Anyway, he was indefatigable right up to his death at age eighty-nine.

His funeral in Calgary was filled with pomp and circumstance and stirring words, after which they put the body of the old trooper on a special coach provided by the CPR and took it north to Edmonton and then to St. Albert. All along the way, people waited and watched. Some waved when he went by, men took off their hats, women made the sign of the cross, children stood silent.

The Man of the Good Heart—so named by the Blackfoot—had died.

The Grave with the Best View

I grew up in the Peace River country so I knew about Twelve Foot Davis and his wonderful grave up on the Peace River hills overlooking the Peace and Smoky Rivers. Made great good sense to me, that a man would choose that lovely spot for a last resting place, and whenever I visited the original grave, I was one big pile of mush. So thoughtful that Peace River Jim Cornwall would remember a promise and bring his friend to this spot to be buried, so lovely, etc., etc.

But then I read Peter Newman's book about the Hudson's Bay Company and had to revise some of my thinking. According to Newman, Davis wasn't primarily interested in the scenic value of the spot. He wanted instead to be buried "with my feet pointing downhill so I can piss on the Hudson's Bay Company."

Twelve Foot Davis was not twelve feet tall. He got his nickname when he discovered that 212 feet (65 m) along Williams Creek in the Cariboo had been staked out by two men. Since each was allowed only 100 feet (30 m) in total, Davis claimed the twelve-foot piece (3.6 m) between them and found enough gold to make himself a tidy sum for those days.

Did he then head back to the US and a comfortable life? Don't be silly.

He decided he liked the north and went over the mountains to the Peace River area. There he became a "free trader," which means he bought furs from the Natives and then traded them to the Hudson's Bay Company for other supplies, which he then used to trade with the Indians for more furs, and so on. It wasn't exactly a get-rich-quick scheme, especially since the Hudson's Bay Company didn't do him any favours, which may account for the comment quoted above. Also, Twelve Foot Davis couldn't say no; if people needed help or supplies, they got it. In fact, Davis left his various supply cabins open at all times just in case people needed to help themselves. He'd get paid eventually, he figured, which is why Cornwall put these words on his friend's grave:

> PATHFINDER, PIONEER,
> MINER AND TRADER
> HE WAS EVERY MAN'S FRIEND
> AND NEVER LOCKED HIS CABIN DOOR.

And that should have been the end of the story—friend keeps a promise and buries friend where he wanted to be. But the gravemarker on the hill became a party place and a favourite target of vandals. Eventually, the town of Peace River had to replace the original with a concrete structure that would withstand the wear and tear that came its way up on that most beautiful spot in the valley. So it looks rather like a bunker now, an impregnable fortress that repels rather than attracts, as unlike the man it marks as anything could be.

Still, the words are there, the hills are there, and a river runs through it.

On the Other Side of the Mountain

Meanwhile, around the corner on the same hill is a cairn with these words:

> IN MEMORY OF WILLIAM GREENE MD DDS
> SAN FRANCISCO—MAY 2, 1874
> EDMONTON—AUGUST 28, 1952
> ONE OF THE FIRST TO FLY
> INVENTOR, EXPLORER, PIONEER

The people of Peace River knew Bill Greene as their quiet dentist, a nice guy who liked to hunt and fish and poke around in the hills. So when this cairn went up with the line that he was "one of the first to fly," a lot of people said, "I beg your pardon? Are you talking about our Bill Greene?"

Yes, as it happens.

Bill Greene grew up in the US and for a while was determined to invent a machine that would fly—just like the Wright brothers and Glenn Curtiss. By 1907, according to his own accounts, he had a biplane that flew or "hopped" fairly well, which would have made him one of the "first" to fly, but he could never get an engine big enough to power his machines. After crashing as often as most people blow their noses—his own words again—he gave up on the idea and moved to northern Canada where he enjoyed having his feet on the ground. "I can close up the office and go away for months with a tent, some grub, and my gun. That's happiness," he told a reporter years later.

When he died, his ashes were scattered from a plane, of course, over the Greene Valley Game Preserve, named for him, of course.

How the West Was Won

When I found the Cecil Denny marker in Calgary's Union cemetery, all I could say was "Wow." It was all there in one hundred words or less—how we came to settle this country and learn to live together, a textbook written in stone:

> IN MEMORY OF CAPTAIN SIR CECIL EDWARD DENNY BT
> SIXTH BARONET OF TRALEE CASTLE, IRELAND
> BORN IN HAMPSHIRE, ENGLAND, 14TH DEC. 1850
> DIED IN EDMONTON, ALBERTA, 24TH AUGUST, 1928
> CROSSED THE PLAINS IN 1874 AS INSPECTOR
> IN THE ORIGINAL NORTH WEST MOUNTED POLICE CO.
> FOUNDER OF FORTS MACLEOD AND CALGARY
> HONORARY CHIEFTAIN IN BLACKFOOT NATION
> INDIAN AGENT, GOVERNMENT ARCHIVIST, EXPLORER,
> PIONEER, ADVENTURER AND AUTHOR
> HE KNEW NOT FEAR.
> A BORN OPTIMIST.

When Cecil Denny heard in 1874 that the Canadian government was recruiting men to form a police force in western Canada, he joined up. He knew beans about the West; he knew even less about the Indians and the illegal liquor trade. He just knew the trip across the Canadian prairies sounded like the adventure he was looking for. And it was, especially when the food ran out and storms killed the horses and travel was so hard as to be almost impossible. Other than that, it was a great adventure for the 274 men who left Manitoba one sunny July morning. And just as advertised, they set about doing police work as soon as they unpacked their bags at Fort

Captain Cecil Denny's inscription in Calgary's Union cemetery tells the story of a life of adventure.

Macleod five months later. Not that there was a Fort Macleod. That came later when Commissioner James Macleod and Cecil Denny decided on a site and began building.

Everything those first NWMP members did, they had to do by the seat of their pants. There were no manuals on "How to negotiate when you don't know the language and culture." There were no established procedures for getting rid of white trash who sold liquor and other rotgut to the Indians. Cecil Denny and the rest just had to figure it out, and by and large they managed quite nicely.

It was just when the bureaucrats in Ottawa got into the act that troubles began. For one thing, they installed Indian agents, some of whom had never worked with Indians. Bad idea. Cecil Denny took on the job for a while, but then Ottawa decreed that he should decrease food rations across the board. What a way to build trust and good relationships, Denny argued back, but it was no use, Ottawa knew best, or so they thought. So that's when Denny embarked on new adventures—exploring, surveying, farming, and writing. His title came about when a half brother died back in the old country, but it didn't make much difference to Denny. He never got to live in a castle or rub shoulders with royalty. He just got to continue living in western Canada with the letters BT after his name, and when he died, he got to have one of the best "books" I've ever found in a graveyard.

The Graveyard That Doesn't Want to Be Found

Frog Lake graveyard is an official historic site, but you have to work hard to find it. The first time I drove through the area, I was practically in Cold Lake before I realized I'd missed a turn somewhere. So it was back down the same bumpy road to the Frog Lake store—that's all there is—and east on a dirt road to the graveyard. No fancy signs along the way. Just keep watching until you see seven black-and-white crosses and one RCMP marker next to a large Historic Sites Board of Canada cairn on a small curve of land next to the road. Then, you'll know you've found Alberta's most important reminder of the North-West Rebellion.

The cairn states simply:

NORTH WEST REBELLION FROG LAKE MASSACRE
HERE ON 2ND APRIL, 1885,
REBEL INDIANS UNDER BIG BEAR MASSACRED:
REV. FATHER LEON ADELARD FAFARD, OMI
REV. FATHER FELIX MARCHAND, O.M.I.
INDIAN AGENT THOMAS QUINN
FARM INSTRUCTOR JOHN DELANEY
JOHN ALEXANDER GOWANLOCK, WILLIAM CAMPBELL GILCHRIST
GEORGE DILL, CHARLES GOUIN, JOHN WILLISCROFT
THEY TOOK PRISONERS MRS. THERESA DELANEY
MRS. THERESA GOWANLOCK

And that's the story, more or less. Disgruntled Indians killed nine white men at the Frog Lake trading post. They took some women prisoner but let them go later. They did all of the above because they were mad at the Indian agent and the government for refusing supplies at various times, and with a frustration fuelled by alcohol, they killed.

Until just a few years ago, the word "massacre" was used whenever Frog Lake was mentioned, but words can be revised. This is what it now says on interpretive panels around the perimeter of the graveyard:

> In the early morning, Indians went about collecting all the arms
> of the white people. After breakfast, the whites were herded into
> the church, a foreshortened mass was said, then the Indians
> tried to move everyone to their camp. But Tom Quinn refused
> to go, the last it seems in a long series of disagreements between

The markers in Frog Lake cemetery say "massacre," but different words are used on the interpretive panels.

he and Wandering Spirit, and the war chief shot him. Whether it was planned to kill the white people, none can say. But when one started shooting, pretty soon everybody was shooting. A few brief moments of fury, dust and smoke and nine people lay dead or dying on the ground. Theresa Delaney and Theresa Gowanlock escaped death because the Indians disdained to kill women.

Whatever the words used, the news scared the wits out of the white population of the prairies, as isolated and unprotected as they were. But Frog Lake was a one-time thing. There were no other battles fought in Alberta during the North-West Rebellion. The rest of the rebellion happened in Saskatchewan.

However, I did find lots of evidence of the North-West Rebellion in Alberta graveyards including this puzzling bit of information on a small gravestone in High Prairie:

IN LOVING MEMORY OF PETER TOMKINS
BORN DEC. 10, 1873 DIED JAN. 21, 1940
VETERAN 1885 REBELLION

I got interested after I did the arithmetic. After all, if Peter had been born in 1873, he would have been twelve years old at the time of the rebellion. Was he a child who was captured during the fighting, or did his dad go off to war and never come back, thus making his son a veteran of sorts? What was the story?

It took some sleuthing. Local historians knew nothing about Mr. Tomkins. Records from Frog Lake mentioned no such name. It was only after I called the Saskatchewan provincial archives that I learned that, indeed, Tomkins (spelled with a p—Tompkins) had been involved in the Riel rebellion. The birth date on the stone is wrong—it should be 1864 or 1865.

He got into trouble when Riel's men found him trying to repair a telegraph pole they had destroyed in order to prevent communication with the outside world. It's hard to defend yourself from the top of a pole so Tompkins was taken prisoner and kept in various locations around Batoche during the last two weeks of fighting. He was freed when Riel surrendered, but later testified against him.

After he became a farm instructor and then land agent in the Peace River country, he had second thoughts about Riel and told his son: "Pete, someday these scissor bills that they've got who put Riel to hang him, they'll be gone and another outfit will spring up and they'll see the mistake that these guys made. They should never have hanged Riel. He never did anything worse than a good Union man would do to his group, and someday they'll build a monument."

The Royal Treatment

Ranchers are Alberta's royalty. They rule over huge tracts of prairie and foothill; they obey the seasons and the sun, not the alarm clock; they can command their subjects with the flick of a rope; they can roll a cigarette with one hand. How cool can you get? Never mind that the life is often dangerous, dirty, and difficult, we still admire it and emulate it. And every chance we get, we mention it on our gravemarkers. This is the Cowboy's Prayer that often appears on more recent markers:

HEAVENLY FATHER, WE PAUSE, MINDFUL
OF THE MANY BLESSINGS YOU HAVE BESTOWED UPON US.
WE ASK THAT YOU BE WITH US AT THIS RODEO
AND WE PRAY THAT YOU WILL GUIDE US IN THE ARENA OF LIFE.
HELP US LORD TO LIVE OUR LIVES IN SUCH A MANNER
THAT WHEN WE MAKE THE LAST INEVITABLE RIDE
TO THE COUNTRY UP THERE, WHERE THE GRASS GROWS
LUSH GREEN AND STIRRUP-HIGH,

AND THE WATER RUNS COOL, CLEAR AND DEEP,
THAT YOU, AS OUR LAST JUDGE, WILL TELL US
THAT OUR ENTRY FEES ARE PAID.

It's such a contradiction—that cowboys should be writing poems and speaking up on their gravemarkers when the heroes of classic cowboy movies said little more than Yep, Nope, and Ma'am. But here's more proof that a home on the range wasn't entirely silent. This is a poem written by Roland Roy Eastman, 1916-1990, and reproduced on his gravemarker at Rosemary:

WE ROAMED THE RANGE TOGETHER,
UNDAUNTED, UNFETTERED SO FREE.
OVER TRAILS THAT ARE NOW FORGOTTEN,
MY BROWN PONY AND ME.
OVER THE HILLS AND VALLEYS,
OUT WHERE THE WILD SAGE GROWS,
OH GIVE ME BACK THAT LIFE SO FREE,
THAT ONLY A COWBOY KNOWS.

Guy Weadick must have sensed that the cowboy thing would be a long-lasting affair. It was he who put on a black, high-crowned cowboy hat and came up from the States to Calgary to sell the idea of an annual party

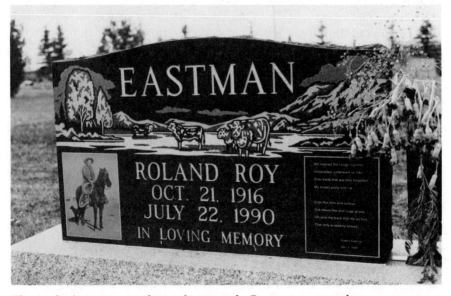

This cowboy's poetry graces his tombstone in the Rosemary graveyard.

that would feature horses—anything to do with horses—and Indians. An unbeatable combination, he said, and he was right. The first Calgary Stampede in 1912 was a huge success, and has been ever since.

Weadick, 1885-1953, got mad at Calgary and the Stampede for a while, but he came back to the country to be buried in the High River cemetery:

ORIGINATOR OF THE CALGARY STAMPEDE
A LOYAL SON OF HIS ADOPTED WEST

At that famous first stampede, Tom Three Persons stayed on the infamous Cyclone longer than anybody else and earned himself the right to put a bucking horse on his gravemarker in the St. Mary's graveyard on the Blood Reserve plus the words:

WORLD'S CHAMPION BRONCO BUSTER
SEPTEMBER, 1912 CALGARY, ALBERTA.

The story is the stuff of legends, literally, since there are now folk songs and poems about Tom's famous ride. He was just an ordinary guy, a local cowboy from the Blood Reserve near Cardston. Nobody expected much from him, but somehow he survived his first two rides and got into the finals.

That's when he drew Cyclone, the outlaw horse that had dumped his last 129 riders, the horse that could go every which way all at once. Tom knew he was a goner. Nobody could ride that crazy horse, but one of Tom's friends advised him not to be fooled by Cyclone. It seems as if he's going to fall over backwards, but he's not. Just hang on, his friend said.

So that's what Tom did, and he won the big prize. World's Champion Bronco Buster. The medal was buried with him years later.

Good News in the Graveyards

I found thirty-six different languages in Alberta graveyards—Welsh, Italian, Ukrainian, Chinese, Arabic, Icelandic, German, etc.,—and that, I think, is the good news that we can read in graveyards. We've come from so many different places and have apparently learned how to live together. Good for us.

Many of those who came with different languages came to "homestead." It's a word unique to western Canada. I didn't know that until I explored Ontario and kept hearing about land "grants." What's this grant stuff? I asked, and learned that other parts of Canada did not parcel themselves out at ten dollars for 160 acres. That's what the Canadian government did in the West to induce settlement.

And it worked. People came from all over the world, especially Europe, to take advantage of the ten-dollar deal. And that's how "homestead" came to be part of our vocabulary, but it means much more than the actual parcel of land. It means a new start, hard work, deprivation, disappointment, struggle, occasional success, family, and community. It means so much that it's hard to carve it in stone. At least that's my theory explaining why it appears on so few gravemarkers. That and the fact that many of the original homesteaders were buried without much ceremony and certainly without big expensive markers. Over the years, their markers simply disappeared.

The Shandro family came to Canada in 1889 from Bukovina, Western Ukraine, and if you want to know how the West was won, listen to this. Anastasia and Stefan had children—how many I'm not sure—but there's a gravemarker in the St. Mary's Russo Greek Orthodox churchyard near Willingdon erected in their memory by their forty-two grandchildren. Part of it says:

> THEY CAME AND FOUND A GOOD LAND,
> THEY PLOUGHED AND SOWED THEIR SEED,
> FAITH IN GOD THEIR STRONGHOLD,
> NEIGHBORLINESS THEIR CREED . . .
> AND NOW THE SONS AND DAUGHTERS
> OF THOSE WHO LED THE WAY,
> ARE PASSING ON THAT SPIRIT
> TO THEIR CHILDREN DAY BY DAY.

The gravemarker that speaks to me of homesteading more than any words could, however, is in the St. Vladimir cemetery near McLennan. I can't even read the name or the inscription because it's in a language I don't know, but I do know the picture. It shows a man in his fifties maybe, dressed in his best white shirt and his best bib overalls. His brow is whiter than the rest of his face because, of course, he usually wears a hat. Make that a cap in view of the overalls.

I know that man, not literally but figuratively. He's my dad, who always had a white brow and whose idea of dressing up was to put on clean overalls. Not that he had much choice in the matter—there wasn't money for much else. He was a homesteader, after all.

Five Famous and One Tired Woman

I love the Tired Woman's epitaph. I never thought I'd find it in sensible old Alberta, but there it was one day in the Okotoks cemetery, a flat marker with this message laughing up at me:

Humour, such as the Tired Woman's epitaph in Okotoks, is the exception rather than the rule in most graveyards.

WEEP NOT FOR ME NOW,
WEEP NOT FOR ME NEVER,
FOR I'M GOING TO DO NOTHING
FOREVER AND EVER.

Good for you, Harriet Elizabeth Connell, 1898-1989, I thought. Go for it. But most women do not wish to call attention to themselves. Just because they taught school for forty years or made fifty quilts a year on behalf of the church, or raised ten kids on a widow's pension is not reason enough to put praise on a gravestone. No, indeed. Just plant some petunias, if you have time, I can hear them saying. Nothing special.

As a result, there's seldom anything special on a woman's gravemarker in Alberta.

Take the Famous Five, the women who girded up their loins and challenged the British North America Act, no less. For years, Emily Murphy was told in her courtroom in Edmonton that she couldn't hear legal cases because she wasn't a "person" according to the BNA Act.

Baloney, she said, or words to that effect, and went right ahead with her courtroom work. But the same tired argument was used against her when organizations across Canada forwarded her name as the first woman to sit in Canada's Senate. No way, the government kept saying. She's not a person. Emily had had enough of this guff. Off went a petition, first to the Supreme Court of Canada and later to the Privy Council of England, asking, "Are women persons?" It was signed by Emily Murphy, Nellie McClung, Louise McKinney, Irene Parlby, and Henrietta Muir Edwards, all from Alberta. The Famous Five, as they became known.

In time, the answer came back. Yes, women are persons. But there's more than one way to keep an uppity woman down. Emily Murphy never did get asked to the Senate. She did, however, get more words on her tomb than anybody else in the Edmonton Mausoleum. I know, I counted:

EMILY FERGUSON MURPHY (JANEY CANUCK)
BELOVED WIFE OF ARTHUR MURPHY, MA.
1868-1933
DECORATED BY HIS MAJESTY KING GEORGE V
A LADY OF GRACE OF THE ORDER OF ST. JOHN OF JERUSALEM
IN 1914. FIRST WOMAN IN THE BRITISH EMPIRE
TO BE APPOINTED A POLICE MAGISTRATE
BEING ALSO JUDGE OF THE JUVENILE COURT FOR ALBERTA
ORIGINATOR AND LEADER OF MOVEMENT ADMITTING WOMEN
TO THE SENATE OF CANADA.
AUTHOR, JURIST, CRUSADER IN SOCIAL REFORMS,
GREAT CITIZEN.

But the other four are good Albertans, staunchly modest to the end. Nellie McClung is buried at Royal Oak in Victoria. Her marker says simply "Loved and Remembered," both of which are true, of course, but so much more could have been said. (Nellie is, of course, claimed by provinces other than Alberta.)

Irene Parlby is buried at Alix. Henrietta Muir Edwards is buried in Edmonton at the Mount Pleasant cemetery. Neither marker says boo about the person it marks.

Louise McKinney shares a gravemarker with her husband in the Claresholm cemetery. His side says "Father," and her side says "Mother."

Can't argue with that, except I'd like to.

The Most Original Tribute

Tristan Jackson of Langdon sent me a homemade tape about a homemade headstone, the one he made for his mother. The tape was absolutely fascinating—he stood in front of a camera and gradually unfolded the story of his mother's death, complete with a surprise ending. The headstone, which I went to see later in the Irricana cemetery, was equally compelling:

JACQUELINE JACKSON-BERTRAM 1940-1992
IN SPACE THINGS TOUCH
IN TIME THINGS PART.

The headstone is essentially a large boulder with a flat front onto which words and pictures have been applied. Jacqueline selected the words before her death, and Tristan sandblasted them into the stone even though he's still not sure what they mean. The pictures, however, are the product of Tristan, his wife, and four kids—pictures of Grandma Jackie's house, stick pictures of the whole family, the outline of a horse that she loved, hand prints from the babies, and so on, all in colour. They are not at all sophisticated, but as Tristan explained on the tape, "I wasn't making it for strangers. I was just trying to pay tribute to her with a good solid job on my part."

So far, the story is one of a thoughtful son who marked his mother well, but suddenly it took a darker turn. "I should have known," he said to the camera. "When she apologized to me that day about stuff that had happened years ago, I should have known. But we're all so chicken to talk about death. I should have stopped the truck and sat her down beside the road and talked. Maybe it would have made a difference. Maybe it wouldn't have, but I should have tried."

A son remembers his mother with this handmade gravemarker in Irricana.

His mom committed suicide. Maybe the homemade headstone is a way of coping with that. I don't know, but it doesn't really matter. It is original, thoughtful, and personal. As Tristan said, "It's easy to pick a headstone out of a catalogue. I didn't want to do that."

Outside the Fence

In years gone by, people who committed suicide were not allowed burial space within a consecrated graveyard. They had to be buried "outside the fence." Everywhere I went, I looked for an example of that cruel idea, but most graves that were once "outside the fence" have been moved inside the fence or the fence has been moved.

Sometimes, the rejection went even further. A rector in a small Alberta town insisted that the coffin of a young suicide victim be left in the porch, not brought into the church proper during the funeral.

Bishop Vital Grandin had a better idea. It is said that he used to allow those "outside the faith" or "outside the fence" to be buried with at least their feet within the consecrated part of St. Albert Catholic cemetery, just in case.

Inside the Fences

The people who decided to make mass graves after the Hillcrest Mine disaster did so because of numbers and haste and expediency, I'm sure, but they couldn't have found a more gripping way to tell the awful story. The first things you see in the Hillcrest cemetery now are short, white picket fences that go on and on, eventually joining to enclose large empty spaces. Well, mostly empty. There's an occasional gravemarker, leaning one way or another, but it's mainly empty space within those wandering walls.

There are four such enclosures marking the areas where the victims were buried after the worst mining accident in Canadian history. On June 19, 1914, 189 men died. They never had a chance. The mine blew with such force that buildings above ground near the mine entrance were flattened and scattered to kingdom come. Imagine what must have happened underground.

It was such an overwhelming disaster that mine and church officials decided to bury the bodies side by side, one foot apart, in four different sections of the local cemetery. Thus, long rows of graves were dug and mass funerals held. The low, white picket fences came later to add their voice to the tragedy.

The picket fence around Caroline on the banks of the Peace River at Dunvegan also does double duty. It marks Caroline, first of all, but it also speaks of isolation, grace under pressure, and unintended results:

IN LOVING MEMORY OF CAROLINE
INFANT DAUGHTER OF ALFRED AND AGNES GARRIOCH
WHO DIED APRIL 20, 1888, AGED 2 DAYS
"FOREVER WITH THE LORD"

Alfred Garrioch had such good intentions and he worked so hard, but things just didn't work out at his Anglican mission at Dunvegan. The Catholic priests had beaten him to the draw as far as religion for the Natives was concerned. His wife, who had grown up in London, England, had a terrible time adjusting to the north. Their first baby survived, barely, but the second one didn't. Their crops were failing, the mission likewise. What to do?

Well, plant some maple seeds, for one thing. I don't think Garrioch was seeking a place in the history books when he planted his seeds, but that's what happened. The maples near the old Anglican mission are lovely now, so unusual for this area that a provincial campground known as The Maples has been created among them.

Nearby in the ever-present, ever-faithful poplars of the Peace River country is Caroline inside her little picket fence box. That's all Garrioch could do for his baby girl—build her a strong fence. The family left the northern mission soon after that, Garrioch convinced that he'd been a total failure in all ways, but the fence and the maple trees kept the faith.

How to Break Your Heart

Death was a constant companion, an ever-present possibility in the bad old days. I often marvel at the way parents seemed to be able to carry on after a child had died. I can't conceive of anything more tragic; yet again and again I read stories like this one in the Dalemead local history book:

> On March 17, 1922, our youngest daughter Ruth was born. This was the year the whooping cough took so many babies and our little one was no exception. She passed away May 3. The funeral was held in the hall and the Dalemead children made wreaths of crocuses that grew so freely on the prairie. Prince and Dan, our best team, carried her to her last resting place.

Wreaths of crocuses—what could be more fitting for a child of the prairies? And Prince and Dan. Who better to carry her?

One Man's War

The old adage about a small town—that you'd better not blink or you'll miss it—applies doubly to Bottrel. It's certainly a small town, maybe four buildings total, and it's so well hidden behind some big trees alongside the road that indeed it's very easy to miss it.

But, like every other small town in the world, it has its stories, its unique experiences. In the cemetery, for example, is an official US army gravemarker for the last known survivor of Pickett's charge in the 1863 battle of Gettysburg:

WILLIAM H. BARNETT PVT. CO. F 11, VA. INF.
CONFEDERATE STATES ARMY
DEC. 6, 1843–JULY 17, 1933

Barnett was one of the Confederate soldiers under Robert E. Lee who galloped up Cemetery Hill near Gettysburg one July morning in 1863, a last-ditch effort to defeat the northern armies once and for all. It didn't work, of course. His side lost, and three months later, Abraham Lincoln was making his famed Gettysburg Address on the slopes where so many from both sides had perished.

By that time, Barnett was back home in Virginia, starting a farm and a family. Eventually, two of his sons moved to Bottrel, and that's where William was when he died in 1933. Thus the burial far from home.

There may have been a wooden marker over his grave at one time, but a fire went through the cemetery years ago and destroyed the old markers. Then the Barnett sons went back to Virginia. William was more or less forgotten until some military historians from Calgary rediscovered him and his story. It was too good to leave alone. This was one old soldier who would not fade away, they decided, and arranged a proper ceremony and new gravestone.

Which is why Bottrel, a mere blink on the map, had six members of a local historical group done up in Confederate uniforms in the graveyard one cold spring morning in 1993, readying their guns for a proper salute, along with a flagbearer holding a Confederate army flag and a trumpeter playing "Taps." It took sixty years, but Barnett finally got a ceremony and a headstone.

The Most Beautiful Graveyards in Alberta

The fog was so thick the morning I explored St. Mary's Russian Greek Orthodox Church at Rabbit Hill near Nisku that even the planes at the nearby Edmonton International Airport had been grounded. It was

Alberta's eastern European settlers established graveyards such as this one at St. Mary's Russian Greek Orthodox Church in the Rabbit Hill district, near Leduc.

wonderful. I like Eastern Orthodox graveyards anyway—they are so loaded with old-fashioned imagery and obvious loving care—but to experience one on a totally silent, almost mysterious morning was an unbeatable combination.

Only the outlines of the church showed up at first, as if a piece of the Ukraine had settled there overnight and would only remain, like Brigadoon, for a day or until the fog lifted, whichever came first. Beyond the church, I could see the first few rows of the graveyard, the bottonee and eastern Orthodox crosses emphasizing their different shapes against the white blanket of fog. I could have been in old Russia or a part of the Ukraine or in another plane of existence. It was absolutely beautiful.

As I walked through the graveyard, I moved from the old country to the new—the markers changed from traditional shapes and designs into the predictable black granite markers seen everywhere; the language changed from Russian or Ukrainian to English; the flowers that decorated the graves were tame petunias of one colour, not silk flowers of every imaginable colour. In some ways, it was a demonstration of good news—how Canada grew and its people learned to get along. But I hope we never lose those first few rows, the reminders of different times and different places.

A piece of the old country graces St. Mary's Russian Greek Orthodox graveyard.

So my nomination for the most beautiful graveyards in Alberta are the old Eastern Orthodox ones that are still cherished by their churches and communities—St. Mary's at Rabbit Hill, St. Mary's Romanian Orthodox Church of Boian near Willingdon, the Russo Greek Orthodox cemetery at Smoky Lake, the old section at Mundare, and the top of the hill in the old Spedden graveyard.

The Best Graveyard in Alberta

There's no contest—the old graveyard in Banff is the best. It holds a veritable Who's Who of Alberta and mountain society. It's surrounded by mountains but not overwhelmed by them. It has wildflowers and pine cones as well as petunias. It has more bronze per square foot and more words per square inch than most, and it has Art. Capital A Art. Poetry, music, sculpture.

In other words, this is a graveyard that does just what the gravemarker for Senator Donald and Stella Cameron advises:

MAKE NO SMALL PLANS.
THEY HOLD NO MAGIC TO STIR MEN'S BLOOD.

The Who's Who of names includes such mountaineering greats as Arthur Wheeler, cofounder of the Alpine Club of Canada, the man who ran his climbing expeditions with such an iron fist that he got the nickname, "He Who Must Be Obeyed"; Tom Wilson, the first white man to see Lake Louise and Emerald Lake—the Indians had known about the wonderful lakes for years and guided Wilson to them; Mary Schaffer Warren, the quiet Quaker from the US who just happened to be writing about alpine flora when she came upon Maligne Lake; Billy Warren, who was with her when she found the lake and later became her husband; Byron Harmon, who seemed to be everywhere in the mountains trying to fulfil his goal of photographing every mountain twice.

Other Banff originals in the cemetery include Billy McCardell, who thought he'd just climb into a certain cave to see what was going on underground and discovered the Cave and Basin; Margaret Greenham, who thought a little mountain school might be fun; Norman Sanson, who thought climbing Tunnel Mountain every week was a blast, even into his eighty-sixth year; Peter and Catharine Whyte, who thought Banff was the best place in the world for a pair of crazy artists; and Bill Peyto, who thought life needed a little spicing up now and then so he carried a live lynx into a bar one day. Mind you, if you go looking for Bill Peyto in the graveyard, you'll have to look long and hard since he's buried much more quietly than he lived—beneath a plain grey Legion marker that identifies him as L/Corporal Ebenezer W. Peyto.

The Brewsters are there too—brothers Jim, Pat, and Jack, and sister Pearl. Jon Whyte is there, a descendant of the artists mentioned above. He was a poet who loved this world, so his epitaph is a circle of the word *earth* repeated over and over again so that you're never quite sure where one earth leaves off and the next begins. Very clever.

That's one of the poems in the graveyard. There's another on the marker of Andrew S. Sibbald, 1888-1945. "The summit attained," it says. What could be more fitting in a graveyard at the foot of Tunnel Mountain? The visual art shows up on all the bronze plaques in the graveyard, many by bronze artist Charlie Beil, and the music is there too in the musical notes carved into the marker for William Cowan, 1862-1910. It's part of the Twenty-third Psalm, the piece about green pastures, I think.

There's one other marker I should mention. I call it the second-best book on an Alberta gravemarker. It belongs to Norman Luxton and his wife Georgia:

NORMAN KENNY LUXTON, 1874-1962
SAILED PACIFIC OCEAN
FROM VANCOUVER TO NEW ZEALAND

IN THIRTY FOOT INDIAN DUGOUT 'TILIKUM' 1902
GEORGIA ELIZABETH, 1870-1965
BORN FORT VICTORIA NORTH (PAKAN)
FIRST WHITE CHILD BORN IN ALBERTA

How's that for an epitaph to catch your attention? It's true. In 1902, Norman Luxton decided to sail around the world with a guy he'd met in a bar. Sounded like the adventure of a lifetime to him. Unfortunately, neither the boat nor the companion were as good as they might have been. Luxton was nearly dead by the time they got halfway around the world, so he came home to Canada, moved to Banff, and began yet another adventure.

His wife, Georgia Elizabeth, was no slouch in the adventure department either. The daughter of David and Annie McDougall, the granddaughter of Rev. George McDougall, she began life in the midst of the smallpox epidemic that killed three of her aunts before it wore itself out. By the time she was a young woman, she was working in her dad's trading post at Morley. There she met an ailing young man who'd come to Banff for rest and relaxation, and the rest is history. It was they who put together the collection of Stoney Indian artifacts that formed the basis of the Luxton Museum, still very much a part of the Banff scene.

The Last Survivor of What?

One day in the Three Hills cemetery, when I was about to give up and drive on to more interesting ports of call, I noticed a small, white marble marker with the words:

JOHN MCALPINE, 1849-1941
THE LAST SURVIVOR OF GENERAL CUSTER

Excuse me? The last time I looked at a history book about Custer's Last Stand, there were no survivors, so what was this claim all about? And what was it doing in a small-town Alberta graveyard?

It took time and a lot of letters, but I finally found out that John McAlpine did indeed serve with General George Custer at the Battle of Little Bighorn in Montana, but as it happened he was two days late for the final battle. He was with the supply trains, and they were held up by rains and muddy roads. He never made it to the battle.

And how did he get to an Alberta graveyard? He homesteaded in the Three Hills area, that's how, and after thirty years as an Alberta farmer, he died there.

This surprising piece of history showed up in the Three Hills cemetery.

The No-Name Graveyard

There are eighteen white metal crosses in the old Fort Saskatchewan jail cemetery, still standing in two more or less straight lines on the river bank, but there are no names. Why not, I wondered? Have the names worn off, do officials think it best to keep them under wraps, what?

Nobody seems to know—that's the amazing part. The local and provincial museums don't have any information. The jail has moved to a new location and has no records. And the government can't help. So there are eighteen unknowns out there.

I don't know why this should have affected me, but it has. I know very well that there are unmarked graves all over the country, but these kept nagging me. Did they mark men who had been hanged? They might have. There wasn't much ceremony or sympathy for people who faced the gallows in the early days. Put them in the jail graveyard and be done with them. Or were the nameless crosses marking men who died of natural causes while in jail but had no family to claim their bodies? That happened too. Families were in other countries, other places. Maybe they never even knew their sons had come to grief. Or maybe they knew and wouldn't have anything to do with them.

Maybe that's why I can't forget those eighteen nameless crosses—they represent so much unhappiness and loneliness and despair.

The Last Word

Trust a cowboy to get the last best words. This is the inscription on the gravemarker in High River for Bill Pender, "Old Time Cowboy, Died 1936":

WHEN THE FINAL SUMMONS COMES
FROM THE COURTHOUSE IN THE SKIES,
AND THE JUDGE OF ALL THE JUDGES,
MAY HE DEEM IT NO SURPRISE
IF I ASK HIM BUT ONE FAVOUR,
HE MAY GRANT IT, NO ONE KNOWS.
SEND ME BACK TO FAIR ALBERTA
WHERE THE HIGHWOOD RIVER FLOWS.

Saskatchewan

✚

Where There Is More
than Meets the Eye

SASKATCHEWAN GETS A BUM RAP.
IT'S NOT THE MIDDLE OF NOWHERE. IT'S NOT ONE BIG FARM
WHERE THE ONLY CONVERSATIONS START AND END
WITH THE WORD "CROP." IT'S NOT ALL FLAT AND BORING.
IT'S NOT POPULATED BY PEOPLE WHO DON'T KNOW BETTER
OR THEY'D GO AWAY. AND SPEAKING OF GOING AWAY,
IT DOES NOT HAVE HIGHWAY SIGNS THAT SAY,
"WOULD THE LAST ONE OUT PLEASE TURN OFF THE LIGHTS?"

Saskatchewan is downright interesting. I challenge any other province to deliver—in one short week—a thunder-and-lightning storm on Cut Knife Hill that made us forget for a moment that the van was stuck in the mud, a visit to the Prince Albert museum that turned up the stuff of which movies are made, and an encounter with Saskatchewan's giant. Did you know Saskatchewan had a giant? Did you know he came from Willow Bunch, and did you know that's where Sitting Bull got most of his groceries while he was in Canada?

I rest my case.

As for its graveyards, they're a lot like Alberta's—for the most part silent, modest to a fault. Time and time again, I'd find a gravemarker, hoping for a bit of the story, but it would give away nothing. W.R. Motherwell, for example, was an interesting guy who came to Saskatchewan from Ontario with plans to revolutionize farming. He figured it should be a profitable and proud occupation instead of the opposite. To make his point, he built himself a grand stone house, which is now a historic park.

But what does his gravemarker in nearby Abernethy say? Nothing, that's what. Just names and dates.

Even in Livelong, they don't write interesting stuff on their gravemarkers. I had never heard of Livelong before I saw a sign pointing to it, but how could I resist? My friend Judy Swan was travelling with me by this time and couldn't believe I'd stop on the basis of a name alone, but I had to know—do people live long in Livelong? Could I find a story or two? But no, it seems as if people there live about as long as anywhere else, and they're just as silent. Judy began to wonder what she'd let herself in for.

The one thing that does make it into graveyards is the North-West Rebellion. It's everywhere. In the northwest are the battle sites—Cut Knife, Duck Lake, Battleford, and Batoche. Maybe it was the storm that followed us or maybe it was the mosquitoes that put us in a fighting mood, but the battle sites were captivating. People pay tons of money to go overseas to see Vimy and Dieppe and others, but they should also see our own battlefields. We fought a civil war on those sites, and we ought to know about it because, as it happens, we haven't finished yet.

The Best Graveyard in Saskatchewan

Batoche is the best. It tells its story without even trying.

Everything is there still—the white clapboard church where Louis Riel kept some of his prisoners, the bumps and gullies where Métis soldiers and government forces advanced and retreated, the clumps of bush that hid them, the banks of the South Saskatchewan River where Gabriel Dumont watched the smokestacks come off the steamer *Northcote*, and finally the cemetery itself. The cemetery was there in 1885. The final battle raged around and over it. And when the guns won, as guns have a habit of doing, Riel and Dumont and the Métis cause were defeated.

This was Canada's only all-Canadian war. This was not, for a change, the British fighting the French, or the Irish fighting the British, or the British fighting the Americans, the fact that they fought on Canadian soil

The Batoche cemetery speaks for itself. It was here that Riel and his men fought a losing battle against government troops.

being almost incidental. This was us fighting us. And there was an "us" by then. We had become the Dominion of Canada on July 1, 1867, but somehow the powers-that-be hadn't given much thought to the people who had been here all along.

So, when the Métis saw the land they had traditionally used being surveyed and carved up into neat little parcels for railways and towns and settlers, they objected. What about us, they asked? What about all those promises? What about our rights?

When nothing changed, Louis Riel formed a provisional government in the Red River area and told Ottawa to get lost. We'll look after our own land and lives, he said. That was 1870, just three years into our dominionhood.

Sounded like rebellion to Ottawa, so with a little bit of negotiation and a lot of soldiers, they put a cap on the unrest. Riel fled to the US, and many of the Métis moved further west into what is now Saskatchewan.

Fourteen years later, land issues were again a matter of disagreement between the Métis and the government, this time aggravated by the disappearance of the buffalo. The Natives were neither here nor there—they couldn't depend on their traditional forms of survival, and they didn't know how to access or were refused government resources. The situation was war asking to happen, or in the case of the North-West Rebellion, a whole lot of little wars asking to happen.

If there is a hero in this most confusing of all wars, that hero has to be Gabriel Dumont. Riel had his crazy moments, and the Canadian government ditto, but Dumont held to one indisputable fact—the Métis people were not being treated fairly. What's more, they were starving. Why couldn't the government see that?

Dumont has the biggest individual gravemarker in the Batoche cemetery: a great slab of rock on the river bank marking the spot where, the story goes, he's buried standing up, the better to see the enemy coming from the river side. But the guide tells us there's another explanation of his position. He wanted to face the river because the river was one thing the whites couldn't change. The river was eternal. It would remain. And it has. Dumont was right.

The plaque on the front of the rock slab marking his grave says:

GABRIEL DUMONT, 1838–1906
BORN IN ASSINIBOIA, RUPERT'S LAND,
HE WON EARLY FAME AS A BUFFALO HUNTER.
ABOUT 1868, HE FOUNDED THE METIS CAMP
WHICH BECAME ST. LAURENT AND IN 1873
BECAME PRES. OF ITS LOCAL GOVERNMENT.
IN 1884, HE LED A PARTY TO MONTANA TO BRING BACK
LOUIS RIEL. HE COMMANDED THE METIS FORCES IN 1885
AND DISPLAYED CONSIDERABLE MILITARY ABILITY.
AFTER THE FALL OF BATOCHE, HE ESCAPED TO THE U.S.
HE RETURNED YEARS LATER
AND RESUMED THE LIFE OF A HUNTER.

Near Dumont is a mass grave for the Métis who fell at Batoche, marked by tall wooden crosses contained within a tall wooden picket fence. No names. Just crosses. There are names, however, on another marker nearby, names of those who fell at Batoche, Fish Creek, and Duck Lake. The first on the list is J. Ouellette, aged ninety years.

We had a ninety-year-old man fighting that battle. Puts it in a different light, doesn't it?

Batoche is a national historic site now, but all the mod cons that go with such a designation—audiovisual presentations, shiny bathrooms, interpretive panels—are located quite a distance from the cemetery, the actual battlefield. It's still able to speak for itself. Don't miss it.

The burial site of Gabriel Dumont. Legend has it that Dumont was buried standing up–the better to see the enemy approaching.

Different Battles, Same War

The North-West Rebellion was not a terribly well-organized affair. It just sort of happened here and there, now and then. The first skirmish occurred at Duck Lake and the Natives won, more or less. The next two were at Fish Creek and Cut Knife Hill. Both were standoffs, although everything depends on your point of view. Only at Batoche was there a clear-cut victory–Major General Frederick Middleton and some eight hundred soldiers put the run on Riel's men, and that effectively ended the rebellion. The clash at Frenchman's Butte a few weeks later didn't change the outcome–Riel was finished.

The massacre at Frog Lake in Alberta wasn't as much a part of Riel's rebellion as it was a part of the rebellion of Wandering Spirit, who had had enough of the white man's law. To that degree, however, it has to belong to what is termed the North-West Rebellion.

See what I mean about disorganized and confusing? Not only that but the word "rebellion" sounds bigger than this actually was. It's true that some of the Native people were fighting back, but they didn't have much to fight with. In a local history book that I bought in Prince Albert, I read the story of Patrice Fleury. He had been around when an inventory of guns was taken early in 1885, just to see how many guns the Métis could muster if needed. They counted some sixty guns in the area, not exactly the biggest armament in the world.

Still, it happened, and men from both sides were killed.

On top of a hill near the reconstructed Fort Battleford is the old police cemetery. A plaque over the massive stone gate honours the NWMP members and volunteers who are buried there, most in unmarked graves, a few with gravemarkers and dates that give away the story:

IN MEMORY OF WM. H. TALBOT LOWRY
BORN DEC. 2, 1854 DIED MAY 3, 1885
THERE SHALL BE NO DEATH THERE
AND GOD SHALL WIPE AWAY ALL TEARS FROM THEIR EYES.

RALPH BATEMAN SLEIGH
BORN JULY 14, 1858
DIED MAY 2, 1885

In other words, both Lowry and Sleigh were killed during the battle of Cut Knife Hill, when war chief Fine Day of Poundmaker's band turned back the government forces.

On a slope beyond the NWMP cemetery, closer to the river, is another burial site. Under a tipilike arrangement of poles, surrounded by wild roses and wolf willow, lie the bodies of eight Indians who were charged with murder after the fighting was over. Wandering Spirit was one of them, and though they had

Plain wooden crosses at Batoche mark a mass grave for the Métis who died during the battle.

no legal counsel throughout their trials, all eight were sentenced to hang, just like that. So they did, no appeal even considered, and the bodies were placed in a common grave on the hillside.

For years, they lay there without a stone or words, but there's a big black granite marker over them now with their names listed in both Cree and English.

Both of these sites in Battleford are memorable because they haven't yet been cleaned up to within an inch of their lives. You can still imagine what it must have been like for white settlers to flee to the fort for protection from what they thought were Indians on the war path. They were so vulnerable, so alone on the wide open prairie all around us. No wonder there was fear. At the same time, you can stand and look at the river and the land on either side, down beside the mass grave, for instance, and imagine how Native people felt about losing all of that. The saskatoons were blooming when we were there, the sage just beginning to perfume the grass. It was incredibly beautiful. But it was no longer theirs. A whole way of life was disappearing. No wonder there was anger.

Cut Knife Hill went one step further in this business of re-creating for us the history and the emotions that went along with the battle. Cut Knife Hill staged a lightning storm that made us feel literally under siege, standing as we were on the highest ridge in the area, and then just in case we hadn't got the message, Cut Knife Hill unleashed its mosquitos. "How could anyone think about fighting with these things coming at them?" Judy asked. Then, because the van was stuck on the dirt road leading to the battle site, she asked, "How are we going to get unstuck?"

Good questions both, but Poundmaker's people fought the govern-ment forces to a standoff at this site, mosquitos and mud notwithstanding. Lt. Col. W.D. Otter chose to "withdraw," although there are those who say he retreated.

As for our retreat, all it needed was my dad's advice from years ago—"Straighten your wheels." Mind you, if I hadn't taken my dad's advice in the first place and made a "run" at the hill, I wouldn't have needed any advice. Still, nothing ventured, nothing gained, I say. Judy was not so sure she shared my philosophy.

As for Chief Poundmaker and his troubles, he went to jail for his part in the rebellion but was released when it looked as if he didn't have long to live. And sure enough, shortly afterward during a celebratory meal with Chief Crowfoot in Alberta, Poundmaker choked on some saskatoon soup and died. Crowfoot was devastated by the loss; Poundmaker was his adopted son, so he had him buried nearby on the Blackfoot Reserve.

However, his body was later moved. This is what it says on his grave now up on top of Cut Knife Hill:

CHIEF POUNDMAKER, 1842–1886
BURIED AT BLACKFOOT CROSSING, ALBERTA JULY 4, 1886
REMAINS OF CHIEF POUNDMAKER BROUGHT HERE
AND INTERRED ON APRIL 18, 1967.

The North-West Rebellion is mentioned on gravemarkers all across Canada, not just at the battle sites. At least the fighting men of Canada realized what an important little war we had back in 1885.

No Wonder Hollywood Couldn't Resist

The story of the Cree Indian, Almighty Voice, has become the stuff of legends, not to mention Hollywood movies.

It seems that Almighty Voice was Almighty Attractive to Women, and when he brought home his fourth wife, he decided to have a wedding feast. To that end, he shot a stray cow. The farmer who owned the cow didn't think it was a stray, however, so he reported the matter to the NWMP at Duck Lake.

Sergeant Colin Colebrook dutifully rode out to Almighty Voice's place thinking the whole matter was pretty routine, but for some reason or other, Almighty Voice shot and killed him. Then he took off into the bush and stayed there for the next nineteen months.

The NWMP mounted search after search, offered rewards, turned themselves inside out to capture Almighty Voice, but nothing worked until one Napoleon Venne, also a Cree, reported the loss of another stray cow. This time, with Venne's help, they found Almighty Voice, but no way would he surrender. Police pumped the woods full of bullets, but he managed to elude both bullets and men. Finally, they brought in two cannons, and that's how they got Almighty Voice. They killed everything in sight with cannon balls—trees, birds, Almighty Voice, and two of his companions. Two more police officers and one volunteer also died during the bombardment. Seven men killed for two stray cows.

Almighty Voice was dubbed "The Man They Needed a Cannon to Kill," and Hollywood soon came calling. The story had all the elements: romance, noble Natives under siege by heartless whites, redcoated Mounties, lots of violence, etc., etc. No wonder they couldn't resist. Two movies resulted: *The Scarlet Trail of Almighty Voice* and *Alien Thunder*.

The NWMP members are buried in St. Mary's in Prince Albert. Almighty Voice lies in an unmarked grave on the One Arrow Reserve. And some of the Venne family lie outside the fence at Batoche cemetery. Could there be a connection?

Sitting Bull's Second Home

The Blackfoot Indians had the right idea when they named the Cypress Hills in southwest Saskatchewan "the hills that shouldn't be." By all the laws of geology and logic, there shouldn't be hills out in the middle of dry prairie lands. But they're there anyway: huge, beautiful, and unexpected. The highest thing between the Rockies and the Laurentians.

Because they are so different, untouched somehow by the glaciers that ground everything else into submission, the Cypress Hills contain flora and fauna not found anywhere else on the prairies. They don't contain cypress trees, but that's about the only thing missing. They are an oasis in the middle of the bald prairie, and as such attract travellers, then and now.

Indians knew about them, of course, and often gathered there. White men came too, especially the whisky traders of the late 1800s who knew the hills and gullies made good hiding places for their illicit trade. It was that illicit trade that led to the awful massacre in 1873 at Farwell's trading post near the US border. It seems some wolf hunters got to drinking together near the trading post, and somewhere along the line one of them accused a nearby encampment of Assiniboines of horse stealing. That was a low blow, but before the Indians, who had also been drinking, could defend themselves, the wolf hunters had their guns out and levelled the Indian village, killing some twenty people. Not only that, but the hunters followed up with rape and pillage. The whole ugly episode reads like ancient Roman or British history, also full of accounts of raping and pillaging, but this was Canada a little over one hundred years ago.

The only good thing to come out of this ugliness was the decision by Prime Minister John A. Macdonald to send a police force that would bring law and order to the great lone land. It would be called the North-West Mounted Police, and its members would wear red coats. He'd heard somewhere that Indians liked red.

Two years later, Fort Walsh was built in the Cypress Hills, and James Morrow Walsh took on the job of keeping the peace.

How he did it boggles the mind because he soon had a much bigger problem than whisky traders. Chief Sitting Bull and some five thousand of his Sioux people were drifting into southern Saskatchewan to avoid the wrath of the US government following the battle at Little Bighorn in Montana, and to avoid being put on reservations.

The first few years weren't too bad. Walsh laid down the law; Sitting Bull and his people kept it. But then the buffalo disappeared. What do you do with five thousand people who haven't enough food?

In the Willow Bunch cemetery is this stone:

A LA MÉMOIRE DE JEAN LOUIS LEGARÉ
FONDATEUR DE WILLOW BUNCH, 1870
1841–1918

The stone gives Legaré credit for founding the town of Willow Bunch, but it doesn't mention that he may have prevented war between Canada and the US. He gave Sitting Bull and the Indians thousands of dollars worth of food, clothing, and blankets from his small trading post at Wood Mountain, and eventually he persuaded Sitting Bull to go back to the States, to accept the reservation and assistance. If Sitting Bull hadn't returned when he did,

the US military was considering a raid on its good neighbour Canada to bring the Sioux to justice.

Incidentally, the government still owes Legaré some forty-eight-thousand dollars for all the aid given to the Sioux in the five years they were here, according to great grandson Edward Legaré, who'd like to see his forefather get more credit for the way he befriended Sitting Bull and prevented bloodshed. Sounds fair to me.

Louis Legaré befriended Sitting Bull and his people, but there is no mention of this on his gravemarker in Willow Bunch.

The military graveyard at Fort Walsh tells this tale of uneasy peacekeeping. The murder remains unsolved.

Walsh also befriended Sitting Bull and admired him, but the Canadian government was not amused. They transferred Walsh out of the territory and admonished the next fort commander to get tough.

It wasn't really necessary. The Sioux didn't have many options. When the buffalo disappeared, they had no food. When the government got tough, they had even less. So they drifted back to the US and onto reserves.

That was pretty well the end of Fort Walsh. It's a national historic park now, a tidy little arrangement of palisades and buildings that look as if they belong in a toybox. But there are two cemeteries nearby–one civilian, one military–to prove that this was once a real place with an important role to play.

The most famous marker in the military graveyard says:

IN MEMORY OF M.N. GRABURN N.W.M.P.
KILLED BY INDIANS NEAR FORT WALSH, N.W.T. 7 NOV. 1879
AGED 19 YEARS.

I'm not sure if Graburn is actually buried at this spot in the graveyard. When his fellow officers found his body in the bush west of the fort, they buried him where he fell and erected a cairn nearby to tell the story. That cairn is still there, surrounded by an iron fence. The whole thing looks suspiciously like a grave, but I don't suppose it matters in the big scheme of things. The cairn explains more of the story:

CONSTABLE MARMADUKE GRABURN, N.W.M.P.
WAS SHOT AND KILLED BY UNKNOWN PERSONS
IN THE CYPRESS HILLS NOV. 17, 1879.
HE WAS THE FIRST MOUNTED POLICEMAN KILLED BY VIOLENCE
SINCE THE FORCE WAS ORGANIZED IN 1873.
STAR CHILD, A BLOOD INDIAN, WAS ACCUSED OF THE MURDER
BUT WAS ACQUITTED IN 1881.

The murder has never been solved, nor understood. Graburn was shot in the back while out checking on some horses.

Familiar Names along the Trail

In St. Mary's cemetery in Prince Albert, I found a small flat stone that read:

SACRED TO THE MEMORY OF MARY
INFANT DAUGHTER OF W.E. AND H. TRAILL
WHO DIED AUGUST 20, 1874
AGED 9 MOS.

It was the second gravemarker I had found for Traill children, and told yet another chapter in the doleful story of the Traills in Canada.

The first generation of Traills who came to Canada from England didn't especially like it. They weren't used to the back-breaking, frustrating work that a farm in the dense bush of Ontario required, and eventually Catharine Parr Traill turned to writing to make some money. In that, she was more successful, the British audience at the time being fascinated with "the backwoods of Canada."

One of their sons joined the Hudson's Bay Company, which in those days was considered a plum of a job. His future seemed rosy, especially when he became chief factor for the trading post at Lac La Biche in what is now northern Alberta but then was just north. Far away. Remote. More backwoods.

Trouble came with the third generation. On the trip west across the country to the new posting, Mary—or Molly as she was known—died of whooping cough. She had to be left behind in Prince Albert. A few years later, her siblings, Catharine Parr and Henry, eldest daughter and infant son respectively, died of scarlet fever. They lie in the Lac La Biche mission cemetery beneath a shared stone that says, "They cannot come to us but we may go to them."

I always marvel at such apparent acceptance, although I know that W.E. Traill did write to his mother later and say he was having a hard time remembering that his children had gone to a better place. He missed them here on earth, he admitted. Incidentally, I found the original Traills in Lakefield, Ontario. Neither Thomas nor Catharine Parr said anything about themselves or the backwoods.

The Other Best Graveyard

Go south, young man, go south, and there you will find Maple Creek. Carry on to the town cemetery and there you will find Horace Greeley, not *the* Horace Greeley of American fame who said, "Go west, young man, go west," but close enough. This is a kin of the other Horace Greeley, and he made his own mark in the world:

HORACE A. GREELEY
SON OF JAMES AND NANCY MARSH GREELEY
BORN IN HUDSON, N.H., U.S.A. SEPT. 17, 1858
DIED AT MAPLE CREEK, SASK. OCT. 21, 1935
CAME TO FORT WALSH, N.W.T. OCT. 27, 1879
CAME TO MAPLE CREEK APRIL 1883
AND RESIDED THERE THEREAFTER.
MEMBER OF THE LEGISLATIVE ASSEMBLY 1898-1905.
MERCHANT, RANCHER AND FARMER
"I'M OFF TO THE LAST ROUND-UP."

Greeley's last line is just one of the many ranching references in this graveyard, not a surprising state of affairs, I suppose, considering that Maple Creek is ranching country. But there are other graveyards in other ranching areas that don't say nearly as much about their passions. Some original soul must have set the tone for this graveyard many years ago, and from then on, it has dared to be different.

For instance, Lindsay Kitchner Doonan, 1917-1988, is buried beneath a message that I hope was heeded:

LAY MY SPURS UPON MY BREAST
MY ROPE AND SADDLE TREE,
AND AS THE BOYS LAY ME TO REST
GO TURN MY HORSES FREE.

Then there's the "sitting rock." It serves as a marker for Lewis Irvine Fleming, 1897-1987, who used to stop and rest on it while when he was riding the range checking the cattle. It was the perfect shape and height for him and what's more, it looked out over his beloved countryside. It meant a great deal to him so that's why it marks his last resting place.

Even women get a word in edgewise in this accepting graveyard. Ann Benstead, 1907-1982, is marked with these words, and even though I never met her, I like her:

> SHE BELIEVED IN HANDS THAT WORKED,
> BRAINS THAT THOUGHT
> AND HEARTS THAT LOVED.

This is not what you'd call a pretty graveyard. The heat poured down on us the day we visited until we began to dry up like the grass and the silk flowers that bloomed better than anything else there. But the graveyard had character. People in this community must be strong enough to live and let live, which is a bit of a contradiction in a graveyard, but there you are.

But What about the Farmers?

Saskatchewan may be the bread basket of the world, but you'd never know it from its graveyards. Hardly a word about farming or wheat pools or elevators, surely the stuff of which Saskatchewan is made. Oh, here and there are shadow-tone pictures on black granite of farmsteads or old trucks, but no long stories about the actual farming experience.

In Rosthern, for example, we found a museum dedicated to Seager Wheeler, 1868-1961, "the wheat wizard," the sign at the museum told us. Seager, it seems, stunned the agricultural world by taking the one-thousand-dollar gold prize at the 1911 New York Fair for best hard spring wheat grown in North America. What's more, he did it four more times.

Great, I thought, and immediately sought out Seager's grave in the nearby Bergthal cemetery. You guessed it—not a word. Not even a decorative wheat design on his black marker. Just names and dates.

I've already mentioned W.R. Motherwell, who came to Saskatchewan from Ontario in 1882, full of brave new ideas for farming in the west. Why not have co-ops, he asked, and then organized some. Why not get involved politically, he asked, and then served as both provincial and federal minister of agriculture. Why not build a beautiful farm home made out of stone instead of a dowdy, wooden one? So he did, and that beautiful home is now a museum near Abernethy. But no hint of any of that on his gravemarker.

Edward Pierce didn't intend to be a farmer when he emigrated to Canada in 1882; he intended to be lord of the manor—Cannington Manor, to be exact. That's what he called his model town, and that's where he encouraged other British immigrants, preferably wealthy ones, to settle. But it turned out that someone had to work. Farming had to be done. A town couldn't exist on thin air.

Indeed, it didn't exist for very long. It's a historic site now, just a few buildings left to mark the experiment, among them the church and the graveyard where Pierce is buried beneath a silent gravemarker.

It wasn't until I got to Sintaluta that I finally found mention of farming:

EDWARD ALEXANDER PARTRIDGE
1862-1931
FIRST PRESIDENT OF THE GRAIN GROWERS GRAIN CO.

I suppose Partridge would be called something of a rabble-rouser now, but he couldn't stand to see farmers get less for their work and crops than they should have. Consequently, he spent a lot of time talking, organizing, and writing about cooperatives, about working together to improve grain delivery and marketing systems.

Eventually, improvements were made, but never enough for Partridge, never the right kind of improvements. He was still an angry man at the end of his days, which may be why—combined with personal troubles—he took his own life.

On a happier note, this is about the best inscription I found in Saskatchewan that relates to farming. I knew this was a farmer speaking as soon as I saw the word "chores." It's on the Czemeres gravemarker in the Fort Qu'Appelle cemetery:

IN MEMORY OF ESTHER, 1914-1992
I'LL MEET YOU WHEN MY CHORES ARE THROUGH,
AND BETWEEN NOW AND THEN TILL I SEE YOU AGAIN
I'LL BE LOV'N YOU . . . LOVE ME.

Saskatchewan Giants

The word "giant" may be used literally or figuratively, but believe me, with Edouard Beaupré, it's used literally.

Born in Willow Bunch in deep south Saskatchewan, he developed normally until the age of seven, when suddenly everything started to grow. In the end, he stood 2.5 m (8.3 ft) tall, weighed 178 kg (396 lb), and wore size twenty-four shoes and size fifty-two pants. The statue in front of the Willow Bunch Museum, a figure built to exact specifications, doesn't look all that big until you look at the size twenty-four feet.

Beneath the statue is his final resting place:

A LA MEMOIRE D'EDOUARD BEAUPRÉ
9 JAN. 1881–9 JUILLET 1904
WILLOW BUNCH–ST. LOUIS, MO
INHUMATION LE 7 JUILLET 1990
PAX

That "pax" is especially suitable, since Beaupré didn't have a lot of peace in his short lifetime and hardly any at all after his death. Giants didn't have many options in the late 1800s. They were recruited by circuses to travel around as part of their freak shows. Now and then, they had to perform, which in Beaupré's case meant he had to fight fellow Canadian Louis Cyr of Québec, who was known as the World's Strongest Man. Not surprisingly, the world's strongest beat the world's tallest.

At the age of twenty-three, Beaupré developed a lung haemorrhage thought to be related in some way to tuberculosis. He died while with the Ringling Brothers Circus in St. Louis, Missouri.

That's bad enough—that a kid who never asked to be the world's tallest man in a circus died far from home. To make matters worse, the circus embalmed his body and continued to display it. The Beaupré family lacked either the money or the know-how to get their big boy back home. So he kept on travelling.

Eventually, the body was stored in a shed in Montréal where some kids found it. They told their folks, who told somebody and somebody told somebody until finally the body ended up at the University of Montréal. What for, I'm scared to ask. There it stayed until Edouard's nephew decided to find his famous uncle and bring him home. He buried his ashes in front of the museum. It took Edouard eighty-six years to get home.

John Diefenbaker was a giant in the metaphorical sense. He was more of a giant killer than a giant when in 1957 and 1958 he took the country by storm and led the Progressive Conservative Party to political victory. That was his finest hour. From then on, he got into hot water one way or another, resulting in the Liberals returning to power in 1963.

Didn't stop John Diefenbaker, however. Known as "the man from Prince Albert," he continued to charm and delight audiences across Canada. Words were his weapon, his soft soap, his delight.

Which is why his gravemarker is so surprising. A plain grey, flat tablet on the lawn in front of the Right Honourable John G. Diefenbaker Centre on the University of Saskatchewan campus, it simply lists the names and dates of John, 1895-1979, and his second wife, Olive Evangeline, 1902-1976.

Diefenbaker, who loved to talk, has a surprisingly brief inscription on his gravemarker on the University of Saskatchewan grounds.

There is the standard government plaque nearby that fills in some of the blanks, but who would have thunk it? Diefenbaker at a loss for words?

Monsignor Athol Murray, 1892-1975, does not have that trouble. He has both a statue and a major gravemarker near the Notre Dame College in Wilcox, where he made his name as an educator and hockey coach. The hockey part of his life is explained more fully on the statue:

> PERE MURRAY COMPLEMENTED THE RELIGIOUS
> AND ACADEMIC MILIEU OF THE COLLEGE
> WITH A VIGOROUS SPORTS PROGRAM.
> THE NOTRE DAME HOUNDS, ACTIVE IN HOCKEY, BASEBALL
> AND FOOTBALL, BECAME ONE OF THE MORE SUCCESSFUL
> AND BETTER KNOWN COLLEGE TEAMS IN THE PROVINCE.
> IN ALL THEIR ENDEAVOURS, PERE ENCOURAGED HIS STUDENTS
> TO AIM FOR HIGH STANDARDS BECAUSE OF HIS BELIEF
> THAT "MEDIOCRITY CANNOT EXIST WHERE THE MIND
> AND HEART INSIST ON EXCELLENCE."

On his gravemarker are the words of St. Augustine:

> SLEEP WELL, GREAT HEART
> YOUR WORKS ENDURE

TO HIM WHO DOES WHAT IN HIM LIES
GOD WILL NOT DENY HIS GRACE.

A Star of David beside the Road

I knew nothing about the Jewish farming settlements in Saskatchewan until I saw the sign beside the road that said Hirsch Community Jewish Cemetery. It was topped by a large Star of David.

What is this, I said, and braked, of course.

The story didn't give itself away in the graveyard. The graves were on the neglected side: many were falling over, concrete grave covers were breaking up, prairie grasses grew wherever they wanted. So, it was clearly a story of abandonment, of people who had moved on. But why?

The information on the gravemarkers was generally written in both Hebrew and English:

BELOVED BROTHER AND SON
MAX RUBACH
BORN IN PINSK, POLAND
DIED JULY 29, 1934 AGED 25 YEARS

The sign at the entrance to the cemetery told more about the name Hirsch and explained why the settlers had come to Canada:

JEWISH IMMIGRANTS WHO MOSTLY CAME
FROM CZARIST RUSSIA, ROUMANIA, AUSTRIA AND POLAND
WERE ASSISTED BY THE BARON DE HIRSCH INSTITUTE
AND THE JEWISH COLONIZATION ASSOCIATION.
THESE COLONISTS WERE MOTIVATED BY A KEEN DESIRE
TO ESCAPE RELIGIOUS PERSECUTION AND RACIAL
DISCRIMINATION WITH THE RIGHTS TO OWN
AND FARM THEIR LAND AND FREELY ADHERE
TO THEIR ORTHODOX FAITH.

So they came to Canada, to Saskatchewan specifically, and named a town for their benefactor. But why had they gone away? Why was this little cemetery so abandoned?

It's the usual story, I guess. It was tough being a farmer—land dried up in the 1930s, money dried up. It was tough being a Jew—there weren't enough teachers, rabbis, to keep the faith alive. There weren't enough Jews to make a community. So the people at Hirsch moved on, some to bigger centres, some to Edenbridge and Wapella and other successful Jewish farming centres.

There's not one building, not one sign of the old town of Hirsch left. Just the graveyard.

First You Find a Boat

"Oh, never mind Grey Owl," the old guys at the Prince Albert museum advised me. "He was a humbug. No more, no less."

Understand that this opinion was not coming from the museum officials. These were just the old guys out front, chewing the fat on a warm summer afternoon, remembering the days when newspapers revealed that Grey Owl was an imposter. He wasn't an Indian at all, the headlines announced. He was just an Englishman named Archie Belaney who came to Canada and let his hair grow.

It was a huge scandal at the time, and for a while Grey Owl *was* put into the humbug category. He's been shined up again, however, by the environmental movement. He may have had his origins mixed up, but his message was strong and clear: conserve the wilderness and wild animals. They are an enormous resource.

He lived his last years in a cabin on Lake Ajawaan in Prince Albert National Park, and when he died April 13, 1938, that's where he was buried. To get there, you have to take a boat and then walk another three kilometres or so to the actual site, a fact that must make Grey Owl very happy. After all, he wanted us to pay attention to the outdoors. What else can we do as we travel over water and land to get to his last resting place?

He's still making us pay attention. Some humbug!

In the Road of a Riot

Regina didn't intend to have a riot. Regina didn't deserve a riot. It just happened that fourteen hundred unemployed men were on their way to Ottawa to protest unemployment, poverty, relief camps, government inaction—you name it—and Regina got caught in the crossfire.

It was 1935, the midst of the Great Depression. People were suffering from hunger and despair. The government had to do something about the unemployment situation, or so the men who got on the trains in Vancouver felt. They'd make Ottawa listen. It was the On to Ottawa Trek.

Ottawa listened all right and told the railway to kick the guys off the trains. If they couldn't get to Ottawa, they couldn't make trouble there. And what kind of trouble could they get into in Regina?

Enough, as it turned out. They were having speeches and a bit of a rally one afternoon when the police and RCMP arrived to arrest some of the leaders. That was the spark and before the fire was out, dozens were injured and one policeman was dead, Charles Millar of the Regina police force. He was more or less beaten to death; the perpetrators were never brought to trial.

Millar, 1894-1935, is buried in the Regina cemetery, not a word on his gravemarker about the way he died.

A gravemarker in Bienfait does a better job of telling a story about worker unrest, albeit unintentionally. There's coal mining in the area, and in 1931 a group of striking miners got together for a parade in Estevan. When the RCMP tried to break up the demonstration, the parade escalated into a protest and then a riot and finally a rout when police fired into the midst of the fighting and killed three men.

The miners were buried in the Bienfait cemetery and marked with a single headstone on which were inscribed a red star and the words, "Murdered by the RCMP."

Later, someone removed the star and words. Then they reappeared, and so it has gone ever since.

Why Must Bad Things Happen?

Since smart people have been trying to figure that out forever, I think I'll leave it alone except to say that graveyards tell again and again that life is uncertain. There are no guarantees. This is what is written on a gravemarker in the Regina cemetery:

> IN LOVING MEMORY OF GEORGE B. CRAVEN
> DAIRY INSTRUCTOR DEPT. OF AGRICULTURE, REGINA
> WHO WAS KILLED IN THE CYCLONE JUNE 30, 1912,
> AGED 28 Y'RS.
> SON OF R.B. CRAVEN R.N.
> THE KINGS EMPIRE VETERANS AUCKLAND, N.Z.

The cyclone hit in late afternoon. Two funnel clouds roared through the heart of Regina and killed twenty-eight people, including George Craven, who had the misfortune to be walking near the CPR roundhouse. He was crushed by a hurtling boxcar, the accounts say. How in the world could a boxcar hurtle?

And yet that's what happened.

In the Saskatoon Nutana cemetery is a brief but familiar message to those who live on the prairies:

ERECTED IN MEMORY OF MY BROTHER
EDWARD WILLIAM MEERES
WHO LOST HIS LIFE ON THE PRAIRIE
DURING A BLIZZARD ON JAN. 14, 1888.
AGED 27 YEARS.

And in Maple Creek, the story is this:

IN MEMORY OF JAMES BARRETT CORRY
WHOSE DEATH WAS CAUSED BY LIGHTNING
AT POINT VIEW, SASK. ON JUNE 17, 1913, AGED 28.

It's not always weather that causes unexpected deaths. This is the story in St. Mary's in Prince Albert:

IN MEMORY OF SERGT. A.E.G. MONTGOMERY
F. DIV. NWMP
WHO DIED AT PRINCE ALBERT AUG. 10, 1890
OF INJURIES RECEIVED THROUGH HIS HORSE STUMBLING
ON PARADE AND THROWING HIM VIOLENTLY TO THE GROUND.
AGED 28 YEARS.

I don't know the story behind this gravemarker in Broadview, but I don't have to know the details in order to know it's not particularly happy:

IN LOVING MEMORY OF CLARA COPE,
BELOVED WIFE OF THOMAS E. COPE
1866–1939 AGED 72 YEARS
A WASTED LIFE FOR CANADA

Just so I don't leave you entirely wrung out, I'll end this section with the inscription from Evaleula Thelma Wilson's grave in Craik. She died July 1912, aged a mere two years, three months, and twelve days, but the words over her are gentler than most, accepting almost all of the good and bad that happens in our lives:

THERE IS NO FLOCK HOWEVER WATCHED AND TENDED
BUT ONE DEAD LAMB IS THERE.
THERE IS NO FIRESIDE HOWEVER DEFENDED
BUT HAS ONE VACANT CHAIR.

More War Memorials Should Be Like This

The cenotaph in Wolseley depicts a soldier in full kit, but for a change he doesn't hold a weapon of any kind. In fact, he's standing behind a cross, which may indicate some kind of Christian acceptance for war or acceptance

This statue of a young soldier stands in the Wolseley cemetery.

of that war at least. But what I like most about this figure is that he looks to be about sixteen. He's just a kid.

I wonder if the sculptor was trying to remind us that we send kids to war, not troops or soldiers or generals or battalions, but kids. Our kids. One at a time.

I like this statue a lot.

The Least Word

Never let it be said that prairie folk use two words when one would do. Over a grave in the Edam cemetery is a homemade black sign that says simply:

BIG JACK HAS GONE UPSTAIRS

And in the Moose Jaw cemetery is a marker for Pte. Alex Ireland, 32 Batt. C.E.F., who died Oct. 12, 1928, at the age of fifty-two years. His marker does not gush:

HE DID HIS BIT

The Last Word

Most epitaphs through the 1800s and early 1900s were of a religious nature—quotes from the Bible, lines from old hymns—but by the mid 1900s, that was all changing. This is on the gravemarker of David Hutcheon Allan, 1883-1948, buried in the Estevan cemetery:

FOR WHEN THE ONE GREAT SCORER
COMES TO WRITE AGAINST YOUR NAME
HE WRITES NOT THAT YOU WON OR LOST
BUT HOW YOU PLAYED THE GAME.

Manitoba

Where Differences Don't Matter but Riel Does

MANITOBA IS AMAZING. IT'S ABOUT AS
MULTICULTURAL AS CANADA COMES, AND YET ALL
THE CULTURES SEEM TO GET ALONG JUST FINE.
YOU DON'T SENSE A LOT OF RACIAL TENSION, YOU DON'T
HEAR EARNEST NEWS ANALYSTS DISCUSSING WHAT
MANITOBA WANTS. AS FAR AS I CAN FIGURE,
WHAT MANITOBA WANTS, MANITOBA GETS,
AND IF NOT, MANITOBA DOESN'T SWEAT IT.

Take the Louis Riel statue, for example. When I was in Winnipeg, it was still standing on the grounds of the legislature, a fierce-looking, black, tortured figure inside two big semicircles of concrete. It wasn't pretty, that's for sure, but prettiness was not the problem. The problem was he didn't have any pants on. His private parts were there for everyone to see, not that you could see much. This statue was what might be termed "modern" art; nothing looked like the real thing. But never mind, the Manitoba Métis Federation didn't like it. A hero of Riel's stature ought to be represented in a more dignified fashion, they said. So the Manitoba government said okay, we'll get rid of it. So they did, just like that.

Seems to me we'd have a lot more huffing and puffing in Ottawa, for example, if a public statue offended some people and had to be removed. Think of the hassle we had over the meat dress at the National Art Gallery. But not Manitoba. It remained calm, did the sensible thing, which is why, I guess, differences are no big deal in Manitoba. In Beauséjour, a French name if ever there was one, I asked a guy in the laundromat why I hadn't found many French names in the town's cemetery. "Because we haven't got many French people here," he said. "We've just got a French name."

"Why don't you change it?" I asked.

"What for?" he asked.

I did encounter one case of ethnic unrest during my Manitoba travels. It happened in a graveyard, of course, but the gentleman who told me a thing or two about Ukrainian settlement in Canada was mostly mad at the CBC, and that's a national pastime in Canada, not specific to Manitoba at all.

Meanwhile back at the legislature grounds, Riel may have been removed but the following remained—speaking of cultural diversity:

- The Wall of Mourning, big black tablets covered with names of Holocaust victims.
- A statue of Taras Shevchenko, 1814-1861, "the national poet of Ukraine, champion of justice and freedom for all."
- A traditional war memorial with a soldier triumphantly holding his helmet aloft, saying, I hope, "I'm home, Mom."
- An untraditional war memorial, a rock under a tree, with the inscription, "There is no way to peace. Peace is the way."

Maybe that last sentiment sums up Manitoba. Then again, maybe it doesn't, but as far as I can figure, Manitoba will not stay awake nights worrying about my perceptions. Manitoba will be just fine, thank you.

The Real Monument for Riel

From the front street, the St-Boniface Basilica looks like the typical massive Catholic church: a towering stone face with three huge arched doorways, columns on either side of the doors that would do Rome proud, a saint carved into the stone above the doors, and a rose window. Yes, a rose window except that this rose window is blank, empty, an unseeing eye.

It's just a facade, you see, a false front like small-town stores used to have. The church burned to the ground in 1968 and rather than replace it

The remains of Louis Riel lie in a churchyard adjacent to Winnipeg's St-Boniface Basilica.

all, the powers-that-be decided to keep the remaining walls and erect a new building inside. Not nearly so grand, the new church seems almost to huddle in the ruins of what used to be.

Do I dare stretch an analogy and suggest that that's how Canada's Native people must feel? Always in the shadow of what might have been? Always surrounded by reminders of a happier past?

Louis Riel is a huge hero in western Canada even though he lost the battle, lost his mind every now and then, and eventually lost his life to the hangman's noose. But none of that seems to matter. He stuck up for his people, first in 1870 when he fought for Métis land rights in the Red River area and then in 1885 when he led, sort of, the North-West Rebellion. I say "sort of" because it seems as if he never really wanted to fight. He could have won more battles than he did, but he always wavered, turned back, delayed, in the process of which he drove Gabriel Dumont crazy. Gabriel Dumont was a warrior. He could have managed a more even fight.

However, be that as it may, Riel's forces surrendered at Batoche in May 1885, and a short six months later, Riel was hanged for treason. The government in Ottawa had had enough aggravation. They thought they'd be done with it after the demise of Riel.

They weren't—not then and not now.

Immediately after his death in Regina, friends and family petitioned to have the body sent back to St. Vital rather than having it buried as per usual on the grounds of the jail. Authorities hemmed and hawed, telegrams went back and forth to Ottawa, but in the end, Riel won. He went back to St. Vital.

Okay, but you can't have a formal funeral, authorities decreed. Once again, Riel won. He had an extremely formal funeral complete with hundreds of mourners who formed a kilometre-long cortege from the Riel home to the basilica. His supporters carried his casket on their shoulders for the entire trip, and Archbishop Taché, no less, presided over the service. Riel would not go away quietly.

The simple red granite pedestal that marks him now continues in the tradition. It's understated, to put it mildly, but it was the first thing that two young moms with kids in tow asked us as we left the graveyard. "Did you find Riel? We've brought the kids to see Riel." We pointed to the red pedestal that says simply:

RIEL
16 NOVEMBRE
1885

Near Riel's simple grave is another no-nonsense one, a white pedestal that marks other members of his family—in particular his father and his maternal grandparents, Jean-Baptiste Lagimodière, 1778-1855, and Marie-Anne Gaboury Lagimodière, 1780-1875. Grandpa Lagimodière was a voyageur and hunter who never stayed home, so his wife, Marie-Anne, decided she wouldn't either. Thus, she became the first (or one of the first, if you'd prefer to be safe about these historical facts) white woman to travel through western Canada, stopping only long enough to have babies, eight of them in all. The second-last baby born to this adventuresome pair was Julie. Julie married Louis Riel Sr., and that's how we got Louis Riel, our unexpected but unforgettable hero.

Hon~ble Is As Hon~ble Does

As soon as I started exploring graveyards in and around Winnipeg, I learned that the Hudson's Bay Company was not just your average fur-trading monopoly. It was The Honourable Hudson's Bay Company, or as the monument makers depicted it, The Hon~ble HBC:

SACRED TO THE MEMORY OF DONALD ROSS, ESQUIRE
CHIEF FACTOR OF THE HON~BLE HUDSON'S BAY COMPANY
WHO DEPARTED THIS LIFE THE 19TH DAY OF NOVEMBER 1852
AGED 54 YEARS.

Another marker in the graveyard surrounding St. John's Anglican Church in Winnipeg explains:

IN MEMORY OF RICHARD HARDISTY OF EDMONTON, NWT
CHIEF FACTOR OF THE HON. HUDSON'S BAY CO.
AND SENATOR OF THE DOMINION OF CANADA
WHO DIED 15 OCTOBER, 1889 AT THE WINNIPEG HOSPITAL
FROM INJURIES RECEIVED IN AN ACCIDENT
AT BROADVIEW, NWT ON 2ND OF THE SAME MONTH
AGED 58 YEARS.

Notice that the Hudson's Bay Company connection gets mentioned first even though Richard Hardisty did all sorts of important things during his lifetime in western Canada. He was the first senator to be appointed from the district of Alberta, for one thing, and he was married to Eliza, a daughter of the missionary Rev. George McDougall. Together, they more or less ruled Edmonton in the early years. However, it's the HBC that gets top billing.

Hardisty was in the Winnipeg area on an official tour of new western settlements. It was a leisurely tour by modern standards—horse and buggy—but somehow the buggy wheel hit a railway track the wrong way and Hardisty was thrown out. He broke his back and died two weeks later.

Eliza got to his side before he died, by train, the history books tell me. They don't tell me if the train that brought her had to use the same track that killed her husband.

But back to the Hon~ble HBC. Even children's graves in Manitoba acknowledge its overwhelming influence. This is what is written on a small white marble grave in the churchyard next to St. Andrews on the Red, not far from Winnipeg:

IN MEMORY OF MARY
THE BELOVED DAUGHTER OF W.J. CHRISTIE, ESQ.
HON. HUDSON'S BAY COMP.
DIED JAN. 14, 1865 AGED 6 YRS AND 1 MO.

Two little markers in the St. John's Anglican graveyard in Winnipeg continue the HBC story with information about William Jeffrey Ward, David Work Finlayson, Marie Rosalie Allan, and Charles Campbell Allan, all children of James Allan Grahame, chief factor, Hon. Hudson's Bay Co. That fact is repeated for each of the four children.

William was born in Norway House, Rupert's Land, in 1865; died at Fort Garry, Red River settlement, 1866.

John Pruden, who died in 1868, breaks with tradition by acknowledging his Native wife on their gravemarker in St. John's Anglican churchyard in Winnipeg.

David was also born at Norway House, 1863; died at Fort Garry, 1866.

Marie was born in Victoria, BC, 1871; died at Winnipeg, 1876.

Charles was born in Winnipeg, 1874; died there in 1876.

Read between the lines and it's plain that Hudson's Bay factors had to move around a lot, this one from Norway House to Fort Garry to Victoria and finally to Winnipeg. There may have been other locations, other deaths, as well, since Charles is listed as the seventh son, Marie the second daughter, etc., so there were other children. The stones also say, again, that it was tough being a child in those days: William and David died within a week of one another. There must have been an epidemic—typhoid? smallpox? The same thing happened with Marie and Charles. They died within three weeks of one another. Another epidemic? A terrible accident?

And finally, the stones suggest that the mother of all these children might have been a Native woman. Her name doesn't appear at all. Lots of Hon~ble Hudson's Bay Co. men took country wives, as they were known. Some honoured them and stayed with them even after leaving the wilderness; others dropped them on their heads and left them behind. The Hon~ble HBC men weren't always that hon~ble. I don't know if that's the case with the mother of the Grahame children; sometimes mothers got left off official records no matter what their origins.

Not so on this stone, also in the St. John's Anglican cemetery in Winnipeg:

JOHN PETER PRUDEN
CHIEF FACTOR HUDSON'S BAY COMPANY
MEMBER OF THE COUNCIL OF ASSINIBOIA
OF THE RED RIVER SETTLEMENT
BORN 1778, MIDDLESEX ENGLAND, DIED 1868
HIS DEARLY BELOVED WIFE NANCY
A CREE INDIAN WOMAN BORN 1785, DIED 1838

This is a new stone, erected by descendants in 1991. I wonder if the original one mentioned Nancy with such pride, but never mind, it's nice to know that the descendants are happy to claim old connections.

The Best Graveyard in Manitoba

When I got to the graveyard at St. John's Anglican Cathedral in Winnipeg, I began to realize what an enormous task lay before me. I was travelling west to east, remember. The West is young, especially Alberta and Saskatchewan, where it's hard to find a gravemarker older than 1900. But Winnipeg, the Red River valley, and Fort Garry go back to the early 1800s as far as settled history goes, which means there are more stories, more people, more wars, more tragedies, more of everything that can be winkled from graveyards. And this particular graveyard, being Anglican and therefore inclined toward a fair amount of tombstone talk, had more than most.

A grey tablet near the church set the scene:

THIS MEMORIAL MARKS THE BIRTHPLACE
OF THE ANGLICAN CHURCH IN WESTERN CANADA.
1812–THE FIRST BURIALS IN THIS CHURCHYARD
WERE MADE SOUTH OF THE PRESENT CATHEDRAL.
1817–LORD SELKIRK MET HIS SETTLERS HERE.
1820–ARRIVAL AT THE RED RIVER SETTLEMENT
OF THE REVEREND JOHN WEST, CHAPLAIN
TO THE HUDSON'S BAY CO. AND A MEMBER
OF THE CHURCH MISSIONARY SOCIETY OF ENGLAND
WHO WAS THE FIRST ANGLICAN MISSIONARY
IN RUPERT'S LAND.
1822–COMPLETION OF THE FIRST ANGLICAN CHURCH
AND DAY SCHOOL, AND ON JULY 21,
FIRST BAPTISM OF TWO INDIAN BOYS,
JAMES HOPE AND HENRY BUDD.

There's more on the tablet but suffice it to say, the Anglican Church was on the scene early and got right to work. Near the official plaque is a gravemarker with proof of that:

> HERE LIE THE REMAINS OF THOMAS BUNN
> LIVERYMAN OF THE CITY OF LONDON.
> WHO DIED 15TH JANUARY 1853 IN HIS 88TH YEAR.
> AND OF PHOEBE HIS WIFE WHO DIED 29TH JUNE 1848
> THEIR MARRIAGE ON SEPT. 8, 1820, AT ROCK DEPOT
> NEAR YORK FACTORY, WAS THE FIRST CONDUCTED
> IN WESTERN CANADA BY AN ANGLICAN CLERGYMAN,
> REVEREND JOHN WEST, M.A.

Just because the church got busy and established itself in western Canada didn't mean we stopped fighting one another:

> CHARLES CONSTANTINE
> SUPERINTENDANT ROYAL N.W. MTD. POLICE
> SERVED IN FENIAN RAIDS OF 1866-70
> WOLSELEY EXP'DN 1870
> NORTH WEST REB. 1885
> PIONEER OFFICER OF YUKON,
> MACKENZIE AND PEACE RIVER DSTS.
> BORN BRADFORD YORKS, ENGLAND, 1849
> DIED AT CALIFORNIA 1912.

Constantine's marker could serve as a directory for Wars We Fought from 1850 to 1900, and his wife's marker, God bless it, could serve as a reminder that it takes two to make a hero:

> HENRIETTA ARMSTRONG, HIS WIFE
> BORN OTTAWA 1858 DIED KINGSTON 1934
> A COURAGEOUS AND CHEERFUL HELPMATE
> DURING MANY YEARS IN THE WEST AND NORTH.

Near Constantine is a group marker, erected by the 50th Battalion Winnipeg Rifles, for men who died in action or died from wounds in the North-West Rebellion of 1885. This is a graveyard, you can see, that marks the government side of any war, not the dissident side.

And speaking of organized military, the legendary Sam Steele is here:

> SACRED TO THE MEMORY OF
> MAJOR-GENERAL SIR SAMUEL BENFIELD STEELE
> K.G.M.G., C.B., M.V.O.
> BELOVED HUSBAND OF MARIE E. de L. HARWOOD

According to Thomas Bunn's epitaph in the St. John's Anglican graveyard, he and his wife, Phoebe, were the first couple to be married by an Anglican clergyman in western Canada.

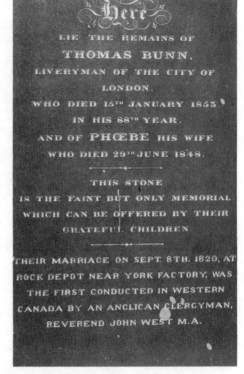

Here

LIE THE REMAINS OF
THOMAS BUNN,
LIVERYMAN OF THE CITY OF
LONDON.
WHO DIED 15TH JANUARY 1853
IN HIS 88TH YEAR.
AND OF **PHŒBE** HIS WIFE
WHO DIED 29TH JUNE 1848.

THIS STONE
IS THE FAINT BUT ONLY MEMORIAL
WHICH CAN BE OFFERED BY THEIR
GRATEFUL CHILDREN

THEIR MARRIAGE ON SEPT. 8TH. 1820, AT
ROCK DEPOT NEAR YORK FACTORY, WAS
THE FIRST CONDUCTED IN WESTERN
CANADA BY AN ANGLICAN CLERGYMAN,
REVEREND JOHN WEST M.A.

4TH SON OF THE LATE
CAPT. ELMES STEELE R.N.
BORN SIMCOE COUNTY,
ONT., JANUARY 5, 1851
DIED PUTNEY, LONDON,
ENGLAND, JAN. 30, 1919
LATE OF CANADIAN ACTIVE
MILITIA, CANADIAN PERMA-
NENT FORCE, ROYAL
NORTH WEST MOUNTED
POLICE, LORD
STRATHCONA'S HORSE
(ROYAL CANADIANS)
AND SOUTH AFRICAN CON-
STABULARY, 1866-1918.

And that's not all. For a man who liked to be in the thick of things at all times, Sam Steele picked the right time to be alive. If there wasn't a newly hatched police service to join (he was the third man to enlist for the NWMP), then there was a rebellion to deal with, there were gold rushes that had to be policed, new towns that needed a firm hand—Fort Steele, for one—riots that had to be controlled, or a world war that demanded his attention. Show him trouble and he was there.

But lest you think that men alone served in Canada's armed forces, listen to these accomplishments listed on a fairly new marker in St. John's:

ALFREDA JEAN ATTRILL R.R.C., S.S.ST.J., F.R.H.S., R.N.
NURSING SISTER LIEUT. C.A.M.C., C.E.F., 1914-1920
SERVED IN FRANCE, EGYPT, MACEDONIA, ENGLAND
AND ON THE SEAS.
STAFF WINNIPEG GENERAL HOSPITAL 1906-1914
NURSE ADVISER WINNIPEG HEALTH DEPT. 1914, 1920-1943
DAME OF GRACE OF ST. JOHN OF JERUSALEM 1966
DAME OF JUSTICE 1967.

SACRED TO THE MEMORY OF
MAJOR-GENERAL SIR SAMUEL BENFIELD STEELE
K.C.M.G. C.B. M.V.O.
BELOVED HUSBAND OF MARIE E. de L. HARWOOD
(4TH) SON OF THE LATE CAPTAIN ELMES STEELE R.N
BORN PURBROOK COUNTY SIMCOE, ONTARIO, JANUARY 5, 1851
DIED PUTNEY, LONDON, ENGLAND JANUARY 30, 1919
LATE OF CANADIAN ACTIVE MILITIA, CANADIAN PERMANENT FORCE,
ROYAL NORTH WEST MOUNTED POLICE,
LORD STRATHCONA'S HORSE (ROYAL CANADIANS)
AND SOUTH AFRICAN CONSTABULARY,
1866 – 1918

Sam Steele was on the scene of many of western Canada's early troublespots and finally came to rest in a Winnipeg graveyard.

It always seems such a contradiction, no matter what churchyard I'm in, to read about so many wars while standing in the most peaceful spot in town. The only noise in the graveyard that day was the sound of blossoms falling from the fat peonies that lined every path. The answer, for a moment at least, seemed so simple. Just don't fight. But that's another thing to learn from graveyards—nothing is simple and not all wars occur on a battlefield:

TO THE MEMORY OF THE HON. JOHN NORQUAY
WHO WAS FOR MANY YEARS PREMIER OF MANITOBA.
BY HIS SUDDEN AND ALL TOO EARLY DEATH
HIS NATIVE LAND LOST AN ELOQUENT SPEAKER,
AN HONEST STATESMAN AND A TRUE FRIEND.
1841–1889
THIS MONUMENT IS A PUBLIC EXPRESSION
OF HIS STERLING WORTH.

The inscription tells much of the story—he was a great speaker, he was premier, he was a native son—but it doesn't explain the "too early death." All I've been able to uncover there is a hint about appendicitis. No suggestion that his dancing feet had done him in; he was, they say, such a good dancer, in spite of some considerable bulk, that he always carried moccasins with him, just in case a dance broke out. What a way to go, I thought, but I can't find any record of that.

History books are much more concerned with the fact, and this is where things get complicated, that Norquay took Manitoba into the railway business. He thought it made sense to run a line south into the States, the better to access markets there. He also thought he had the prime minister's okay on the idea and, more to the point, a promise of financial support. But no to both ideas. Sir John A. Macdonald pulled the rug out from under him, leaving both the province and a number of investors with huge debts. And that was the end of that, not to mention the end of Norquay's political career.

Ironically, Sir John A. Macdonald's son, the Honourable Sir Hugh John Macdonald, 1850-1929, also a former premier of Manitoba, is buried within hailing distance of Norquay. Not that the son was responsible for the sins, or otherwise, of the father, but it does seem a bit too close for comfort.

There are many more familiar names in this graveyard crowded with history—Luxton, Galt, Richardson, Sifton, Inkster, Sugden—but there are also the homelier tales, the ones that always stop me in my tracks, the ones about children, of course. A grey tablet lists Mary Jane, Isabella, Janet, and Flora Bannerman. All died before the age of twelve, and the inscription asks:

> HOLY EARTH, TO THEE WE TRUST
> THESE BONNY HEAPS OF PRECIOUS DUST
> KEEP THEM SAFELY, SACRED TOMB
> TILL FOND PARENTS ASK FOR ROOM.

What a Difference a Word Makes

All it takes to change an inscription from ordinary to extraordinary is a single word. This, for example, is what it says on yet another gravemarker in the St. John's Anglican cemetery in Winnipeg:

> SACRED TO THE MEMORY OF MY MOTHER
> MARGARET NAHOVWAY SINCLAIR
> THIS LAST TOKEN OF LOVE AND AFFECTION
> IS ERECTED BY HER WANDERING BOY COLIN 1897

Probably an Hon~ble Hudson's Bay Company man, I thought when I first saw this stone, one of those incredible men who wandered northern Canada in search of furs and profit for the company store. But no, I was completely wrong. Colin Sinclair did not go to ground; he went to sea—not that he intended to.

During his lifetime, John Norquay, a former premier of Manitoba, was always ready to kick up his heels.

Colin was the Sinclairs' youngest child, only nine years old. His Hudson's Bay Company dad wanted him to go to Scotland as the other children had, to stay with relatives and get an education. Mrs. Sinclair resisted. He was her last chick, he was too young, etc., etc. It would likely have remained a stalemate for a few more years except that Colin went with his dad to York Factory one day where dad had to do some business with the captain of a ship bound for Scotland. During the shipboard negotiations, the youngster fell asleep. It was a sign as far as dad was concerned. He left Colin right where he was and let him sail for Scotland.

Apparently, Colin adjusted. In fact, he grew downright fond of ships and sailing, and at age eighteen, went to sea and stayed there for the next fifty years. Not once did he sail into home territory, not once did he write, so the Sinclairs had to conclude he had been lost at sea.

It wasn't until he was eighty-one years old, seventy-two years after falling asleep at the wrong time, that he returned to the Red River area. There he found his mother's grave and erected the monument that marks her now, the monument from her wandering son.

The Most Ministers per Square Churchyard

It's tempting to say that the Winnipeg area must be extra holy because it has so many church leaders in its cemeteries, but I guess I'll have to yield not to temptation and say instead that Winnipeg was headquarters for much of the missionary work throughout western and northern Canada. Therefore, its cemeteries have more ministers than most.

Catholics and Anglicans were well established by the 1820s, but it was 1851 before the Presbyterians finally got their first minister, Rev. John Black, and their first church, now called the Old Kildonan in Winnipeg. Maybe that's why men such as Rev. George Bryce, 1844-1931, worked so hard in the next few years. He is buried in the Old Kildonan churchyard beneath a stone that includes the following facts:

> FOUNDER OF MANITOBA COLLEGE 1871
> ORGANIZED KNOX CHURCH WPC 1872
> A FOUNDER OF MANITOBA UNIVERSITY
> DEDICATED NINETY CHURCHES
> A HISTORIAN OF WESTERN CANADA

Near Rev. Bryce is Rev. James Robertson, first pastor of Knox Church in Winnipeg, 1874-1881, and superintendent of western missions, 1881-1902.

> THE STORY OF HIS WORKS IS THE HISTORY
> OF THE PRESBYTERIAN CHURCH IN WESTERN CANADA
> AND WHILE WESTERN CANADA ENDURES,
> THAT WORK WILL ABIDE.

As usual, I can't resist the wife's story:

> ALSO IN LOVING MEMORY OF MARY ANNE COWING 1839-1908
> BELOVED WIFE OF THE REV. JAMES ROBERTSON
> WHO DENYING HER HEART ITS CLAIMS,
> WITH FIDELITY, PATIENCE AND COURAGE FOR TWENTY YEARS
> KEPT HER LONELY WATCH OVER HOME AND CHILDREN
> THAT HIS WORK FOR WESTERN CANADA MIGHT BE DONE.
> AS SHE SHARED HIS SACRIFICE,
> SHE SHARES HIS GLORY.

I should hope so, and speaking of wives who served beyond the call of duty, there's also Sadie Stringer, who trained as a nurse before ever she'd marry young Isaac. After all, her intended intended to bring the Gospel to what were then called the Eskimos of northern Canada. If she were to survive up there, she'd need training, she figured. And she was right. Two of her children were born in the north country far from doctors and hospitals. As far as I can tell, she calmly choreographed the whole affair and told her husband what to do. She is not mentioned on her husband's handsome marker in St. John's graveyard:

SACRED TO THE MEMORY OF ISAAC O. STRINGER
ARCHBISHOP OF RUPERT'S LAND
SOMETIME BISHOP OF YUKON
FIRST MISSIONARY TO THE ESKIMO OF HERSCHEL ISLAND
1866–1934

He too managed remarkable feats of survival in this forbidding climate. On one occasion, lost in a wilderness of wind and snow, hungry and tired, he boiled his rawhide boots. "Palatable, feel encouraged," he said in his diary. Two days later, he was still lost but wrote, "Breakfast and dinner of rawhide boots. Fine. But not enough." After fifty-one days, he stumbled into an ·Inuit camp and was taken back to the mission. Ever afterwards, he was known as The Bishop Who Ate His Boots.

John Hudspith Turner was not quite so fortunate. This is what it says under a picture of an igloo on his gravemarker in St. John's Anglican cemetery:

IN PROUD AND HALLOWED MEMORY
OF JOHN HUDSPITH TURNER, M.P.S.
BELOVED HUSBAND OF JOAN MIRIAM
CANON OF ALL SAINTS CATHEDRAL AKLAVIK N.W.T.
AFTER LABOURING JOYFULLY FOR 18 YEARS IN BAFFIN LAND
MAKING LONG JOURNEYS OVER FROZEN SEAS
TO ESKIMO CAMPS AND DEVOTING HIMSELF
TO THE TRANSLATION OF THE SCRIPTURES
INTO THE NATIVE TONGUE,
HE ENTERED INTO THE PRESENCE OF HIS LORD
ON DECEMBER 9TH, 1947, AGED 42 YEARS.

He entered into the presence of the Lord because he left the safety off his gun and accidentally shot himself in the head. That happened on September 24, 1947, in a northern outpost so isolated that it took a week for a nearby Inuit family to make their way to a Hudson's Bay post at Arctic Bay to radio for help. Then, it took another two months before the Canadian army and an RCAF rescue team could complete one of the most incredible rescue missions ever attempted in Canada's north. It reads like a James Bond novel except that it was real: appalling cold, impossible landing conditions, a terribly sick man, his pregnant wife and two little kids, and heroic men who somehow got them out.

"Operation Canon" was a success, but the Canon himself didn't make it. He died about two weeks after the rescue, and two weeks after that his wife had a baby girl, their third daughter. There's an incredible picture of

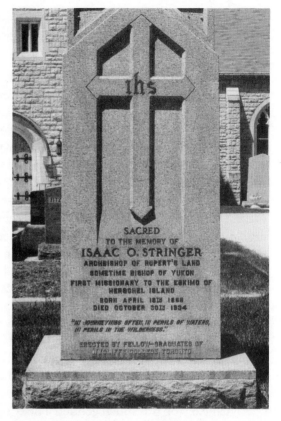

The gravemarker of Isaac O. Stringer neglects to tell us that he was known as The Bishop Who Ate His Boots.

the first daughter, then about three years old, watching her father being loaded on the plane that's taking them all to Winnipeg. She's wearing fur from head to foot; only her little face is uncovered. She's crying.

The Amazing Technicolor Day

One sunny Sunday in Manitoba, I braked five times for graveyards and in the process found myself in five different countries. It was great.

The first stop was a Jewish cemetery. Most of the epitaphs were written in Hebrew, and a ceremony taking place in a newer section of the graveyard was being conducted in Hebrew. Later, someone told me that the ceremony was likely the unveiling of a headstone, which takes place six months to one year after a death. But at the time all I knew was that I could be almost anywhere in the world. The chanting of the Kaddish, the prayer for the dead, would sound the same everywhere; the stones would read the same.

One gravemarker in English explained:

OUR REVERED FATHER
ISRAEL ISAAC KAHANOVITCH
CHIEF RABBI OF WESTERN CANADA
HUMBLE AND KIND
FOR OVER FORTY YEARS
SERVED HIS PEOPLE AND RELIGION
HIS COMMUNITY AND THE HOPES OF ISRAEL

WITH A STEADFAST FAITHFULNESS AND LOYALTY.
BEING SUMMONED TO ETERNITY
ON THE ELEVENTH DAY OF TAMUZ 1945

The next stop was happenstance. As I drove north of Winnipeg, I noticed a lot of cars ahead, then a lot of folding chairs, then a lot of people all dressed up, then a graveyard. I braked, of course.

Most of the markers in the graveyard were in Russian or Ukrainian, but the central cairn explained in English that this was the Winnipeg Ukrainian Greek Catholic cemetery. Now all I had to do was find someone to explain all the activity.

I picked the wrong person to ask, or maybe it was the right one because I won't easily forget what he said. It was a celebration of Pentecost, he told me, which was to include a special ceremony in front of their war memorial to "Fallen Heroes." The Legion would be marching, speeches would be made, the porta-potties would be necessary, but most of all my tour guide wanted me to take away the message that we Canadians don't know our history.

We don't know that Ukrainians were interned in Canada during World War I, and the CBC is no good because they won't show the documentary about Ukrainian internment. Tell them, he said. His English wasn't too good but I got the message, and since then I've seen more stories on internment camps in Canada. Again, it was a Canada I didn't recognize.

The next stop was much gentler. The congregation inside St. Andrews on the Red Anglican Church were singing "How Firm a Foundation," and the birds were singing in the graveyard. We could have been in an English country churchyard: the markers were in English, many contained a Bible verse, many referred to the Hudson's Bay Company. One broke me right up with the message that Eliza Peers died 1864, aged twelve years, "the only beloved and dutiful daughter of Augustus Peers." No mention of the mom.

Rev. William Cockran is buried there. He got the church built and was so taken with its location on the St. Andrews Rapids that he asked to be buried within sound of them. But he died in Portage la Prairie, some 128 kilometres away. It would have shown disrespect in those days to carry the coffin to its final resting place by horse and buggy, so his faithful parishioners had to organize relays of men to carry it on their shoulders. It took the better part of three days with overnight stops in two of the churches he had established, but he got his wish.

My next stop was St. Peter's Dynevor Catholic Church, where, I had been told, the well-known Saulteaux chief Peguis is buried. I braked in front of the church and guess what? It was Peguis Day. Indians from all over the district were there dancing, drumming, singing, playing with their little kids, generally having a grand time.

Peguis was chief of the Saulteaux back when Lord Selkirk was trying to establish his settlement, and if it hadn't been for Peguis and his people, Selkirk's settlers might have perished. In fact, Selkirk is quoted on a cairn at the site as saying in 1817, "Peguis has been a steady friend of the settlement ever since its establishment and has never deserted its cause in its greatest reverses."

A new gravemarker near the church commemorates Peguis thus:

> IN MEMORY OF PEGUIS
> CHIEF OF THE SAULTEAUX INDIANS
> AND GRATEFUL RECOGNITION OF HIS GOOD OFFICES
> TO THE EARLY SETTLERS. ONE OF THE FIRST CONVERTS
> TO CHRISTIANITY OF HIS RACE.
> HE DIED IN 1864 AND HIS BODY RESTS IN THE OLD CEMETERY
> OF ST. PETERS CHURCH NEAR SELKIRK
> WHERE HE WAS A DEVOUT WORSHIPPER.

The Peguis party was tempting, but it was time to head north to Gimli, the district that once upon a time was an independent Icelandic country within British North America. Surely Gimli would have more multicultural goodies for us but alas, no. The graveyard was standard, the town likewise except for a rather mean-looking Viking statue down by the lake. It was then that I remembered—Scandinavians don't say much. This too was a cultural experience.

And that was the end of my most multicultural day. Well, almost. We had Texas Fried Steak in Lac du Bonnet that night. Only in Manitoba, you say? Pity.

All You Ever Wanted to Know about Manitoba

In my day, many moons ago, I learned two things about Manitoba: it had Selkirk settlers and it had floods. Neither event is prominent in the graveyards, however.

I did finally find mention of "Selkirk settlers" in the Old Kildonan cemetery in Winnipeg. The inscription on the tomb of Flora Livingstone, a native of Argyleshire, Scotland, 1805-1865, says, "One of Lord Selkirk's Colonists," and Donald Murray, 1800-1888, born in Sutherlandshire, Scotland, admits to being "One of the Selkirk Settlers."

Lord Selkirk was the Scottish philanthropist who decided to bring poor Scottish crofters to the Northwest Territories. We had land in those days. They didn't. There were other considerations in the scheme, of course. He was a big shareholder in the Hudson's Bay Company and thought he could kill two birds with one stone, i.e., give the landless Scots a new lease on life and in the process supply locally grown food to the HBC rather than import it.

Neither intention worked out, not at first anyway. The first Selkirk settlers in Canada froze, starved, moved again and again, died of disease and fatigue; some even died in a battle now known as the Seven Oaks Skirmish. It used to be called the Seven Oaks Massacre, but it's been downgraded because it was kind of an accidental war. In June 1816, Métis Cuthbert Grant and his men were transporting pemmican and other supplies through Selkirk territory to a North West Company post. Governor Robert Semple rode out with some of his men to tell the Métis to get

lost, and somehow a gun went off—Semple's, they think now—and the battle was on. Twenty-one men died, all but one from the Scottish side.

Selkirk came a year later to settle the disputes, but they were settling themselves in that the North West Company and the Hudson's Bay Company eventually amalgamated. Now there was no need to shoot at one another.

Grateful Selkirk settlers and their descendants erected this tribute to the Saulteaux chief Peguis in the St. Peter's Dynevor cemetery north of Winnipeg.

And what happened to Cuthbert Grant, who led this mini-revolution? Good question.

The Disappearing Grave

To find Cuthbert Grant, I went to the small town west of Winnipeg that used to be called Grantown but is now known as Saint Francois Xavier. The name change should have been my first clue.

Next I went to the Catholic church where Grant is supposed to be buried. It was locked tight, and even when two friendly gents from the farm nearby unlocked it and let me look around, I couldn't find any sign of Grant's tomb. Nor was he buried in the graveyard nearby, although there was at least one gravemarker that mentions his name:

> JOSUE BRELAND
> DIED AUG. 18, 1971 AGE 86 YEARS
> GREAT GRANDSON OF CUTHBERT GRANT,
> "WARDEN OF THE PLAINS."

It took the lady in the teahouse next door to set me right. "He's likely buried beneath the highway," she said. "He was once upon a time buried beneath the Catholic church but there was a flood, the church floated away, and things got kind of mixed up from then on."

"It's too bad," she added. "He should have been the Métis hero instead of Riel. He was a good administrator and wise leader."

The Most Beautiful Graveyard in Manitoba

It was almost dusk when we finally found Neepawa's cemetery, a time of day that made it even more beautiful: long light giving dimension to the abundant flowers, hedges shaped just so, markers that behaved themselves. But it was also big, a lot bigger than we had imagined. How could we find Margaret Laurence's grave and her stone angel before dark?

As it turned out, the stone angel was easy to spot. It's big—about 3.5 metres, it stands on the brow of a hill overlooking the town, and it's white marble. That's exactly how Margaret Laurence described it in her book *The Stone Angel*, except that the real one, the one in Riverside cemetery, gazes with kindness upon the person buried beneath her. Margaret Laurence gave her stone angel sightless eyes looking nowhere.

Maybe it was catching, this sightless business. We couldn't for the life of us find Margaret Laurence. We asked two women who were busily rearranging flowers in a vase. "Her kids brought her back here to be buried,"

I explained. No, that couldn't be, they told me, because she was never married. They were wrong, but I moved on without comment.

The next pair that I asked looked blankly at me, "Who's Margaret Laurence?" It wasn't until we came upon a young woman who had obviously taken some Canadian lit in her day that we made progress. "She's right over there," she pointed, "with her grandparents. Look for the name Wemyss."

Sure enough. Not a word about her accomplishments, however. Not a single hint that she was someone we should know and cherish. Just her name and dates, 1926-1987.

A Home Away from Home

I'm still looking, but so far I haven't found a single person who admits to being a Barnardo boy or girl on his or her gravemarker. There is an official cairn near what used to be the Russell Industrial Farm that tells this much:

BARNARDO HOMES NATIONAL INC., 1888-1907
BURIED HERE ARE:
ALF W. RENWICK, DIED 1896, AGE 18
CHARLES ERNEST WARRINGTON, DIED JUNE 18, 1901,
AGE A FEW HOURS
GEORGE WILLIAMS, DIED AUGUST 15, 1890, AGE 23
JOHN UNDERWOOD, DIED MARCH 23, 1903, AGE 19

The baby was the child of the horticultural instructor at the farm; the older boys must have been some of the young men brought from Britain to be trained for work on farms in Canada. There's no indication as to why they died.

Actually, the homeless boys who came to the industrial school near Russell seem to have been the lucky ones. At least they were older and had some notion of what was expected of them before they went out into the backwoods of Canada. But many of the first children who came, anywhere from age five up, went directly to Canadian families who may or may not have used them well. That was the trouble. There was very little supervision of the program at first. Some children were treated like little slaves. Most were separated from brothers and sisters. Some weren't even allowed to go to school.

Facing page: The stone angel in the Riverside cemetery in Neepawa gazes with kindness at those who rest there, unlike the sightless statue in Margaret Laurence's story.

The idea to move children from the streets of London and distribute them in Canada like so many cards in a deck came from Dr. Thomas Barnardo, who really did want to provide better homes and a future for children who had neither. But he couldn't be everywhere at once, and some of his charges went from the frying pan into the fire.

Some, to be fair, did just fine, but they don't seem to be speaking up on their gravemarkers either. It is not, apparently, a source of pride in Canada.

Murder and Mercy in Manitoba

I couldn't tell from the signs around the town of Notre-Dame-de-Lourdes whether it was French in name only or whether the population was also French. The Shell station, for example, promised "Avec Service," but the seed plant was stolidly the Notre Dame Seed Plant.

The graveyard told me clearly, however, with its row upon row of markers in French for people from France, Switzerland, Belgium, and Luxembourg. The graveyard also told me this story:

A LA MÉMOIRE DE
NOTRE CHÈRE FRÈRE
HENRI ROCK DU CHATELARD, SUISSE
MORT D'UN ASSASSINAT A HAYWOOD LE 14 OCT. 1916
À L'AGE DE 25 ANS.
PRIONS POUR LUI.
R.I.P.

In other words, Henry Rock came to Canada from Switzerland only to be killed by an assassin, all of which sounds terribly un-Canadian. However, that's exactly what happened.

I don't know whether Mr. Rock chose to become a travelling salesman—it wasn't exactly an easy life—but at any rate, that's what he was doing. He was going door to door in the countryside, selling spices and household goods on behalf of the Rawleigh Company. As was the custom of the day, he stayed with friendly folk along the way except that one of the folk turned out to be less than friendly. He let Henry stay the night, then robbed and killed him. And lest you think that murderers always got their due in those bad old days, think again. This particular one served only a few years in jail.

On a happier note, there's a grotto across the street from the cemetery with a plaque in front of it that includes the word "poliomyelitis." It's the first time I've ever found it mentioned in or near a graveyard even though many people died during the epidemics in the 1940s and 1950s. The plaque explains that the grotto was built to thank the Virgin Mary for protecting the children of the community from the dreaded disease.

The Last Word

I give the last word in Manitoba to a mystery. This is written on a stone in the Old Kildonan graveyard in Winnipeg. Does anyone know the end of the story?

ERECTED IN MEMORY OF SAMUEL HENDERSON
WHO LEFT HIS HOUSE SOUND AND WELL JULY 4, 1864
AND DID NOT RETURN,
NOR AFTER THE MOST DILIGENT SEARCH
HAVE ANY TRACES OF HIM BEEN FOUND.
HE WAS AN HUMBLE MINDED CHRISTIAN.
AGE 74 YEARS.
A NATIVE OF ORKNEY.

Ontario

✝

Where Canada Gets More Complicated

I WISH I COULD BE LIKE
THOSE TERRIBLY CLEVER JOURNALISTS
WHO LAND IN UNFAMILIAR TERRITORY
AND KNOW EVERYTHING ABOUT THE PLACE
THAT'S WORTH KNOWING
WITHIN A FEW HOURS OR DAYS.
I WAS IN ONTARIO FOR SEVERAL WEEKS,
BUT DARNED IF I KNOW ANYTHING ABOUT IT
EXCEPT THAT IT'S TOO BIG AND COMPLEX
TO KNOW ANYTHING FOR SURE.

There was the day I ran out of gas, for example. A nightmare, you might think, to run out of gas on one of Ontario's freeways, but the gods were with me. I coughed to a stop at the main intersection of Elmira, Elmira being a Mennonite town where horses are more important than cars, so important indeed that they get their own gravel lane on streets and highways.

Horses, it turns out, don't mind a car that's stalled in the main intersection; they just trotted obligingly around us. And when I went looking for gas, I found it at the second house down the street. "Yeah, sure," the young man said. "I'll just get my dad's lawnmower can. That'll take you to the service station."

And it did, and then we went for two orders of apple pandowdy at a local restaurant, and lived happily ever after.

Or until we got to Niagara Falls a few days later. There, we were told that every other tourist in the world was in town that night so our hotel room would be $145, "take it or leave it." We took it but I, for one, could have spit nails, not that anyone would have noticed what with the loud-speaker next door blaring all night long about the splendours of Miniature World. "Come in now, open all night, view the small wonders of the world." Yeah, right.

See how Ontario presented itself as an uncomplicated entity, a place where everyone thinks alike and behaves according to my expectations? Ha. How do these journalists do it anyhow?

Later, Judy and I saw *Cyrano de Bergerac* at the Stratford Festival. I still don't know how we got there. One minute we were on the road to Kitchener, the next we saw a sign that said thirty kilometres to Stratford. Since it was so close, and there were no signs to Kitchener, what could we do? The most efficient tourist system in the world got us accommodation and tickets faster than we could say howdy, and there we were, watching the not-so-lovely Cyrano long for the lovely Roxanne, knowing he'd never have her because she measured success by excess. That is, she thought true love was demonstrated by an excess of flowery words and silly tributes delivered by handsome men with teeny tiny noses.

The term "success by excess" caught my attention, and even though it had everything to do with love and such stuff, I concluded it also applied to Ontario. Success is excess here, I decided as I listened to Roxanne carry on, glad that I had finally found a description to fit all, and then I fell asleep, having driven to excess that day, which is the only way to drive in Ontario.

I didn't sleep long, believe me. The play was wonderful. And being the nice westerner that I am, I wanted Cyrano to know that he could bring his big nose out west any day, and we'd love him out here where appearances don't matter so much.

Am I mixing my metaphors? Am I confusing a play with real life? Do I realize that *Cyrano de Bergerac* was not written in Ontario for Ontario? Yes to all of the above, but there's an interesting echo in that success and excess line.

I was not as disorganized as all of this makes me sound. I couldn't be. Ontario has had more people than any other province for most of its history; therefore, there are an awful lot of graveyards to check out. Second, I was coming from Alberta. We have one hundred years, tops, of history in our graveyards, but Ontario has 250 years at least, which adds to the number of graveyards and the complexity of the stories in all those graveyards. In other words, I had to know more wars, more places, more names, more dates. My lists had lists!

And then the director of the Ontario Historical Society asked if I had read Alberta's Cemetery Act? Well, no, I had to admit, I hadn't. "Better do it," he said, "before somebody comes along wanting to change the rules about old cemeteries and what can be done with the land." So I had to add present-day politics to the lists.

It seems that the Ontario government had recently proposed changes to the province's cemetery act that would have allowed commercial development of old graveyard sites, many of which are valuable inner-city pieces of land. The Historical Society was up in arms; so were many citizens. It was an eye opener for me. Graveyards are not usually high on political agendas—except at Hallowe'en when local governments catch heck for letting vandals do their worst again. But here graveyards were the concern of high-priced government departments, editorials, Sunday sermons, and consultants. It was a signal to me that in Ontario graveyards are not just quiet corners of the world; they are Politics.

With that sure knowledge ringing in my ears, I decided to get Political and choose the biggest cemetery in the biggest city as the best graveyard in the province. After all, didn't someone once say that Success is Excess?

The Best Graveyard in Ontario

Mount Pleasant in the heart of Toronto is amazing—drive through its imposing castlelike gates and you're in another world. No more traffic, no more noise, no more drivers' dirty looks. You're in a park, folks. Just because there are a few gravemarkers here and there can't change that fact. This is exactly what the planners had in mind in 1876 when they decided to make themselves a "rural cemetery" in the style of the most famous rural cemetery of all—Mount Auburn cemetery in Cambridge, Massachusetts.

Until Mount Auburn was developed in 1831, graveyards had been rather nasty places—generally jammed into small churchyards, often unkempt and unloved, almost certainly unsanitary. People who had no church affiliation were tough out of luck and ended up in unmarked graves in potter's fields or farmers' fields. There was a potter's field, for instance, in Toronto at the corner of what is now Yonge and Bloor, about the busiest, shiniest corner you can find in the city now. A plaque at Mount Pleasant talks about that first graveyard:

IN THIS AREA OF THE CEMETERY LIE BURIED
MANY OF THE INHABITANTS
OF THE EARLY TOWN OF "MUDDY YORK."
THEY WERE ORIGINALLY BURIED IN THE POTTER'S FIELD
A PLOT OF SIX ACRES IN YORKVILLE.
THE REMAINS OF 364 PERSONS WERE REMOVED
TO THIS LOCATION AND SOME 984 OTHERS
WERE REMOVED TO THE TORONTO NECROPOLIS
BETWEEN THE YEARS 1851 AND 1881.

Next time you descend the steps into the bright lights of the underground passages at the corner of Yonge and Bloor, think of the stories the nearby earth could tell.

So Mount Pleasant was developed because there was a need for more burial spaces, and it was developed as a park because that was the emerging cemetery style at the time. Which means it's lovely: more trees than you've ever heard of, flowers and shrubs, quiet winding roads, benches here and there for contemplation. But what a job for the graveyard explorer. Had Judy and I not had maps, we'd be there still. Some 81 hectares (200 acres), some 168,000 graves.

What did we find? Not as much as I expected, but I was looking for words and stories, remember. Gravemarkers in Mount Pleasant tell more by their size, shape, and design than by actual words. For instance, there are individual family mausoleums that are bigger than your average downtown apartment. Thus do we know that the Massey family and the Eaton family, to name just two, had more money than the rest of us. But no words. No explanation of how this all came about.

Size is demonstrated in a number of group monuments as well, such as the Independent Order of Oddfellows monument, the St. Andrews monument, the 48th Highlanders' Memorial monument, and a Salvation Army monument with these words written beneath the carving of a huge wave:

IN SACRED MEMORY OF 167 OFFICERS AND SOLDIERS
OF THE SALVATION ARMY

PROMOTED TO GLORY FROM THE EMPRESS OF IRELAND
AT DAYBREAK FRIDAY, MAY 29, 1914.

That was the terrible, foggy, cold night when the passenger ship, the *Empress of Ireland*, collided with another ship in the middle of the St. Lawrence. It was all over in fifteen minutes. Only 465 people survived; 1,014 died including 167 Salvationists enroute to London for a Salvation Army Congress.

The Fitch monument tells its story in size and elaborate design as well. There's a bust of a most handsome fellow, mounted between black granite columns. But the epitaph also spells out some of the tale:

IN MEMORIAM
LIEUTENANT WILLIAM CHARLES FITCH
ROYAL GRENADIERS
BORN AT TORONTO, SEPT'R 10TH, 1858
KILLED IN ACTION AT BATOCHE, N'W'T' MAY 12, 1885.

In Saskatchewan and Manitoba, the story of the North-West Rebellion is told to a large extent by Indian and Métis graves, especially in Batoche. In Toronto, it's told from the other side of the guns.

Here's another east-west comparison. In the West, the story of immigration from eastern European lands is recounted in small prairie graveyards full of little white wooden crosses with Russian or Ukrainian writing on them. In Toronto is a massive piece of grey granite with information on it about the man who encouraged the "men in sheepskin coats" to come to Canada:

CLIFFORD SIFTON, 1861–1929
PATRIOT STATESMAN SPORTSMAN
A LOYAL HUSBAND
AN INDULGENT FATHER
A TRUE FRIEND

John Reginald Thorn is remembered with an impressive monument, but the most impressive thing of all is his gallant farewell:

JOHN REGINALD THORN, AGED 20 YEARS
ELDEST SON OF CONSTANCE E. AND MAJOR J.O. THORN,
QUARTERMASTER QUEEN'S OWN RIFLES OF CANADA
ACCIDENTALLY KILLED BY HIS HORSE FALLING UPON HIM
WHILE ACTING IN THE Q.O.R. PAGEANT ON MONDAY NIGHT,
JUNE 20TH, 1910
"TELL MOTHER I'LL BE ALL RIGHT IN THE MORNING."

Unlike western Canadian grave-yards, the Mount Pleasant cemetery in Toronto recounts the North-West Rebellion through the epitaphs of those who fought on the government side.

John was riding in a military pageant at the exhibition when his horse fell backwards on him, impaling him on the pommel. At first, his injuries didn't seem that serious, which is why he said as he left the grandstand, "Tell Mother I'll be all right in the morning."

Tommy Thompson's last words are also famous. On his gravemarker, under the carving of a tree and a walking stick—the one he always used as he inspected his beloved parks—are the words:

THOMAS "TOMMY" W.M. THOMPSON, B.S.A.
METROPOLITAN TORONTO'S FIRST PARKS COMMISSIONER
OCT. 15, 1913–MAR. 1, 1985
"PLEASE WALK ON THE GRASS."

The musician Glenn Gould, 1932-1982, is buried in a newer part of Mount Pleasant, marked simply with a stone and a plaque. I didn't realize at first that the spindly tree behind the stone was significant, but it is:

THIS TREE HAS BEEN PARTICULARLY CHOSEN
BECAUSE FROM ITS WOOD ARE MADE
THE SOUNDING BOARDS OF SOME PIANOS.

It's a Sitka spruce erected in Gould's honour by those who attended the Glenn Gould Conference, September 1992.

A young man's last message to his mother is repeated on his gravestone in Mount Pleasant cemetery.

But greater by far are those gravemarkers that give nothing away—just names and dates. Foster Hewitt first used the most Canadian of all phrases, "He shoots, he scores." That is not on his gravemarker. Egerton Ryerson saw to it that every child in Ontario had the right to go to school. It doesn't mention that on his gravemarker. Drs. Banting and Best isolated insulin as a treatment for diabetes. Silence on their gravemarkers. Robert Simpson opened a store, then a whole bunch of stores, then a catalogue. His gravemarker is tall but entirely silent. Dr. Augusta Stowe-Gullen was the first woman to graduate in medicine from a Canadian medical school. She was also a champion of women's issues. Not a word about any of that on her drawer in the Mount Pleasant mausoleum. Charles Conacher has a wonderfully original gravemarker, the slash on one corner resembling a hockey blade. But that's the closest the gravemarker comes to mentioning Conacher's hockey days.

And nowhere on John Smith's grave does it say that because he died in 1898 at the age of thirty-one, his five-year-old daughter had to go to work. Not that she minded. She took to it like a duck to water and ruled the movie world from then on as Mary Pickford.

Even Mackenzie King, prime minister of Canada for twenty-one years, is silent. There's a government plaque nearby that admits to his political past, but his actual grave gives away nothing but his dates, December 17, 1874–July 22, 1950.

What a modest lot we Canadians are, although that's changing too. Check out the newer sections of Mount Pleasant; words, statues, symbols are making a comeback. In fact, if you want to experience this change first-hand, wander through Mount Pleasant some sunny afternoon. It's got it all, including a reference to the BNA Act, of all things, an unexpected piece of politics in the graveyard. On a rock, in a newer section, is this plaque:

> THIS SUGAR MAPLE WAS PLANTED . . .
> ON APRIL 17, 1982, TO COMMEMORATE
> THE PATRIATION TO CANADA
> OF THE CONSTITUTION.

The Other Best Graveyard in Ontario

Lundy's Lane in Niagara Falls is not at all like Mount Pleasant. It's not quiet, rural, orderly, or conducive to contemplation, but it tells wonderful stories, and that's where I come in.

In fact, Lundy's Lane is an improbable collection of stuff that seems to work in spite of itself. There's the Queen Victoria water fountain as you pass the church enroute to the cemetery. Originally built of eighty-two large limestones—one for each year of the Queen's life—it used to supply water on three levels for dogs, horses, and humans. Unfortunately, it no longer works. But it's there any-

This message from Toronto's first commissioner of parks, Tommy Thompson, seems only fitting.

way, an interesting reminder of the importance of queens and horses in our earlier days.

The graveyard itself is dominated by the huge Soldiers monument, just one of the many war references throughout this cemetery. This particular piece of stone honours twenty-two soldiers who died during the battle of Lundy's Lane:

> ERECTED BY THE CANADIAN PARLIAMENT
> IN HONOUR OF THE VICTORY GAINED
> BY THE BRITISH AND CANADIAN FORCES
> ON THIS FIELD ON JULY 25, 1814
> AND IN GRATEFUL REMEMBRANCE OF THE BRAVE MEN
> WHO DIED ON THAT DAY
> FIGHTING FOR THE UNITY OF THE EMPIRE.

That date is important. It was one of the last battles fought between the British and the Americans in the War of 1812. Why were they fighting? It's hard to figure out now, but as far as I can tell, the bottom line is that they thought it was necessary at the time. We were British subjects. We had to keep US troops out of Canada. So we did, and we died, as people in wars always do. That's the lesson of graveyards—that those who died in war are not forgotten, but sometimes the reasons for the war are.

Lundy's Lane was just an innocent trail through the bush past Bill Lundy's place near Niagara Falls until the British and Canadian commanders decided to get serious about fighting one another. So they drew the line at Lundy's Lane and started shooting. It was an awful battle, hundreds of dead and wounded on both

Wood from the Sitka spruce, such as the one planted near Glenn Gould's grave, is used in the construction of some pianos.

sides, but in the end, the good guys won, although I'm not sure that sentence would read the same in an American textbook.

Probably an American textbook would make more of the fact that Capt. Abraham Hull of the United States Army was buried where he fell, which means that he lies among his enemies in Lundy's Lane. Aside from the stars and stripes fluttering in front of his plain grey marker, his last resting place doesn't look much different from any others.

Laura Secord's grave stands out, however. It has lots of words, as well as a bust of the famous patriot:

TO PERPETUATE THE NAME AND FAME
OF LAURA SECORD
WHO WALKED ALONE NEARLY 20 MILES
BY A CIRCUITOUS, DIFFICULT AND PERILOUS ROUTE
THROUGH WOODS AND SWAMPS AND OVER MIRY ROADS
TO WARN A BRITISH OUTPOST AT DE CEW'S FALLS
OF AN INTENDED ATTACK
AND THEREBY ENABLED LIEUT. FITZGIBBON
ON THE 24TH JUNE, 1813, WITH LESS THAN 50 MEN
OF H.M. 49TH REGT., ABOUT 15 MILITIAMEN
AND A SMALL FORCE OF SIX NATIONS AND OTHER INDIANS
UNDER CAPTAINS WILLIAM JOHNSON KERR
AND DOMINIQUE DUCHARME, TO SURPRISE AND ATTACK
THE ENEMY AT BEECHWOODS (OR BEAVER DAMS),
AND AFTER A SHORT ENGAGEMENT
TO CAPTURE COL. BOERSTLER OF THE U.S. ARMY
AND HIS ENTIRE FORCE OF 542 MEN
WITH TWO FIELD PIECES.

There it is, in 125 words or less, the story of another battle in the War of 1812. Legend has it that Laura took along her cow to provide a cover for the dangerous mission, but most formal historians discount the cow. Too slow, they say. She'd never have made it through miry roads with a cow trailing along. Maybe a milk pail to fool the American soldiers but not a whole cow!

Too bad. It was one of the best parts of the Laura Secord story. One of the lesser-known parts of the same story is that the Secords came upon hard times after the war so Laura petitioned the king for a pension in compensation for her brave deed. It took awhile but in 1860, some forty-seven years later, she received one hundred pounds. She was eighty-five then.

Lundy's Lane is not just about war, thank heavens. There are also stories such as the one below—a natural for a graveyard where you can almost feel the mist from the falls and can certainly hear the traffic of tourists everywhere else in the city:

IN MEMORY OF JOHN BURCH, ESQ.
WHO DEPARTED THIS LIFE MARCH 7TH, 1797,
IN THE 55TH YEAR OF HIS AGE.
THE FIRST INTERMENT IN THIS YARD.
JOHN BURCH WAS ONE OF THE EARLIEST
LOYALIST PIONEERS IN THIS AREA IN 1786.
HE MADE THE FIRST COMMERCIAL USE
OF NIAGARA POWER BY ERECTING SAW AND GRIST MILLS
ON THE SHORE OF THE UPPER NIAGARA RAPIDS.

While John Burch was building his grist mill, Rebecca Biggar's folks were just getting there:

REBECCA C. BIGGAR
FIRST WHITE CHILD BORN ON NIAGARA FRONTIER
SEPT. 26, 1786, 8 D'YS AFTER HER PARENTS WALKED
FROM NEW JERSEY TO BENDER FARM
DIED OCT. 8, 1880
HER PARENTS INTERRED IN LUNDY'S LANE.

Did you hear the story in those few words? Rebecca's mother had a baby eight days after she walked—walked!—to her new home. Had she been walking all summer? Is that why Rebecca proved to be such a healthy person, living, as she did, to the ripe old age of ninety-four?

There are other good stories in Lundy's Lane and a museum right next door to answer your questions, but an equally good reason to stop there is that Lundy's Lane is not a tourist attraction. It is blessedly quiet and inexpensive and real.

Twice the Biggest Gravemarker

No contest. The biggest gravemarker in Ontario is the Brock monument just down the road from Niagara Falls. It's a huge thing—a column some fifty-six metres high located on an escarpment above the Niagara River. Very impressive. Very unlike Canadians, who don't generally mark one another with such ceremony, but then Capt. Isaac Brock was not Canadian. He was British, commander of the British and Canadian forces who managed to squeak out a victory against American forces on October 13, 1812, the same war that played out in Laura Secord's pasture a year later and Lundy's Lane two years later.

Laura Secord's story is recorded on her gravemarker in Lundy's Lane cemetery in Niagara Falls.

TO PERPETUATE
THE NAME AND FAME OF
LAURA SECORD,
WHO WALKED ALONE NEARLY 20
MILES BY A CIRCUITOUS, DIFFICULT
AND PERILOUS ROUTE THROUGH WOODS
AND SWAMPS AND OVER MIRY ROADS
TO WARN A BRITISH OUTPOST AT
DE CEW'S FALLS OF AN INTENDED ATTACK
AND THEREBY ENABLED LIEUT FITZ GIBBON
ON THE 24TH JUNE, 1813, WITH LESS
THAN 50 MEN OF H. M. 49TH RECT.,
ABOUT 15 MILITIAMEN AND A SMALL
FORCE OF SIX NATION AND OTHER INDIANS
UNDER CAPTAINS WILLIAM JOHNSON KERR
AND DOMINIQUE DUCHARME, TO SURPRISE
AND ATTACK THE ENEMY AT BEECHWOODS
OR BEAVER DAMS, AND AFTER A SHORT
ENGAGEMENT TO CAPTURE COL. BOERSTLER
OF THE U. S. ARMY AND HIS ENTIRE FORCE
OF 542 MEN WITH TWO FIELD PIECES.

Actually, I can't quite understand how Brock got the glory that day. He was killed during the battle, at which point another British commander took charge, Maj. Gen. Roger Hale Scheaffe. He changed tactics and managed to get the Americans between a rock and a hard place. That is, he had them pinned on the edge of the escarpment—advance and be killed or jump off the cliff.

Isaac Brock got the monument, however. In fact, he got two monuments. The first one was erected in 1824, and fourteen years later, two Americans who were still mad about the licking they took, crossed the river and blew it up. Undaunted, Upper Canada put up another one—even bigger:

UPPER CANADA HAS DEDICATED THIS MONUMENT
TO THE MEMORY OF THE LATE
MAJOR-GENERAL SIR ISAAC BROCK, K.B.
PROVISIONAL LIEUT. GOVERNOR AND COMMANDER
OF THE FORCES IN THIS PROVINCE
WHOSE REMAINS ARE DEPOSITED IN THE VAULT BENEATH.
OPPOSING THE INVADING ENEMY, HE FELL IN ACTION
NEAR THESE HEIGHTS ON OCT. 13, 1812
IN THE 43RD YEAR OF HIS AGE.
REVERED AND LAMENTED BY THE PEOPLE WHOM HE GOVERNED
AND DEPLORED BY THE SOVREIGN
TO WHOSE SERVICE HIS LIFE HAD BEEN DEVOTED.

Incidentally, the word "deplored" also means to lament greatly, to regret deeply. It doesn't, in this instance, mean that the sovereign didn't like him.

If All Else Fails, Pick Up a Pitchfork

That William Lyon Mackenzie, 1795-1861, managed to die in his own bed in his own house in the city that had to endure his famous rebellion is amazing indeed. Two of his companions in arms during that short-lived but memorable rebellion in 1837 were hanged in public for their so-called treason. But Mackenzie hightailed it out of town when he saw his cause was lost, hid out in the US for ten years, then came home and went right back to politics and newspaper writing. He was Ontario's equivalent of Québec's Louis Joseph Papineau, both of them passionate men who wanted their province, their country, to determine its own future, not wait for instructions from England.

Mackenzie especially resented what he called the Family Compact, the tightly knit group of men who appointed one another to all the important positions, who thought patronage was ordained by God, and if not God, then England. Same difference, in fact.

That was why Mackenzie set out from Montgomery's Tavern one night with a bunch of similarly disenchanted men, some with guns but most armed with pitchforks and other useless weapons. They were going to take government house and make it into a truly representative governing body. Instead, they were taken later by government troops. Some rebels died, most fled. It was one of the most miserable military battles ever fought on Canadian soil, but perhaps Mackenzie knew what he was doing. After all, he was a newspaperman. He knew the value of public opinion. And suddenly, the citizens of Ontario began to notice how little say they had in their own affairs.

None of this is mentioned on William Lyon Mackenzie's gravestone in Toronto's Necropolis cemetery. The only information provided is on the wall at the entrance to the graveyard, where it lists some of Toronto's early VIPs, including Mackenzie, who was, they say, "A Celebrated Reformer."

Generations of War

The Jarvis mausoleum in Toronto's St. James Anglican cemetery is instructive in so many ways. First of all, it's a museum of war. Most of the wars we fought in the last two hundred years are mentioned in one way or another on the walls. The Jarvis men, generation after generation, did their duty and fought and died all over the world. The inscriptions do not try to justify this everlasting fighting. They don't have to. War, it seems, was not questioned centuries ago. It was just done.

Second, because women didn't do war, they don't get much space on the walls of the mausoleum. It tells us something about our values then and how things are different now, sort of. This is what is said about the first Jarvis:

> JARVIS, WILLIAM, UEL
> WAS OFFICER IN QUEEN'S RANGERS DRAGOON BRIGADE.
> HE SERVED WITH THAT CORPS DURING
> THE REVOLUTIONARY WAR. WAS SECRETARY OF STATE
> OF THE PROVINCE OF UPPER CANADA DURING
> THE ADMINISTRATION OF GOVERNORS SIMCOE, RUSSELL,
> HUNTER AND GORE 1792-1817.
> BORN IN STANFORD, CONN. 1756
> DIED AT YORK, UPPER CANADA, 1817.

Because he fought on the British side during the US War of Independence, he had to get out of the States when the shooting stopped, which for him meant Canada. Here, he got the usual United Empire Loyalist dispensations—land, money, a good job.

His son carried on the family tradition, taking part in all the big ones, even the small one started by Mackenzie, see above.

> LT. COL. SAMUEL PETERS JARVIS
> ELDEST SON OF WILLIAM
> SERVED DURING THE WAR OF 1812, 1813, 1814.
> WAS PRESENT AT QUEENSTON HEIGHTS, LUNDY'S LANE,
> STONEY CREEK, DETROIT (MEDAL AND CLASP)
> COMMANDED THE GUARD WHICH ESCORTED
> THE AMERICAN GENERAL WINFIELD SCOTT AS POW.
> DURING THE REBELLION OF 1837,
> HE RAISED AND COMMANDED THE MILITIA REGT.
> KNOWN AS THE QUEEN'S RANGERS.
> PRESENT AT THE CUTTING OUT OF THE
> STEAMER CAROLINE AT FORT SCHLOSSER,
> WAS COMMANDER OF THE GARRISON TORONTO
> AND JUDGE ADVOCATE OF THE COURT MARTIAL
> TO TRY THE AMERICAN PRISONER GENERAL SUTHERLAND
> AND WAS FOR MANY YEARS CHIEF SUPERINTENDENT
> OF INDIAN AFFAIRS.
> BORN 1792, DIED 1857.

Now, if that doesn't lead a student of history into the wilds of Ontario in the 1800s, I don't know what will.

The third generation did his share:

MAJOR GENERAL SAMUEL PETERS JARVIS
82 REGT. INDIAN MUTINY
COMMANDER OF FORCES IN RIEL REBELLION
UNTIL WOLSELEY CAME.
DURING KAFFIR WARS OF 1878
SENT OUT ON SPECIAL SERVICES TO SOUTH AFRICA.
BORN 1820, DIED 1905.
BURIED NEAR BATH, ENGLAND.

The fourth generation, Samuel Peters Jarvis, 1903-1970, does not mention war on the walls of his family vault. Whether that's because he didn't fight in a war, or didn't want to mention it, I don't know, but taken together, the Jarvis inscriptions should be compulsory reading for all of us.

That's exactly what James Counter Norsworthy, 1846-1936, contends on yet another gravemarker that gets into the subject of war, one in the Ingersoll cemetery that commemorates his son and two other young relatives who died in World War I. "They fought the good fight," the inscription concludes. "Read the history of your country and understand."

NOT FOR FAME OR REWARD,
NOT FOR PLACE OR RANK
NOT LURED BY AMBITION
OR GOADED BY NECESSITY
BUT IN SIMPLE OBEDIENCE TO DUTY
AS HE UNDERSTOOD IT,
MAJOR NORSWORTHY SACRIFICED ALL–
SUFFERED ALL–DARED ALL–AND DIED.

Guns at Eight Paces

In between wars, there were duels. Can you believe it? Even in sensible old Canada, we fought duels. One rainy, murky morning in 1817, Samuel Peters Jarvis (Jarvis generation #2) met John Ridout on a field approximately where College and Yonge Streets come together now. Why they were shooting at one another is never explained sufficiently in history books other than to say there was "bad blood" between the two families. Anyway, John and Samuel faced one another across eight yards and were told by their seconds to turn and then fire on the count of three. John made a mistake and fired on the count of two, completely missing his target. According to proper duelling procedure, Jarvis was then allowed a free shot, as it were. He used it to kill John pointblank, and that's another part of our noble history.

In the front hall of St. James Cathedral in Toronto is the gravestone of John Ridout. Notice the creative wording for "death by duel":

IN MEMORY OF JOHN RIDOUT
HIS FILIAL AFFECTION, ENGAGING MANNERS,
AND NOBLENESS OF MIND
GAVE EARLY PROMISE OF FUTURE EXCELLENCE.
THIS PROMISE HE GALLANTLY FULFILLED
BY HIS BRAVE, ACTIVE AND ENTERPRISING CONDUCT
WHICH GAINED THE PRAISE OF HIS SUPERIORS
WHILE SERVING AS MIDSHIPMAN
IN THE PROVINCIAL NAVY DURING THE LATE WAR.
AT THE RETURN OF PEACE,
HE COMMENCED WITH ARDOUR
THE STUDY OF LAW,
AND WITH THE FAIREST OF PROSPECTS,
BUT A BLIGHT CAME,
AND HE WAS CONSIGNED TO AN EARLY GRAVE
ON 12TH JULY, 1817, AGED 18.

The Only Royal Church

By the time we got to Her Majesty's Chapel of the Mohawks outside of Brantford, I was getting gun shy. Everywhere I went, I learned about another battle, another opportunity to shoot at somebody. I never realized what a nasty bunch we were. We shot at everything in the early days, and then, if we belonged to the right side, we came home and claimed our land.

The Mohawk Chapel looked peaceful—a white clapboard church with a polite spire, a carefully tended graveyard around the church, trees to shade tourists on a hot summer day, a white fence enclosing it all. But my heart sank when I read the interpretive panel outside the church. This lovely little church in the wildwood came about because of—are you ready—war.

Joseph Brant and other members of the Six Nations of the Iroquois fought with England in the American War of Independence between 1775 and 1783, and when England lost, they lost—their land, their homes. So England said, Come on up to Canada and we'll give you land around the Grand River in southern Ontario. And that's how the Mohawks got some 308,000 hectares in reserve.

They got the church a year later by appealing to the British crown, which is why it's the only church outside the United Kingdom with the title "Royal." Brant is buried there in a big long above-ground tomb:

> THIS TOMB IS ERECTED TO THE MEMORY
> OF THAYENDANEGEA, OR CAPTAIN JOSEPH BRANT.
> PRINCIPAL CHIEF AND WARRIOR OF THE SIX NATIONS INDIANS,
> BY HIS FELLOW SUBJECTS, ADMIRERS OF HIS FIDELITY
> AND ATTACHMENT TO THE BRITISH CROWN.
> BORN ON THE BANKS OF THE OHIO RIVER, 1742
> DIED AT WELLINGTON SQUARE, U.C. 1807.
>
> IT ALSO CONTAINS THE REMAINS OF HIS SON,
> AHYOUWAIGHS, OR CAPTAIN JOHN BRANT
> WHO SUCCEEDED HIS FATHER AND DISTINGUISHED
> HIMSELF IN THE WAR OF 1812–1815.
> BORN AT THE MOHAWK VILLAGE, U.C. 1794
> DIED AT THE SAME PLACE, 1833

Because the church is the oldest surviving Protestant church in Ontario, the graveyard has some lovely old-fashioned gravemarkers, this one for Eliza Wallace, died 1835 in her 28th year, victim of goodness knows what kind of war:

> OUR GENTLE ELIZA, THOU ART GONE TO REST
> OH MOTHER EARTH, PRESERVE HER SACRED DUST
> AND LET HER PILLOW BE THE HALLOWED BREAST
> TILL THE LAST MORNING'S TRUMP SHALL WAKE THE JUST.

Betsy Fowles died August 27, 1877, "aged 96 y'rs, 3 m's and 2 d's." Her inscription explains matter-of-factly:

> SHE TOOK THE CUP OF LIFE TO DRINK
> TOO BITTER 'TWAS TO DRAIN,
> SHE CALMLY TOOK IT FROM HER LIPS
> AND WENT TO SLEEP AGAIN.

For Heaven's Sake

I couldn't believe what I was hearing as I stood beside Jean de Brébeuf's grave at the reconstructed mission of Sainte-Marie Among the Hurons, near Midland. The grave is just a patch of smooth dirt inside a wooden fence inside a restored primitive church, but the guide is earnestly explaining to us tourists how the experts know that Brébeuf is actually there, even though his bones were removed from the corpse back in 1649 or thereabouts. There were enough bones and some flesh remaining in the old gravesite, he

A corner of the reconstructed mission at Sainte-Marie Among the Hurons. Partial remains of Jean de Brébeuf are believed to be buried here.

explains, to allow them to verify that, indeed, it was Brébeuf, even though it was some three hundred years later. They also turned up some extra bones and flesh, which confused them for a while, but it turned out that Gabriel Lalemant was buried there as well. It was a stroke of luck to find them both like that, he confides.

As for the bones that were removed back in 1649, they are in various locations, he tells us cheerfully—some next door at the Martyrs' Shrine, some in the basilica in Québec City, some with Catholic church officials.

And then, as if we haven't just heard the most incredible discussion of body parts, he asks jauntily, "Any questions?"

We're afraid to ask.

Jean de Brébeuf came to Canada in 1625, not to get rich on furs or fish, but to bring the word of God to the Native people. We're not comfortable talking like that any more, but in the early days of Canadian settlement, all the Christians were doing it. Bringing God to the heathens. Jean de Brébeuf and his fellow Jesuits were among the first.

They tried hard and had some success with the Hurons, eventually establishing the mission of Sainte-Marie in 1639. But it was not to be—Brébeuf and Lalemant were away from the mission one day when they were captured by the Iroquois, tortured, and killed. Rather than suffer the same fate, the remaining Jesuits decided to abandon Sainte-Marie, burn it to the ground, and make for the safety of another mission on Christian Island. Before they left, however, they somehow found the bodies of Brébeuf and Lalemant, removed the bones for the martyrdom they knew would follow, and buried the remains in the mission.

Don't ask me how they did that, and don't ask me where the bones were for the next three hundred years. Ask the guide at Sainte-Marie Among the Hurons next time you're there.

But when the original mission site was rediscovered in the bush alongside the Wye River, and the decision was made to excavate the site and rebuild, the subject of bones came up again. The archaeologists found buildings and stockades and water canals but no grave for Brébeuf and Lalemant. Not until 1954 did a small lead plaque show up with Jean de Brébeuf's name on it:

FR. JEAN DE BRÉBEUF
BRULE PAR LE IROQUOIS
17 MARCH 1649.

Eight men died between 1642 and 1649, all of them connected to the Jesuit order of the Catholic Church: Jean de Brébeuf, Gabriel Lalemant, Isaac Jogues, Antoine Daniel, Charles Garnier, Noël Chabanel, Jean de La Lande, and René Goupil. Canonized in 1930, they are all honoured in the Martyrs' Shrine next door to the old mission, their relics displayed within the Shrine Church, their deaths explained on monuments throughout the grounds. This is what it says for René Goupil, for instance:

ST. RENE GOUPIL
PUT TO DEATH AT AURIESVILLE, NY SEPT. 29, 1642.
HE WAS THE FIRST OF THE MARTYRS.
HE HAD BEEN CAPTURED WHILE ENROUTE TO STE. MARIE
TO TAKE CHARGE OF THE HOSPITAL THERE.

Later Rounds on Behalf of Heaven

By the 1800s in Ontario, it wasn't nearly so dangerous to be a man of God. In fact, if you were Bishop John Strachan, you had the best of both worlds: you were more or less the king of the Anglican church and by extension awfully powerful in the secular world as well.

Strachan first came to the attention of the citizens of York (now known as Toronto) in 1813 when American soldiers sailed into the harbour, sent the few local soldiers packing, and declared that the town was theirs. It was all part of the war between the US and England that went on in fits and starts between 1812 and 1814.

When the American troops began burning buildings, including the houses of Parliament, and ransacking homes, Strachan got up on his hind legs and told the American commander in no uncertain terms to cut it out. You may do your worst, he thundered in his best brimstone-and-fire voice, but you'll always know that you did not keep your word as gentlemen.

That was the ultimate threat, I gather. There was no more looting.

From then on, John Strachan led a charmed and influential life. If he wasn't on every government committee and social list, then his parishioners or ex-students were, and they made sure they knew what he wanted before any decisions were made.

When he died, he was buried in the vault beneath the chancel at the Cathedral Church of St. James in Toronto, and a memorial on a nearby wall explains:

NEAR THIS SPOT REST THE MORTAL REMAINS
OF JOHN STRACHAN, FIRST BISHOP OF TORONTO,
WHO DEPARTED THIS LIFE NOV. 1, 1867
IN THE 90TH YEAR OF HIS AGE
AND THE 29TH OF HIS EPISCOPATE.
HIS CONSPICUOUS LABOURS, FORESIGHT AND CONSTANCY
IN THE SERVICE OF THE CHURCH
AND OF THE COMMONWEALTH
AS AN EDUCATOR, AS A MAN OF RELIGION,
AS A STATESMAN, FORM AN IMPORTANT PORTION
OF THE EARLY HISTORY OF WESTERN CANADA.

Most men of the cloth got special notices and special places in graveyards—not quite as grand as Strachan's but grander than most, at any rate. In the St. Andrews Presbyterian cemetery in Williamstown is a stone of substance that says:

IN MEMORY OF REV. JOHN BETHUNE
PASTOR OF THE CONGREGATION
OF THE KIRK OF SCOTLAND IN GLENGARRY.
HE DEPARTED THIS LIFE AT WILLIAMSTOWN
ON 23 SEPTEMBER, 1815 IN THE 66TH YEAR OF HIS AGE
AND IN THE 44TH OF HIS MINISTRY.

Yes, he is related to the famous Dr. Norman Bethune—he is his great great grandfather. But it turns out he doesn't need any help in the fame department. A Scot who emigrated to South Carolina by choice, he became a Canadian by golly when he was kicked out of the US after fighting on the British side during the War of Independence. That didn't seem to bother him. He settled down on his grant of land in Glengarry County and started churches—four of them, to be exact, which earned him the respect, admiration, and love of Presbyterians in Upper Canada, who, until then, had not had their own church. Naturally, he got the name of "Father of Presbyterianism in Canada."

And just to keep our genders equal, there is in Canada a "Mother of Methodism," also referred to as the "Founder of North American Methodism." This is what is says on her gravemarker next to the Blue Church in Prescott:

> BARBARA HECK, 1734-1804
> BARBARA HECK PUT HER BRAVE SOUL
> AGAINST THE RUGGED POSSIBILITIES OF THE FUTURE
> AND UNDER GOD BROUGHT INTO EXISTENCE
> AMERICAN AND CANADIAN METHODISM
> AND BETWEEN THESE HER MEMORY WILL EVER FORM
> A MOST HALLOWED LINK.

Gender Equity in the Backwoods

Susanna Moodie was one grouchy lady—didn't like Canada, didn't like roughing it in the bush, didn't like the straitened circumstances that followed her everywhere after moving here. And she didn't hesitate to share her feelings in her two most famous books: *Roughing It in the Bush* and *Life in the Clearings*.

By contrast, her sister Catharine Parr Traill was much more cheerful about Canada in her books: *The Backwoods of Canada* and *The Female Emigrants' Guide*. It's not easy to move from a genteel life in England to a pioneer life in Canada, she said in effect, but it had its moments.

In spite of their differences, both sisters wrote well, their books serving as valuable records of the way we were in early Canada. But does any of this make it onto their gravemarkers?

You probably know the answer by now. No, their accomplishments are not mentioned on their tombstones. Catharine Parr Traill is buried at the Hillside cemetery in Lakefield—just names and dates—1802-1899. Susanna Moodie is in the Belleville cemetery, again just names and dates—1803-1885.

But her gravemarker at least reveals something about that famous grouchiness. One side of the family gravemarker tells this story of two young sons:

JOHN STRICKLAND
DROWNED IN THE BAY OF QUINTE
JUNE 18, 1844 AGED 5 Y'RS, 8 MO'S.
ALSO GEORGE ARTHUR
DIED AUG. 8, 1840 AGED 1 MONTH.
CHILDREN OF J.W. AND SUSANNA MOODIE

John went fishing one day and got into water over his head. George was sickly, as they used to say, and failed to make it. No wonder Susanna had her down times.

Bring on the Cats

In a graveyard near Glen Allen in Waterloo County is an inscription that begs a whole lot of questions:

IN MEMORY OF LADY GRATTON HOLT
WHO SAVED HER AREA FROM SMALLPOX

And just how did she do that? Well, according to the story handed down to her descendants, she read an article in a scientific journal from Ireland about a vaccine that had been developed to protect people from smallpox. Then she read some more and learned that the magic vaccine was available in Toronto but in limited supply only. Not enough for a whole community. Why not make their own, she wondered? So she sent her son-in-law off into the bush to walk some 149 kilometres to Toronto to get some vaccine, and when he got back with it, she rounded up the neighbourhood cats.

That's how the story goes.

She incubated the vaccine in the cats, vaccinated family and friends, and "saved her area from smallpox."

Through the years, historical researchers and journalists have tried to verify this cat business by studying the cat population of Glen Allen around 1845 when all of this was supposed to be happening. But cats were cats then; nobody bothered to count them.

So the story stands.

The Longest Way Home

Sophia Cameron's dying request was "Take me home," so her husband did just that even though he had to go halfway around the world and bury her four times in the process.

She's "home" now in the graveyard next to Salem United Church in

Summerstown. The words on her worn marker barely hint at the story:

ERECTED BY JOHN A. CAMERON
TO THE MEMORY OF MARGARET SOPHIA HIS WIFE
WHO DIED AT CARIBOO, B.C. OCTOBER 22, 1862
ALSO HER DAUGHTER ALICE AGED 14 MONTHS

Sophia should have known when she married John Cameron that they would not likely stay close to home. He had already taken part in the California and Fraser River gold rushes, making just enough money to keep him coming back. Thus when gold was discovered in 1860 in the Cariboo, they were off.

From that time on, there was nothing but grief for Sophia. Baby Alice died. Another baby was stillborn. Typhoid hit the mining community of Williams Creek, where they were living. The winter of 1862 came early, and it came hard. It was too much. Sophia died October 22, 1862, asking only that she be returned "home."

John vowed to carry out her last wish, but first he had to work his claim a bit more. They were nearly there, he thought, so he buried Sophia temporarily near an abandoned shack in the community. Burial #1. And sure enough, two months later, he and his partners struck gold. Lots of gold. It was one of the richest seams in the area.

With gold in his pockets (and in the coffin, some said), John Cameron disinterred Sophia's coffin and

It took four burials, but Sophia Cameron finally made it "home" to the Salem United Church cemetery in Summerstown.

took it by sled and ship to Victoria. Burial #2. There he waited some six months to get a ship that would take him and his cargo to the Panama Canal. Again, he had to wait for another ship so it was Burial #3.

Finally, Sophia was laid to rest among her people, Burial #4, and that should have been the end of that. RIP. But for some strange reason, rumours kept circulating that Cameron had killed his wife or sold her into slavery or otherwise disposed of her, and then put gold into the casket. Some people just couldn't believe that a man would go to such lengths to carry out a wife's last request.

There were so many rumours that Cameron finally had to disinter his wife's casket one last time and open it to prove, once and for all, that she was there.

She was. But this is one story that just won't die, if you don't mind a pun. It is said that while the casket was open, he poured out the alcohol that had preserved his wife's body all this time, and grass never grew on that spot again. It's a great story, but I have to tell you that grass grew everywhere in the very tidy, well-maintained Summerstown graveyard.

Uncle Tom Moves North

Uncle Tom, the chief character in one of the most famous books about slavery in the United States, was a Canadian. It seems that the American author Harriet Beecher Stowe met Josiah Henson of Dresden, Upper Canada, in 1849, and after hearing his story was inspired to write the famous *Uncle Tom's Cabin*. It sold three thousand copies on the first day of publication, three-hundred thousand within the year, and millions since then.

All because one Rev. Josiah Henson decided in 1830 that he'd had enough of slavery, discrimination, and violence. He'd try the country to the north.

Not that Canadians were faultless in our behaviour. We had slaves in Canada. Some came with the first French settlers in Lower Canada; still others came with the United Empire Loyalists after the American War of Independence in 1783 when, technically, it was still legal. That law had been challenged along the way, though, and we just weren't into slavery like the southern US. Thus, even before we made the whole business illegal in 1834, slaves made their way to Canada via the underground railway, hoping for better times here. Henson was one of them.

He wasn't satisfied with simply escaping, however. He decided to get practical and offer job training to others fleeing into Canada, many of whom lacked the skills it would take to survive here. Thus was born the British-American Institute, a vocational school, a community, and a support for blacks in Upper Canada. No wonder Henson had such a fund of interesting stories to tell Harriet Beecher Stowe.

He's buried beside his house and school near Dresden, the two buildings now a historic site. His grave says nothing of his interesting and important past, wouldn't you know. Just tells us that he died in 1883, aged ninety-three years, ten months, and five days. The final line is nice, however. Maybe he was referring to Canada when he had these words added:

THERE IS A LAND OF PURE DELIGHT

Judy was totally disgusted one morning because somehow we missed the road she thought we should be on. Judy was the navigator and a good one, but somehow we were on a secondary road going goodness-knows-where. It was then that a small log church showed up beside the road with a sign over the door that said, African Methodist Episcopal Church, Oro, 1849. I braked, of course, and a plaque near the church explained:

BETWEEN 1830 AND 1850 SOME 24 NEGRO FAMILIES
WHO HAD FLED FROM SLAVERY IN THE UNITED STATES
TO FREEDOM IN CANADA WERE SETTLED IN ORO,
MOSTLY ON THE CONCESSION RUNNING NORTH
OF SHANTY BAY KNOWN AS WILBERFORCE STREET.
IN 1849, THEY ACQUIRED THIS PIECE OF LAND
FOR A BURYING GROUND AND BUILT HERE
THIS AFRICAN EPISCOPAL CHURCH.

I don't think we could ever find that little church again, but what good fortune to chance upon it like that and get one more piece of the story of black immigration to Canada.

Another piece turned up for us in the Sarnia graveyard:

IN MEMORY OF PETER PENNINGTON
COLOURED
BORN IN MARYLAND ABOUT AD 1827
DIED AT SARNIA, 18 SEPT. 1884
GUIDED NORTH. HE FOLLOWED HERE FOR 25 YEARS
THE CALLING OF FISHERMAN.
HAVING NO CHILD OR KNOWN RELATIVE
BEQUEATHED HIS SMALL BEQUEST OF ABOUT $1000
IN EQUAL PORTIONS
TO THE SEVERAL CHARITIES OF THE TOWN.

It's the only time I've found the word "coloured" on a gravemarker, but I must admit I was more interested in the last few lines. They almost sound Biblical—the fisherman who helped others.

Murder Most Foul

As far as I can figure, Ontario doesn't like to mention the word "murder" in its graveyards. Not once did I find it, not even on the gravemarker of the Donnellys, the most famous multiple murder Canada has ever had. Nor was it even hinted on the tombstone of one of our most famous Fathers of Confederation, a man who believed in saying it like it was.

In the case of the Donnellys, the original gravemarker in St. Patrick's churchyard near Lucan certainly said MURDERED in big loud white letters on a big black granite pedestal. Said it five times:

> JAMES DONNELLY, MURDERED FEB. 4, 1880
> JOHANNAH DONNELLY, MURDERED FEB. 4, 1880
> THOMAS DONNELLY, MURDERED FEB. 4, 1880
> JOHN DONNELLY, MURDERED FEB. 4, 1880
> BRIDGET DONNELLY, MURDERED FEB. 4, 1880.

The word "murdered" appeared five times on the original Donnelly gravestone in St. Patrick's churchyard near Lucan, but tourists carried most of it away as souvenirs.

But when the gravemarker became a tourist attraction and people came from near and far to gawk and, what's more, to chip pieces off the stone or the church or the fence nearby, the church and community decided to erect a less inflammatory stone. Which is why the Donnelly stone is now a generic grey granite with five names, one date of death—February 4, 1880, no mention of cause of death, and the hope that their souls rest in peace.

The Donnellys moved to Canada from Ireland in the mid-1800s and squatted on land in the area north of London. Nothing would move them from that land, nothing and no one. They beat up anyone who challenged them, burned buildings, killed livestock, and generally terrorized the whole area. Besides defending their new turf, they fought old wars, feuds that they brought with them from Ireland. If it wasn't one thing they fought over, it was another, and there were lots of them to do it—father, mother, seven sons, one daughter, and a niece, Bridget.

The district took this guff for some twenty years, only once catching a Donnelly in the act. Father James went to jail for a while, but his sons and wife kept up the good work while he was away. Community members finally decided to take matters into their own hands. So a bunch of them got likkered up one night and went out and killed a few Donnellys. Just like that. It didn't stop all the trouble, but it stopped most of it. And when the local men were later acquitted of murder, the community breathed a huge sigh of relief, which is why they weren't thrilled to bits when tourists started cluttering up their graveyard and church. Enough already, which is why the gravemarker is more or less silent now.

Someone was always mad at George Brown. He was a newspaperman who didn't hesitate to express his own opinions in his own newspaper. He was a politician who wasn't always kind to other politicians. He was a citizen of Upper Canada who thought Lower Canada (Québec) had more than its share of influence and colonial goodies. And finally, he thought Canada might just as well organize itself into a federation and get it over with. Thus, he became one of our Fathers of Confederation. But none of the above led to his untimely death. Rather, he was shot by a former employee who was armed with resentment, liquor, and a gun. That is not mentioned on his gravemarker in Toronto's Necropolis, but his accomplishments are listed:

GEORGE BROWN, A SCOTTISH IMMIGRANT,
FOUNDED THE GLOBE. THROUGH HIS NEWSPAPER,
HE EXERTED A VERY GREAT INFLUENCE
ON THE EARLY DEVELOPMENT OF CANADA.

HE WAS THE ARCHITECT OF THE REFORM PARTY,
WHICH LATER BECAME THE LIBERAL PARTY.
BOTH AS A JOURNALIST AND AS A POLITICIAN,
HE SPOKE OUT FOR RESPONSIBLE GOVERNMENT
AND FREEDOM OF THE INDIVIDUAL.
HE WAS ELECTED TO THE PARLIAMENT
OF THE PROVINCE OF CANADA IN 1851
AND SOME YEARS LATER, AS LEADER OF THE LIBERAL PARTY,
HE ENTERED INTO A COALITION WITH JOHN A. MACDONALD
OF THE CONSERVATIVES
TO PROCEED WITH THE CONFEDERATION
OF THE CANADIAN PROVINCES.

Television gives us all the violence we can stomach, and more, these days but back in the 1800s, hangings were a favourite public entertainment. Certainly, George Bennett, a.k.a. George Dixon, had a big audience the morning he was scheduled to pay the ultimate price for having killed George Brown, and he was up for it. He spoke without faltering as he stood at the foot of the gallows: "Gentlemen, I am going to die, and I am innocent of the crime . . . It would have been a shameful thing to have done such an act, as Mr. Brown did not deserve it. He was a most popular man throughout the world, and he went to his death through an oversight on my part. I could not control the event. There was liquor in me, and the accident occurred, and the result was the fatal act."

With that, he signalled the hangman, and the crowd held its breath.

He hanged. That's the end of that story.

Not Quite the End of the Story

Sometimes, there's such a flood of adjectives on a gravemarker that it hardly seems possible one person could be that wonderful. This is just part of what it says on the grand tombstone for Nicholas Flood Davin in Ottawa's Beechwood cemetery:

THIS MEMORIAL HAS BEEN ERECTED
BY HIS FORMER PARLIAMENTARY ASSOCIATES
AND OTHER FRIENDS AS A LASTING PROOF
OF THE ESTEEM AND AFFECTION
WHICH THEY ENTERTAINED FOR ONE WHOSE CHARACTER
WAS STRONGLY MARKED BY SINCERITY AND FEARLESSNESS:
WHOSE MIND BY VIVACITY AND CLEARNESS
OF COMPREHENSION, AND WHOSE CLASSICAL SCHOLARSHIP

AND WIDE CULTURE UNITED TO HIS BRILLIANT ORATORY
AND SINGULAR WIT MADE HIM EMINENT IN DEBATE
AND DELIGHTFUL IN SOCIETY.

Wow. Davin, 1843-1901, had a way with words, which is why he was at various times in his life a journalist, author, politician, and lawyer. As a lawyer, his most famous case was the defence of George Bennett, the man who was eventually hanged for the murder of George Brown. Davin was eloquent in his defence, but it wasn't enough.

So he went west and founded the *Leader* newspaper in Regina in 1883, just in time for the North-West Rebellion. Again, Davin called on his wit and words to get him into the thick of things. He disguised himself as a priest and talked his way into Riel's cell so that he could interview him.

The newspaper did famously, but Davin couldn't resist a go at politics, and it was politics that did him in eventually. Already depressed over an election loss, he spoke to a group in Winnipeg who would not be charmed by his legendary charm, and it was too much. Davin shot himself.

There Were Ninety and Nine

If it hadn't been for a heartbroken sister in Scotland, we would never have had the following inscription on a gravemarker in Fergus:

IN MEMORY OF GEORGE
DIED MAY 2, 1851, AGE 32
ELDEST SON OF ANDREW CLEPHANE, ESQ.
LATE SHERRIFF OF FIFESHIRE, SCOTLAND
BROTHER OF THE AUTHOR OF "THE NINETY AND NINE."

George Clephane came to Canada from Scotland in 1841. Here, it was hoped he'd "make" something of himself, something he hadn't done to the satisfaction of his disgusted sheriff father back in Scotland. However, George was a bit too fond of "the drink" and a bit too used to the regular remittances from home to get overly serious about life. He simply enjoyed himself until one stormy spring night in 1851, when he set out on horseback to ride to town. Whether his horse slipped or whether he simply fell off, no one knows, but he lay for hours beside the road in the pouring rain. The town doctor found him, but it was too late. George, the black sheep of his family, had died in far-off Canada. The doctor paid for a simple white headstone.

And that would have been that except for Elizabeth, his younger sister back in Scotland. She was so devastated by George's death, far away from home and loved ones, that she wrote a poem in his memory. The first verse went:

> There were ninety and nine that safely lay
> In the shelter of the fold;
> But one was out on the hills away,
> Far off from the gates of gold,
> Away on the mountain wild and bare,
> Away from the tender shepherd's care.

After she died almost twenty years later, the poem was published in a local paper. Again, that would have been that, except for the fact that two famous American evangelists were travelling through Scotland at the time. One of them, Ira Sankey, saw the poem, cut it out, and set it to music. "Note by note, the tune was given," he explained later.

And that's the tune still sung in Protestant churches everywhere—all because a sister loved her weak, wayward brother.

First but Not the Biggest

I've always wanted to know more about Sir John A. Macdonald's family life and less about his everlasting politics and deals and drinking. Years ago, I made myself read a two-volume biography of our famous first prime minister, hoping to learn some of the homelier details, but there was barely a nod to home and hearth. Just politics. Ye gods.

So I looked forward to finding his gravesite. Surely there'd have to be some indication of the other side of his life.

Well, there was, but still not enough.

He's buried in the Cataraqui cemetery in Kingston. It's not a particularly impressive grave, nothing that would stop you in your tracks and make you say, Wow, that must be a prime minister. There's a sturdy pedestal marker, a fairly fancy iron-grille fence, an official government plaque, but it's not nearly as impressive as Laurier's grave or Peter Verigin's, to name just two.

Inside the fence are buried his mother Helen and his father Hugh. Sir John A. himself, 1815-1891, is there along with his first wife, Isabella, 1809-1857, and an infant son, Hugh, who died in 1848. I had already found son #2 in Winnipeg so I knew he wouldn't be there, but where was wife #2, Susan Agnes Bernard, and their daughter Mary?

Wife #2 is the one remembered fondly in the West because, it is said, she so admired the Rockies on a train trip west that she asked to have a

Sir John A. Macdonald and some of his family are buried in the Cataraqui cemetery in Kingston.

chair placed on the cow-catcher so that she might sit out there and enjoy the scenery close up. Such a wonderful piece of public relations in a day and age before we even knew relations were public. I hope there is at least a hint on her gravemarker—wherever it is—that she had some very interesting moments.

I did find out later that Agnes and Mary are both buried in Eastbourne, England. Agnes's epitaph does mention Canada and Sir John A. Macdonald, but it's all very official and stiff. Not at all like a woman who rode on the cowcatcher. Daughter Mary was an invalid all her life, both mentally and physically disabled. Her care occupied Lady Macdonald's life right to the end.

Mary's Seven Sons

That's one thing our graveyards tell us over and over again—that we used to have much bigger families than we do now. In Sarnia, for example, I was looking for the grave of our second prime minister, Alexander Mackenzie, but I found this first:

MARY STEWART FLEMING
RELICT OF ALEXANDER MACKENZIE
OF PERTHSHIRE, SCOTLAND
CAME TO CANADA WITH HER FAMILY OF SEVEN SONS, AD 1847
AND DIED IN SARNIA 16 FEB. 1861 AGED 66 YEARS.

This was the prime minister's mother, her achievement of seven sons given as much notice as the achievements of said sons. Good for her.

There's supposed to be some magic in the fact of seven sons, especially if the seventh son is the son of a seventh son, and so on. Such rare birds were encouraged to go into medicine in that they were supposed to have special healing talents. By contrast, seventh daughters were expected to be witches. Such a deal.

We had one other seventh son in our history, Lord Selkirk, who outlived six brothers and thus inherited enough money to buy half of Manitoba and a lot of PEI.

But back to Alexander Mackenzie, who in spite of being one of seven sons did not enjoy a particularly blessed or happy life. It's true he was prime minister for a while after Sir John A. Macdonald, but his efforts to build a railway without going into debt or patronage got him nowhere at all. So he retired to the back benches and stayed there.

The Dionnes' Five Daughters

However, seven sons, one after the other, pale beside five daughters all at once. The Dionne quintuplets, born in 1934, were the most exciting news we'd ever had—five little girls who had to be fed by eye dropper and kept warm in the kitchen oven. Five little girls who not only survived but turned out to be incredibly cute and good for business and a sure way to keep Canada on the map.

The fact that the little girls and their parents weren't enjoying all of this as much as the rest of us didn't register. Canada claimed them; Canada profited by them; Canada came to see them. They lived in a huge palace of a place in Corbeil called Quintland, complete with one-way mirrors where tourists could shuffle by and get a look. Imagine. We wouldn't do it to baby elephants in the zoo nowadays.

Quintland is a health centre now, the Dionne house is a museum in nearby North Bay, and the five little girls are now three grown-up, somewhat bitter women. Emilie died first. Her grave is in the Corbeil cemetery:

À LA DOUCE MÉMOIRE
DE EMILIE DIONNE
NÉE LE 28 MAI 1934
DÉCÉDÉE LE 6 AOÛT 1954
À L'ÂGE DE 20 ANS
RIP

Emilie was the first of the Dionne quintuplets to die, but there is no reference to the famous five on her gravemarker near Corbeil.

The gravemarker is about the nicest in the cemetery, but there's no other clue that this was one of the famous quintuplets. The parents are nearby—Oliva, 1903-1979, and Elzire, 1909-1986. They too are silent about their part in the biggest story Canada ever had. Marie died in 1970 in Montréal.

How to Be Noticeably Silent

As I've mentioned already, most Canadian prime ministers are anything but prime ministerial in their last resting places—more likely to be modest like the rest of us. The one exception is Sir Wilfrid Laurier, who has an enormous monument at the entrance to Notre Dame cemetery in Ottawa. On a grey granite base stand eight lifesized female figures in black granite, all of them suitably saintly and beautiful, guarding, I guess, the sarcophagus that stretches along the top of the structure.

It's so impressive it doesn't need words, or so it seems, for all it says is:

LAURIER 1841-1919
LADY LAURIER 1841-1921

Facing Page: Wilfrid Laurier's grave in Notre Dame cemetery in Ottawa expresses itself in size and grandeur rather than words.

Lester B. Pearson reverts to the modest mode. He was prime minister of Canada from 1963-1968 and winner of the Nobel Peace Prize in 1957, but he's not outstanding in his field, if you don't mind an old joke. What I mean by that is his gravemarker is no bigger, no better than the others around him in the Wakefield cemetery. There is a small Canadian flag flapping in the petunias in front of him, but that's all. Mind you, he wanted it that way. According to the stories I hear, he was out walking with some friends one day in the Gatineau hills north of Ottawa and came upon this small rural cemetery on top of a hill overlooking a wide green valley. "What do you say, boys?" Pearson said, or words to that effect. "Shall we be buried here?" And so they were and are.

A Royal Puzzle or a Royal Pain

It's a lovely mystery, and what makes it even more appealing is that it will never be solved. Agatha Christie couldn't have done better.

On a standard grey column in the Cambridge cemetery are the following words, decidedly unstandard:

MILICENT MILROY, A.M.M.M.
P. ST. DAUGHTER OF JAMES AND HELEN JANE MILROY
1890-1985
WIFE OF EDWARD (VIII)
DUKE OF WINDSOR
1894-1972

I beg your pardon? The Prince of Wales? The same prince who wouldn't be king because he wanted to marry Wallis Simpson?

Yes, the same.

Reporters, researchers, and historians have all had a go at this story, but no one has been able to determine for sure whether Milicent was simply full of baloney, whether she made up a good story to cover certain indiscretions in her youth, or whether she really did marry the prince. The thing was, she was so reasonable, so believable. A school teacher for thirty-five years, she seemed normal in every other way—except for this business about the prince. Whenever someone asked for proof, pictures, documents, etc., she'd say she couldn't reveal anything until she was dead. They don't want me to, she'd say.

But, she would add, I have a box of pictures and information hidden away that will tell all, after my death. But her house was broken into the week after she died, and furniture and household goods were carted off. So

In death as in life, Milicent Milroy held to her claim to be the wife of the Prince of Wales.

was the box, if ever there was one, because it wasn't there when people went looking.

Speculation mounted. Maybe it was Buckingham Palace that came calling in the middle of the night, just to make sure the prince's secret would remain that way? After all, a man who had worked for Milicent told the local newspaper that he had seen the pictures of Milicent and the prince. What's more, he had seen the marriage certificate. And he too seemed like a perfectly reasonable man.

You figure it out.

Anyway, the marriage was supposed to have happened in 1919 when indeed the Prince of Wales visited southern Ontario, and in the course of his official appearances went to several local schools. That would explain how he came to meet Milicent. A son is also supposed to have happened, and when Milicent's mother died in 1943, her obituary mentioned a "foster son" named Ernest. Nobody seems to know much about Ernest except that he died in a car accident some years later, but Ernest would have been about the right age to be the issue of Milicent and her prince.

And so the plot thickens.

Incidentally, the A.M.M.M. on the stone stands for the rest of her name, Agnes Mary Maureen Marguerite, and the P. ST. stands for Princess of the Royal House of Stuart, a distinction that came from her father's side of the family.

Travellers in Our Midst

Canadians are travellers. We have to be; we live in a huge country. I'll never forget an Ontario auntie of mine asking, as we drove the endless miles in northern Alberta, "Does it never end?"

No, Auntie, it doesn't. We always have miles to go before we sleep. Thus, travel in a variety of ways shows up in our graveyards, as is the case with the Reverend Father whose unhappy travel story is told in the North Bay cemetery:

IN LOVING REMEMBRANCE
OF REV. FATHER PETER EUGENE MARY BLOEM P.P.
OF NORTH BAY, ONT.
BORN IN HEERLEN, LIMB, HOLLAND, 1861
ORDAINED PRIEST 1883
CAME TO NORTH BAY, ONT, CANADA IN 1887
WHERE HE WAS FATALLY INJURED
WHILST TRYING TO BOARD A TRAIN
FEBRUARY 3, 1896
AND DIED THE SAME DAY AT MATTAWA, ONT.

Our first travellers were the Natives. Then came the explorers, who could not have managed their amazing work without the Natives; yet it is the explorers who get the credit. Such is the way of the world, at least as it shows up in our graveyards. This is what it says on the gravemarker of Simon Fraser, 1776-1862, buried in the St. Andrews cemetery:

IN MEMORY OF SIMON FRASER,
EXPLORER WHILE IN THE EMPLOY OF THE NORTH WEST CO.
HE CONDUCTED IMPORTANT EXPLORATION
AND PIONEER WORK PRINCIPALLY IN THE AREA
NOW KNOWN AS BRITISH COLUMBIA
WHICH HE HELPED TO SECURE FOR THE BRITISH.
HE LED THE FIRST EXPLORING EXPEDITION
TO DESCEND THE GREAT RIVER WHICH BEARS HIS NAME
REACHING THE GULF OF GEORGIA ON JULY 2, 1808.

Sir Alexander Mackenzie had the idea first, that there must be a way across the mountains to the Pacific Ocean, but in 1789, he found a river that led to the Arctic Ocean instead. The river became the Mackenzie, and Mackenzie went home to the British Isles to fame and fortune. He's buried there, but there's a mouldy old marker in Prescott that mentions him and other members of his family:

SIR ALEXANDER MACKENZIE
ONE OF THE MAKERS OF CANADA
BORN 1763 AND WAS BURIED AT AVOCH, SCOTLAND, 1820
ALSO RELATIVES RODERICK AND DANIEL MACKENZIE
COUSINS WHO WERE WITH HIM
AT DISCOVERY OF MACKENZIE RIVER IN 1789.

A terrible story of travel is told on a memorial in Toronto's Mount Pleasant cemetery:

IN MEMORY OF THOSE WHO LOST THEIR LIVES
IN THE FIRE WHICH DESTROYED
THE PASSENGER STEAMSHIP NORONIC
SEPTEMBER 17, 1949.

The cruise ship was spending a night in Toronto harbour before carrying on to other destinations along the Great Lakes. In the middle of the night, a passenger discovered a fire on board and for some awful reason, the city fire department didn't get there right away and the ship didn't warn its passengers. By then it was too late. Of the seven hundred on board, some 119 died. They could see shore; they just couldn't get there.

Sons from the Other Side

Not all sons who lie in distant lands were on the Allied side in the two world wars. Some German soldiers ended up in prisoner-of-war camps in thirty-six locations in Canada, and some of those men died while they were here. At first, they were buried in the communities near the camps. For instance, Medicine Hat in Alberta had eighteen buried in their Hillside cemetery. Some there died of disease. Others died as a result of murder within the camps. Still others were hanged for those crimes.

It took a mother to put a different face on the POWs in the little cemetery. She came from Germany in the 1950s to visit her son's grave and stayed for two weeks, putting flowers on all the graves, reblacking the names, haunting both the cemetery and the city. Years later when all the graves were relocated by the German War Graves Commission to the Woodland cemetery in Kitchener, she came to that too. Just because her son was on the opposite side of that terrible war didn't mean he wasn't missed in other lives and other places.

A large flat marker in one corner of Woodland explains:

IN THIS CEMETERY SECTION
REST 187 GERMAN WAR DEAD

1914-1918 1939-1945
THEY WERE BROUGHT TOGETHER IN 1970
FROM 36 LOCATIONS ACROSS CANADA.

And Now for Something a Little Different

As a rule, we Canadians are pretty conservative in our graveyards, never straying too far from black granite and RIP, but there are lovely exceptions.

The Memorial cemetery at the McMichael Canadian Art Gallery in Kleinburg is one such exception. Here are buried six members of the Group of Seven, which actually was a Group of Eight, but who's counting? The artists who are there, marked by stones of various sizes and shapes, include: Arthur Lismer, Frederick Varley, Lawren Harris, A.Y. Jackson, Franz Johnston, and A.J. Casson.

Notice that Tom Thomson is not there. He was not officially a member of the Group of Seven because he died before the group was so named. He's buried in his family's plot in the cemetery beside Leith United Church:

TOM THOMSON LANDSCAPE PAINTER
DROWNED IN CANOE LAKE JULY 18, 1917,
AGED 39 YEARS, 11 MONTHS
AND 3 DAYS.

The remains of prisoners of war who died in Canada were brought together and buried in the Woodland cemetery in Kitchener.

His death was a huge mystery. Still is. After all, he was an experienced outdoorsman who could canoe and swim with the best of them. Yet he was found drowned in Canoe Lake in Algonquin Park. Murder was murmured but never proven.

You don't often find a secret code on a gravemarker, but there's one in the Rushes cemetery near Crosshill. Actually, there are two. The original white limestone or marble marker is terribly worn now, hard enough to read at the best of times but almost impossible in its present state, so someone has obligingly reproduced the famous cryptogram on a modern grey granite stone nearby. It's still hard to figure out, the letters and numbers seemingly unconnected, but when you crack the code, you find a memorial for the two wives of Dr. S. Bean.

> TWO BETTER WIVES A MAN NEVER HAD.
> THEY WERE GIFTS FROM GOD AND ARE NOW IN HEAVEN.
> MAY GOD HELP ME, SB, TO MEET THEM THERE.

In the Belleville cemetery is a puzzle of another kind—a tombstone with finger spelling on it. That is, the name of the deceased, John Barrett McGann, is not written with letters of the alphabet but with depictions of hand and finger positions. McGann, 1810–1880, was a teacher and principal at the school for the deaf in Belleville.

And sometimes, we go right ahead and tell the whole story. I can't begin to

Dr. Bean had two good wives, and he wanted their memorial to say so. This is the puzzling result in the Rushes cemetery near Crosshill.

reproduce everything that is written on the Han Wen-huan stone in Beechwood in Ottawa. There's just too much. But it concerns a Chinese family who moved to Canada. Han Wen-huan was born in China in 1906, served with distinction in the military there from 1925 to 1949, and then moved with his wife, five sons, and three daughters to Canada where:

ALL OF THEM HAVE RECEIVED AT LEAST A MASTER'S DEGREE
WITH MOST OF THEM ACQUIRING DOCTORATE DEGREES.
IN HIS LATE YEARS, HAN EXPRESSED THE SENTIMENT
THAT THE WINDING TRAIL OF HIS LIFE
HAD LEFT HIM FINALLY WITH NOTHING UNSATISFIED.

What great good news!

Time, Gentlemen, Please

Graveyards are all about time: not enough time, the exact time, more time, the end of time. After all, just about every gravemarker includes at least the date of death—time—and the age of the deceased—time.

Eveline Louisa Gill's marker in the Lakefield Church cemetery is typical of a child's grave. It says she "departed this life May 24, 1862, at the age of 10 y'rs, 1 mo. and 24 d'ys."

I can't read the date of death on Elizabeth Webster's gravemarker in the Fergus cemetery, but I can read that she "died after a sickness of 36 hours from scarlet fever, aged 9 y. and 4 m."

Here's an inscription in the South Lancaster cemetery that gets precise about the time of day:

TO THE MEMORY OF MARGARET McEDWARD
BORN IN THE EVENING OF THE 22 NOV. 1850
DIED IN THE MORNING OF THE 31 AUG. 1871

William Pierce's gravemarker in the St. Mary Magdalene Cemetery in Picton misses the day entirely. He's known as the man who never died:

WM. PIERCE
DIED FEB. 31, 1860 AGED 73 YEARS.

Why does mention of time make it into the graveyard so often? It is, according to Mazo de la Roche's gravemarker in St. George's churchyard in Sibbald Point Provincial Park, because "Death interrupts all that is mortal." In which case, we should pay attention to the warning on Deborah Freel's grave in Butler's Burying Ground in Niagara-on-the-Lake. She died in 1816, aged seventy years:

The man who never died is remembered in the St. Mary Magdalene cemetery in Picton.

WM. PIERCE.
Died
Feb 31, 1860.
Aged
73 years.

MY DEAR CHILDREN,
THINK ON GOD AND
HIS COMMANDMENTS
AND HE WILL THINK
ON YOU.
OBSERVE YOUR
YOUTH, DON'T LOSE
NO TIME,
LESS GOD SHOULD
TAKE YOU IN YOUR
PRIME.
THEREFORE, IN TIME,
SERVE GOD ABOVE
AND, IN THIS WORLD,
FIX NOT YOUR LOVE.

Surprisingly, the man who should mention time on his gravemarker does not. Sir Sandford Fleming, who surveyed potential railroad routes all over Canada, including some over the western Rockies, invented what is known as Standard Time. Divide the world into twenty-four equal time zones, he suggested to an international conference convened to deal with problems of time. Good idea, they said, and that's how a Canadian came to be the one to invent time.

His gravemarker in Beechwood cemetery in Ottawa is silent on that matter however. It includes the standard items of time:

SIR SANDFORD FLEMING
BORN JANUARY 7, 1827
MARRIED JANUARY 3, 1855
DIED JULY 22, 1915.

The best expression of time comes from a poet, of course, since the rest of us just put in time, waste time, fritter it, lose it, want it. This is part of what poet Archibald Lampman wrote about time for a plaque at the entrance to Beechwood cemetery in Ottawa:

HERE THE DEAD SLEEP–THE QUIET DEAD. NO SOUND
DISTURBS THEM EVER, AND NO STORM DISMAYS.
OUR CENTURIES TO THEM ARE BUT AS STROKES
IN THE DIM GAMUT OF SOME FAR-OFF CHIME.
UNALTERING REST THEIR PERFECT BEING CLOAKS
A THING TOO VAST TO HEAR OR FEEL OR SEE
CHILDREN OF SILENCE AND ETERNITY,
THEY KNOW NO SEASON BUT THE END OF TIME.

Lampman is buried in Beechwood, marked only by a boulder with his name on it.

The Last Word

The front of the Ferguson stone in the North Bay cemetery contains the accomplishments of John, 1862-1946, the founder of North Bay and an active member of the community all his life. So the stone tells us, but I like the side panel where I learn this about Duncan McIntyre, 1885-1913, son of John and Jeannie Ferguson:

NORTH BAY'S FIRST BORN CITIZEN
HIS LAST WORDS AND MESSAGE:
"BE GOOD TO ONE ANOTHER."

Québec

✝

Where Graves Aren't Always in Graveyards

QUÉBEC VERY NEARLY DEFEATED ME.
I'M NOT CATHOLIC, AND I DON'T SPEAK FRENCH,
A COMBINATION THAT HANDICAPPED ME MIGHTILY.
I THOUGHT I'D BE OKAY BECAUSE I CAN READ FRENCH,
BUT I QUICKLY LEARNED THAT READING WASN'T MUCH HELP
SINCE MOST FRENCH CANADIAN CATHOLIC GRAVES DON'T
SAY MUCH. NAMES, DATES, AND RIP. THAT'S ABOUT IT.

Then, too, I couldn't seem to find the graves of the high and mighty. In English-speaking Canada, you go to the nearest graveyard, look around for the tallest monuments, and you've found some of the big names at least. But in Catholic Québec, that didn't work. For instance, why wasn't Louis-Joseph Papineau resting beneath a big monument somewhere with words of praise above him? And where was Jeanne Mance? I kept seeing her name on street signs and buildings but not in the graveyard. How come? And why couldn't I find René Lévesque, for heaven's sake? He died only a decade or so ago.

The answer lies in the distinct nature of Québec. There, I've said it, the word "distinct." My part of the country bristles at the very mention of that word for fear that to claim "distinction" is to claim "superiority." No way, we say as we climb our high horses, that any part of the country is better than our part.

But if the word "distinct" is taken to mean "different," simply that and no more, then Québec is distinct. And that being the case, I had to look for burial sites outside of graveyards—in cathedrals, for example, or in the bend of a busy city street. Burial is not confined to private spaces in Québec; it's done right out in the open.

Mind you, I contradict myself immediately by beginning with a traditional cemetery, but what a cemetery.

The Best Cemetery in Québec

I choose Mount Royal in Montréal even though a little bird is sitting on my shoulder saying, "You liked Grosse Île better." It's true, I was enormously moved by Grosse Île, and I'll tell you more about it shortly, but Mount Royal cannot be denied.

It is huge—almost seventy hectares, it has every kind of monument, tree, bird, and flower you could ever imagine, and it tells story after story. Some stories are the big five-star kind—prime ministers and generals and captains of industry. This is Montréal, after all. Other stories are ordinary tales of heartbreak and sorrow, which, of course, are not ordinary either. This is the epitaph for Evalina Francisca Xavier, died 1887, aged two years:

> THY HANDS ARE CLASPED UPON THY BREAST
> WE HAVE KISSED THY LOVELY BROW
> AND IN OUR ACHING HEARTS WE KNOW
> WE HAVE NO DARLING NOW.

So many years later, I can still feel the anguish of that family over the loss of Evalina. What an honour they did her with their choice of words.

Hugh Allan, one of the big names, doesn't have as many words on his gravemarker as Evalina does, but sometimes it takes only one word to hint at a larger story. In Hugh Allan's case, that word is "knight."

Allan was one lucky fellow. At the height of one of Montréal's cholera epidemics, he hitched a ride on a "plague boat" from Trois Rivières to Montréal. He had business to do, people to see, so he decided to take the chance. But when the boat got to Montréal, health officials wouldn't allow it to dock until the dead and dying had been removed. That made no sense at all to Hugh Allan, so he bribed the owner of a small boat to take him ashore. Money talks. Hugh Allan got himself safely ashore and safely away from the plague.

He went on to fame and fortune. By the end of his career, he owned railways, ships, banks, politicians, influence, a huge house on the slopes of Mount Royal, and a knighthood. Sir Hugh Allan. His son must have followed in his footsteps because I see the word "knight" after his name on the huge marker in Mount Royal as well.

But on a flat marker within the family plot is another story, this one about the third-generation Hugh Allan, born 1896:

KILLED WHILE ON PATROL DUTY OVER THE GERMAN LINES
6TH JULY, 1917, AGED 20 YEARS.
BURIED IN COXYDE, BELGIUM
"TIME WOULD HAVE BROUGHT HIM IN HER PATIENT WAYS
SO HIS YOUNG LIFE SPOKE TO PROSPEROUS DAYS,
TO FULLNESS OF AUTHORITY AND PRAISE.
HE WOULD NOT WAIT SO LONG A BOY
HE SPENT HIS BOY'S DEAR LIFE FOR ENGLAND
NO HONOUR OF AGE HAD BEEN MORE EXCELLENT."

The words remind me of Evalina. All of us, great and small, have to make sense of our children's deaths. Otherwise, how could we continue to live?

Sir Alexander Tilloch Galt, 1817-1893, also has a big, handsome marker in Mount Royal. An official government plaque above his name indicates that he was a Father of Confederation. All very impressive, but like Sir Hugh Allan's, there's more than meets the eye:

SIR ALEXANDER TILLOCH GALT, G.C.M.G.
BORN 1817, DIED 1893.
ELLIOTT TORRANCE, HIS WIFE
BORN 5TH NOVEMBER 1828,
DIED 25TH MAY 1850.
AMY GORDON TORRANCE, HIS WIFE
BORN 23RD MARCH 1834
DIED 6TH APRIL 1911.

I got interested when I did the arithmetic. The first Mrs. Galt died at age twenty-two. It sounds like childbirth, but there's no indication. Then apparently Galt married the younger sister. Did she have children, I wondered? What's the story?

Turns out the story is much more interesting than any of my guesses.

The first wife did die in childbirth, leaving a son named for her. A year later, Galt married the younger sister, but because there were restrictions in Canada at the time about men marrying their deceased wife's sister, they had to go to New York for the ceremony.

People were amazed at the time that Galt was even allowed near the Torrance sisters since Papa Torrance kept a stern eye on his eight daughters. In fact, he had a high brick wall built around their home and finished it off with a layer of broken glass to further discourage would-be suitors. Maybe it's a mark of Galt's ability that he was able to breach the defences not once but twice!

Anyway, Galt and his second wife had twelve children, only two of whom died in infancy, quite a good record for those days, and they raised Elliott. In turn, Elliott discovered the potential of western Canada, pioneered coal mining, irrigation, and railways in southern Alberta, and kept up the standards set by his father. Father and son accomplished; sister and sister had thirteen babies.

It was women's lot in those days to have children and look after the home. That's just how it was, and I'm not going to get into a philosophical snit over it, but we should also know about women like Hannah Lyman, 1816–1871:

> HER NOBLE WORK MOST WORTHILY DONE
> WAS THE MOULDING BY HER INSTRUCTION AND INFLUENCE
> THE MINDS AND HEARTS OF MANY OF HER OWN SEX
> BY WHOM HER MEMORY WILL EVER BE TENDERLY
> AND GRATEFULLY CHERISHED.

It turns out she ran a highly regarded school for young women in Montréal. So highly regarded were her school and her teaching methods that she ended up as principal of the prestigious Vassar Women's College in the US. She'd likely be called a feminist nowadays, but in the 1800s in Montréal, she was described as "a true-hearted woman," which meant, I'll bet, that she stayed safely within what were perceived to be "feminine" concerns. Had she run a business in competition with the Allans and the Galts of the day, what do you bet she'd have been called a "false-hearted woman."

Another woman who took refuge in teaching was Anna Harriet Leonowens, 1834–1915:

> DUTY WAS THE GUIDE OF HER LIFE
> AND THE LOVE OF HER HEART.

TO HER, LIFE WAS BEAUTIFUL AND GOOD.
SHE WAS A BENEDICTION TO ALL WHO KNEW HER,
A BREATH OF THE SPIRIT OF GOD.

If only the lovely epitaph could have mentioned in passing that this Anna was the original Anna of *Anna and the King of Siam*. Widowed with two little kids in Singapore in the 1860s, she answered an ad for a governess for the King of Siam's sixty-four children. From then on, her life followed the movie script, more or less, except that the movie never mentioned that Anna ended up in Montréal with a married daughter, and that's how come she's in Mount Royal.

Near Anna, whose stone tells too little, is a stone that tells almost too much:

TO THE MEMORY
OF 52 GERMAN EMIGRANTS BURIED HERE
AND ALSO OF 45 MORE
WHO ARE INTERRED IN THE CATHOLIC CEMETERY
HAVING LOST THEIR LIVES ON JUNE 29, 1864
BY THE PRECIPITATION OF A TRAIN OF 11 CARS
WITH 500 GERMAN EMIGRANTS
THROUGH THE OPEN DRAWBRIDGE
OVER THE RICHELIEU RIVER.
RUHET IM FRIEDEN DES HERRN.

There it is—the whole story. By some terrible mistake, the drawbridge was open when the train came along. The train poured into the river, and ninety-seven people died.

There's some poetry on the Drummond grave nearby that maybe helps:

THE SHADOWS PASS, I SEE THE LIGHT
O MORNING LIGHT, HOW CLEAR AND STRONG.

The Drummonds, George, who died in 1865 and Elizabeth, died 1906, have the most beautiful Celtic cross I've found anywhere, elaborately carved, and framed by huge trees in a shady corner of Mount Royal. I would have stayed longer in the trees' cool shade except that I wasn't alone. The young couple who were there already obviously planned to stay for a while, so I carried on. So did they, I have no doubt.

All across the prairies, I kept looking for gravemarker stories about farming—without much luck, as I've already explained. Imagine my surprise when I found this cautionary tale in memory of John Dods, Esq., 1807-1861, in the Mount Royal cemetery:

FOR MANY YEARS, PRESIDENT
OF THE MONTREAL AGRICULTURAL SOCIETY
AND WELL KNOWN THROUGHOUT CANADA
AS A SCIENTIFIC, ENERGETIC AND SUCCESSFUL FARMER.
MANLY, STRAIGHTFORWARD, KIND-HEARTED AND INTELLIGENT,
HE WAS BELOVED BY ALL WHO KNEW HIM.
A HUMBLE CHRISTIAN, HE WALKED WITH GOD
AND DEATH FOUND HIM NEITHER UNPREPARED NOR AFRAID.
HE FELL A SACRIFICE IN THE CAUSE
TO WHICH HIS LIFE WAS DEVOTED.

What happened to Mr. Dods, Esq.? I asked as soon as I got back to the cemetery office, the friendliest, most helpful cemetery office in Canada incidentally. A clerk checked, then showed me four small words that explained his untimely demise: Gored by a bull.

Sir Arthur William Currie also experienced some problems with the cause to which his life was devoted. His handsome gravemarker says:

ERECTED BY FORMER MEMBERS
OF THE CANADIAN CORPS
IN MEMORY OF GENERAL SIR ARTHUR WILLIAM CURRIE
G.C.M.G., K.C.B., V.C., L.L.D., D.C.L.
GENERAL OFFICER COMMANDING CANADIAN CORPS
IN THE FIELD 1917-1919
PRINCIPAL AND VICE CHANCELLOR
MCGILL UNIVERSITY, 1920-1933
"THEY SERVED TILL DEATH—WHY NOT WE?"

Currie came home from World War I a hero. He had kept the Canadian forces together and trained them well. As a result, they fought valiantly. The country was proud of them and proud of Canada. It was the first time we had stood on our own two feet as an independent nation, not a mere colony of Great Britain.

But in 1928, that all changed when a newspaper in Port Hope reported that Currie had needlessly sent his troops into battle on the last day of war, and that both civilians and soldiers had died because of it. Currie sued for libel and won, but two weeks later, the newspaper appealed. Currie was at his desk at McGill when he heard the news, and he collapsed. It was just too much for that old soldier to have to go through again. Even though the appeal was dismissed, Currie never really recovered. He died a few years later.

There are many more big and little names in Mount Royal. I can't begin

This beautiful, carved Celtic cross, in Montréal's amazing Mount Royal cemetery, was erected in honour of the Drummond family.

to list them all here, but there's a map and a list of Who's Who at the office. It's a good way to continue your explorations. Let me caution you, however, that a lot of the famous names say nothing. Absolutely nothing. Must we be so Canadian?

- Sir George Simpson, whose gravemarker admits he was a knight by the time he died. But that's all; no dates even. I had hoped to see the nickname "The Little Emperor" on his grave because that's what he was for the Hudson's Bay Company in Canada, but no such luck.

- Honoré Beaugrand, who was mayor of Montréal during the terrible smallpox epidemic in 1885 that killed over three thousand Montréalers. Beaugrand instituted mandatory vaccination and got into huge trouble over it—riots and civil disobedience—but he was right. No clues at all to the eventual honours that came his way.

- The Molson family, who have the most interesting collection of mausoleum and other structures in their own corner of the graveyard, not to mention a remarkable door that matches the Molson beer label. But there are no words to tell us why this should be.

- Henry Birks and sons and daughters, listed on a long, beautifully designed tablet, but again no words.

- Four generations of the Dawson family listed on a big obelisk mounted on a tall pile of rocks. Perhaps the rocks tell the story, since the Dawsons surveyed some of the rockiest parts of Canada. But I had hoped the gravemarker might say something about Sir William's famous statement when the organ was first played in his church. "No kist o'whustles will lead us in the worship of our God," he said. With that, he left his pew in the Erskine Presbyterian Church and never darkened its doorway again, believing as he did that instrumental music did not belong in a church. He was principal of McGill University from 1855 to 1899. These dates are mentioned on his grave, but nothing about his stand on music. Nothing about Dawson City being named for son George Dawson, one of the most indefatigable explorers and anthropologists this country ever had.

· One of Canada's prime ministers, who must have belonged to the Dawson school of no-nonsense. Sir John Joseph Caldwell Abbott admits only that he was "Premier of Canada, June 1891 to Dec. 1892."

· And finally, Howie Morenz, the Montréal Canadien hockey player who was so popular that the Montréal Forum was filled to the rafters for his funeral in 1937. Although buried at Mount Royal, he's not even listed under his own name. He lies with members of his wife's family under the name of Stewart.

The Other Best Cemetery in Québec

When you go to Grosse Île, take hankies. It is the most moving place.

You have to take a tour boat from Berthier-sur-Mer, a small village on the south side of the St. Lawrence, and it's not long before a rocky piece of land shows up in the middle of the wide river. This is Grosse Île. Then, it's not long before a tall Celtic cross appears on the highest part of the island, a rock upon rocks. This is the memorial that marks thousands of people who wanted a new life in a new country:

SACRED TO THE MEMORY
OF THOUSANDS OF IRISH EMIGRANTS
WHO, TO PRESERVE THE FAITH,
SUFFERED HUNGER AND EXILE IN 1847-1848
AND, STRICKEN WITH FEVER,
ENDED HERE THEIR SORROWFUL PILGRIMAGE.

In other words, Grosse Île is a graveyard. It doesn't really look like it. There are a few white crosses and gravemarkers scattered about, but there are buildings as well and wild flowers and cheerful guides, and if you didn't

So many would-be immigrants to Canada died on Grosse Île that the island became one big graveyard. A Celtic cross stands in their memory.

know the story, you'd never guess that this pretty little island held so much unhappiness.

A cholera epidemic devastated Europe in 1832. In order to prevent the same thing happening in Canada, government officials decided to set up isolated quarantine stations where overseas passengers could be screened for the disease. Grosse Île was perfect—an island located downstream from the two main ports of Québec City and Montréal, but not so far away that supplies and equipment and workers couldn't get to it.

So a rough hospital was quickly built, as well as hotels, homes for the staff, a church, and most important, a fence around a neutral zone. You see, once the passengers were sorted—the sick ones to the hospital side of the island, the others to the hotels at the other end—there was no visiting back and forth. No contact. A mother could not slip over to see her sick baby. A husband couldn't visit his wife. Guards patrolled the area to make sure the sick ones stayed in isolation and vice versa.

Once in the hospital, you either lived or died. If you lived, you were allowed to return to your family and back on the ship. If you didn't, you were buried then and there on the island. Thus did Grosse Île become one huge graveyard.

Fifteen years later, an even worse epidemic came along with the thousands of Irish emigrants who fled their homeland because of famine and political turmoil. They were crowded into dirty, slow ships. Many died enroute. Many more died when they got to Grosse Île. It was an awful situation—people whose only hope was a new life in a new land cut down by an old disease. The medical superintendent on Grosse Île reported at the height of the epidemic that as many as fifty a day were dying on that little island. Priests and ministers tried to keep up with proper burial services, but the services got shorter and shorter. Eventually, trenches had to be dug, bodies lowered into them side by side, dirt piled on top. Then the dirt ran out, and ships had to bring extra from shore. It was a nightmare.

The disease this time was typhus.

On a substantial grey pedestal marker near the western graveyard are the words:

IN THIS SECLUDED SPOT LIE THE MORTAL REMAINS
OF 5,424 PERSONS WHO FLYING FROM PESTILENCE
AND FAMINE IN IRELAND IN THE YEAR 1847
FOUND IN AMERICA BUT A GRAVE.

It wasn't only the emigrants who died. Also listed on the gravemarker are the names of six doctors who "died of typhus fever contracted in the faithful discharge of their duty upon the sick." And on the huge grey twelve-metre cross that overlooks the island are the names of forty-four priests who served there, six of whom died.

There is no special mention of all the children who were orphaned as a result of the epidemic, but again, there were thousands. Some of them were so young they didn't even know their names. They were unknown, alone, in a strange land. Some were adopted by Irish families who lived through the terror; others were taken into French Canadian homes. One man at the dedication service in 1909 for the huge Celtic memorial told reporters that he was one of the unknowns—a no-name baby adopted by a local French Canadian family. But he praised his adoptive family for keeping alive the fact that he was Irish. That much he knew.

Irish president Mary Robinson visited Grosse Île in the summer of 1994. When she laid a wreath at one of the mass graves, she spoke of "the summer of sorrow," that awful summer of 1847 when so many Irish emigrants died on an island at the entrance to Canada.

The story of Grosse Île turns up in other parts of Québec as well. On a wall of the Holy Trinity Anglican Cathedral in Québec City is a plaque to the memory of John Robert N. Symes, Esq., died Meaford, Canada West, 1858:

HE WAS MAGISTRATE AT GROSSE ÎLE 1847
DURING THE SHIP FEVER
AND ON SEVERAL OCCASIONS
CHURCH WARDEN OF THIS PARISH.
HIS CONSTANT AIM WAS TO DO GOOD.

The simplest monument of all is a big black stone, standing alone—but not lonely, there is the most awful crush of traffic whizzing by—near the Victoria Bridge in Montréal. The words say:

TO PRESERVE FROM DESECRATION
THE REMAINS OF 6,000 IMMIGRANTS
WHO DIED OF SHIP FEVER AD 1847-48

While building the bridge in 1859, workers kept unearthing bones, the remains of typhus victims who died enroute to Canada and were buried in the handiest, closest place to the ship—the river bank. It was a creepy and sad experience because many of the workers were immigrants. So one day they decided to at least mark the site. They hoisted a huge boulder, which had been blasted out of the river bottom, onto a concrete base and named it The Irish Rock.

And there it stands today, still marking the place.

That Blasted Battle

One lesson we all learn in Canadian history is that, in the middle of the night on September 13, 1759, General James Wolfe took his British soldiers up the steep banks of the St. Lawrence River at Québec City, surprised the sleeping French forces on top of the hill, and whomped them thoroughly.

This is called, we are taught, the Battle of the Plains of Abraham, and this is why we became a British colony. Unfortunately, the more informal discussions usually included the fact that France got whipped; therefore, what are we doing worrying about French language rights and other sissy stuff? We beat them, didn't we?

The thing is the English barely beat them. Wolfe was lucky; the Marquis de Montcalm, the general of the French forces, was not. Most historians now agree that he could have easily defeated the British if he hadn't rushed into battle. Besides, France wasn't that keen on having Canada. We were something of a nuisance, or as Madame de Pompadour, King Louis XV's mistress, said, "We can be happy without Canada."

Nobody knew then that the Battle of the Plains of Abraham would be seen as pivotal in Canada's history. In those days there were battles all the time between France and England. Who was to know this one would count more than all the rest?

Both generals died in the battle. Wolfe's body was taken back to England, but Montcalm's remained in Canada, first in a bomb crater near the Ursuline Convent, then later reinterred beneath the chapel of the Ursulines—minus his skull, I gather, since the skull is on display at the Ursuline Museum, or it should be by now. When I was there in the summer of 1994, "malheureusement," a young nun said to me, he was not available. He was put away for the term, she said, because the museum was undergoing renovation.

Better reminders of the battle are the cliffs that we tourists can now safely and comfortably view from above, steep prickly slopes that must have been the very devil to climb, especially in the dark. How the soldiers managed, I can't imagine, but they did and that's what made the difference.

Interestingly, the only monument to the two generals in Québec City is a shared one, located behind the Château Frontenac. The Count of Dalhousie, who had the monument erected many years later, must have been a canny old politician for the words on the plaque are written entirely in Latin, thus circumventing the whole language thing. One of the translations is:

> VALOUR GAVE THEM A COMMON DEATH,
> HISTORY A COMMON FAME,
> POSTERITY A COMMON MONUMENT.

The Other Blasted Battle

Turning a loosely organized batch of Canadian colonies into a nation was another major battle—just ask George-Étienne Cartier. It was he who, more than anyone else, brought Québec around to the idea of belonging to a confederation of Canadian provinces, equal but different. So what happened on the very first day of nationhood?

The governor general announced with great pomp and ceremony that John A. Macdonald would be made a Knight Commander of the Bath, "Sir" John from now on. As for Cartier, who had played an equal if not greater part in bringing off nationhood, he would be made a plain old Commander of the Bath. No "Sir" for him.

It was an incredibly thoughtless piece of bad politics, and Cartier understandably said No Thanks. All or nothing, he said. The trouble was there were no more knighthoods lying around; the quota was filled. A knight would have to die before Cartier could be so honoured.

It took time, but the light finally went on. Why not give him an even higher honour, make him a baronet? There were openings in the baronet ranks. So Cartier became Sir George-Étienne Cartier, BT.

None of this shows up on the Cartier family pedestal in Montréal's Côte des Neiges cemetery. George-Étienne is identified simply as G.E. Cartier, 1814-1873.

Speaking of Body Parts

The Roman Catholic church honours the "relics" of its saints; therefore, Québec has more body parts here and there than most other Canadian provinces. I began to get the picture when I visited St. Joseph's Oratory in Montréal, a church/shrine/basilica that is so big it seems unreal. Bigger than St. Paul's in London, bigger than St. Patrick's in New York, or so I read in a booklet that I picked up in the church gift shop, also bigger than most.

And all because one small French Canadian member of a religious order, Brother André, decided that St. Joseph, patron saint of the little guy, deserved a wonderful shrine and he was the little guy to do it. And he did. His is a wonderful story of prayer and perseverance.

When he died in 1937 at age ninety-one, his tomb was given a place of honour in the oratory, of course. Pilgrims come from far and near, some on their knees all the way up the long long staircases, to pray before him and show their respect. And after the pilgrims do that, they go around the corner and check out his heart.

This is the hard part for a simple westerner—the heart displayed in a reddish jar behind a decorative iron grill. But there it is, as big as life, and I'd better get used to it because there's more.

At the shrine of Sainte-Anne-de-Beaupré, which is just as incredible as St. Joseph's Oratory—how do French Canadians decide which wonderful church to attend?—we were told about the relic of Sainte Anne that they are proud to possess. It's a piece of her forearm displayed in a solid silver reliquary.

But there was more, much more. The Cathedral Notre-Dame-de-Québec in Québec City takes the cake for bones, and I'm not being disrespectful. It's just that bones are discussed as easily inside the basilica as the weather is discussed outside. For instance, François de Laval, the first bishop of Québec and a man who made a huge difference to both the church and state in Canada, is buried in a beautiful corner of this beautiful church. But, the guide says matter-of-factly, he's been in four different graves since his death in 1708. They know it's him, though, because on one of the unearthings, they checked and sure enough, they had the right guy. And so on. Some of us tourists are wishing him permanence at last!

But that's nothing. We descend a long circular staircase to the lower regions of the basilica and find ourselves beside a long black granite wall with one word on it—"ossuaire." It means, the guide explains calmly, a place for bones. There are the remains of some eight hundred to one thousand men, women, and children behind that wall, he says, bodies that used to be in Catholic cemeteries that were closed years ago.

I'm almost afraid to look but, it turns out, there's nothing to see. The area is sealed. But there's more. Beyond the bone wall is a pleasant, bright area, all marble and discreet lighting. This is the mausoleum for nuns, priests, bishops, and archbishops. It's full; bishops and archbishops are now buried in St. Mary Queen of the World in Montréal. But this used to be the last resting place for all the big names in the church. Each drawer has a name and various symbols on it: tassels according to rank, maple leaves for the first Canadian-born cardinal, Elzéar Taschereau, and so on.

And lest I forget, there are relics of Catholic martyrs here too, pieces of Jean de Brébeuf, Charles Gaimer, and Gabriel Lalemant, although I only saw a sign indicating the presence of relics; I didn't actually see any.

Finally, the guide explained that Samuel de Champlain, the man whose statue is all over the place in Québec, died on Christmas Day, 1635, and was buried behind the church chapel . . . except that the original church burned, and then there was an earthquake and a few wars, and things got a bit mixed up in the graveyard, and nobody's sure where Champlain is any more. They're looking, however, he told us cheerfully. Lots of digging going on. Very interesting, he said.

Only in Québec, you say?

Well, not really. You see, there's still the bone story concerning John Rowand, who lived most of his life in Alberta, and is in the Québec chapter only because he was buried in Mount Royal, Montréal:

> SACRED TO THE MEMORY OF JOHN ROWAND, ESQ.
> A CHIEF FACTOR IN THE SERVICE
> OF THE HUDSONS BAY COMPANY
> DIED MAY 31, 1854,
> AT FORT PITT, SASKATCHEWAN RIVER
> AGED 65 YEARS.

John Rowand's bones travelled a long way before coming to rest beneath this monument in Montréal's Mount Royal cemetery.

John Rowand more or less ruled the West back in the days when the Hudson's Bay Company ruled the West. Every now and then, his boss George Simpson rowed into the territory to check on him, but that wasn't often, and besides, they were friends. Simpson thought Rowand was just fine, and paid no attention to the complaints from Native workers that Rowand was a cruel taskmaster.

One day, Rowand decided he'd better pack it in. He was sixty-five. Time to take it easy. Time to move back to Montréal and find suitable husbands for his unmarried daughters. On the first night out, he told his son that he wanted to be buried in Montréal, *if* the time ever came, not that he thought it would.

It did—the very next morning, and contrary to his dad's wishes, young Rowand had him buried at Fort Pitt. After all, how do you haul a body across Canada by canoe and horseback? But Simpson back in Montréal heard about his friend's last wish, and Simpson was no faint heart. He travelled west, had Rowand disinterred, boiled his body down to the bones, packed the bones into a tidy package, and began the trip back to Montréal.

However, he got the feeling that the Natives travelling with him weren't keen on his package, just as they hadn't been keen on the original. "I was afraid they might from a superstitious feeling drop it over board at some time," he wrote in his journal. So he had it shipped to York Factory and from there to England and from there back to Montréal.

It took four years to make the round trip, but Simpson was true to his word. Rowand was buried in Montréal, mostly.

Unrepentant to the End

When it comes to unrepentant, this story takes the prize. I don't know the details other than that Indian tribes fought one another, aided and abetted by guns provided by the first European traders and settlers. As a result, this happened:

> HERE, ON HISTORIC CAPE DIAMOND
> JUSTLY RETALIATING HURONS
> BURNT CAPTURED IROQUOIS ALIVE
> BUT EVERY BURNING IROQUOIS
> SANG HIS DEFIANT DEATH-SONG
> QUITE UNFLINCHINGLY
> TILL HIS LAST DYING BREATH.
> 17TH CENTURY.

Read that on a plaque as you stand on the Plains of Abraham in Québec City, and tell me we don't have an interesting history.

You have to work a little harder to get the story of unrepentant Charles Chiniquy, but it's equally amazing. His grave in Mount Royal cemetery looks and sounds pretty normal:

> CHARLES CHINIQUY
> DOCTEUR EN THEOLOGIE
> PASTEUR DE L'EGLISE PRESBYTERIENNE
> APOTRE DE LA TEMPERANCE DU CANADA
> 1809-1899

He was a pastor of the Presbyterian Church and an apostle on behalf of temperance, the words tell us. It all sounds so noble, so reasonable, but it wasn't at all. Not at all, and the fact that Chiniquy is buried in the Protestant cemetery right next door to the Catholic cemetery only adds fuel to the flames.

What a guy. He began his crazy career as a Catholic priest, a charismatic, rooting tooting Catholic evangelist who could sway huge audiences to his cause of temperance. Down with drink was his message, and thousands bought it. But even as he charmed the birds out of the trees with his eloquence, so did he charm the ladies into the bushes, and that got him into trouble with the church. The bishop of Montréal, Ignace Bourget, warned him to be careful of "personnes du sexe," but Chiniquy bounced from one scrape to another, covering his tracks with words—always words—until finally the Catholic Church excommunicated him in 1856.

Never mind, he could still talk a blue streak, and the Presbyterians welcomed him into their fold several years later. To his temperance talk, still popular with the masses, he added a bit of Catholic-bashing and that too brought in the audiences. He was the televangelist of his day—made money and converts wherever he went, not that the converts, or the money, lasted. He was such a scoundrel but managed to get away with it all.

Before he died, it was rumoured that the Catholic Church sent him a letter offering forgiveness if he'd recant, but he said No Thanks, Jesus Christ was good enough for him. And then two nuns were supposed to have snuck into his house to give him one last chance at everlasting life, but that too was rejected.

So Chiniquy died and was buried in the Protestant cemetery, not that that was the last of him. Legend has it that he was buried standing up, and as they placed the last shovelful of dirt over his coffin, the coffin was rent down the middle, split by divine retribution.

It would be just like Chiniquy to have the last word, although things look pretty calm around him now.

As if the Catholic Church didn't have its hands full with Chiniquy, along came Joseph Guibord to add to their woes. None of this would have happened, incidentally, if the church hadn't been as all powerful as it was in Québec in the 1700s and 1800s. The church was the state and vice versa.

Not everybody agreed with this sharing of power. Some, like the members of the Institut Canadien, thought the church had no business telling them what they could and couldn't read, for instance. The institute was a literary and discussion society. They had their own library, and that's how they got into trouble with Bishop Ignace Bourget because some of the books in that library were on his "Index of Forbidden Books." One of them was Darwin's *Origin of Species*; another was Victor Hugo's *Les Misérables*.

The institute defied the bishop; he, in turn, announced that henceforth any members of the institute would be denied the sacraments "even at the point of death."

I don't suppose Guibord wanted to be the first to challenge the bishop's ruling, but he was unlucky enough to die shortly after the decree, and sure

The bishop won in the end, but Joseph Guibord's supporters succeeded in having his remains buried in consecrated ground in Montréal's Notre-Dame-des-Neiges.

enough, he was denied burial within consecrated ground. His wife sued the church on the grounds that her husband had been a Catholic and was therefore entitled to Catholic burial; the institute supported her suit, and the whole nasty thing wound through the courts for the next five years. Eventually, Guibord won, if win is the right word, and his body was removed from the vault in the Protestant cemetery and taken to the Catholic Notre-Dame-des-Neiges.

But if you think the decision was accepted with good grace, think again. The army was called out, some twelve hundred men, to prevent violence enroute to the cemetery. And the coffin was encased in cement as it was lowered into the ground, the better to prevent desecration. There was such passion about this small dead man who had defied the church. It's hard to believe in the 1990s, but that's the way we were.

Guibord's grave was eventually marked by a huge boulder, but no name or dates were applied. He's entirely silent after all his troubles, even though the day I was there, there was a single red plastic rose on his rock. Someone souviens.

What's more, the church had the last word after all. The bishop deconsecrated the ground in which Guibord was buried and told his Catholic followers in a pastoral letter that from henceforth, the ground that held Guibord would be "cursed ground."

The Megantic Outlaw

When I went to the Gisla cemetery in the Eastern Townships of Québec, I hoped against hope that Donald Morrison's grave would say something, anything that would help me tell his story. But all that distinguished his grave were the petunias blooming bravely in the grass in front of his plain red granite marker. He was the only one who had petunias, however, so I decided petunias would have to do.

Earlier that day, I had stopped at a local museum. When I asked the people there about interesting gravemarkers in the area, they immediately said as one, "The Megantic Outlaw." Did I know about him?

No, I didn't, but as far as I can tell from their fond memories and the few written accounts of the story that exist, it went something like this: Donald Morrison and his folks came from Scotland and settled in the area around Lake Megantic in the townships. They wanted their own land so Donald went west to make his fortune. He didn't make a fortune apparently, but he did send enough money home for his folks to make regular mortgage payments to a certain landowner in the area.

Trouble started when the landowner didn't give the Morrisons receipts for the payments. So when Donald came home seven years later and asked for title to the land, the landowner refused. No receipts, no proof, he said. So there were court challenges and arguments and finally a fight, in the course of which Donald killed the bad guy. There are those who say it was a fair fight and Donald would have been acquitted of any charges on the basis of self-defence, but he chose to run instead. By now, he didn't trust the courts to deliver justice.

So for weeks, months, years—the time gets longer as the story ages—Donald hid out in the woods, sheltered and fed by his Scottish neighbours, who understood the justice of his cause. Police constantly laid traps, tried to surprise him, but Donald got very good at hide-and-seek. Besides, his neighbours used to warn him away. One story goes that police suddenly appeared at a house where he was enjoying a good meal. The lady of the house shoved him under the bed, spread her skirts over the hiding place, and told the police to get lost. Meanwhile, she spoke Gaelic to her family. The police didn't understand but Donald did, so he knew when it was safe to come out. It was a pretty good scam for a while, the classic struggle between good and evil.

Eventually of course Donald was caught, found guilty, and put in jail where he died. But his story hasn't died. He's the Megantic Outlaw forever and ever in that area, a hero to the folks, and that's why he's the only one in the graveyard who has petunias.

Speaking of Heroes

Louis Cyr once lifted a platform with eighteen fat men standing on it. Why he did this, and why eighteen fat men just happened to be standing on a platform, I don't know. But it's one of the accomplishments of Louis Cyr that is always mentioned in accounts of his life.

The other accomplishment that's always mentioned is the horse feat. While in England on tour, he hitched himself to two horses, one going south, the other going north. Each horse was driven as hard as possible in its respective direction, but Cyr held them to a standstill. I'm not quite as impressed by this as by the fat men on a platform story. Seems to me the horses might have cancelled one another's power, but never mind. The point is that Louis Cyr was one strong man. The strongest in the world, they said at the time.

And the neat thing is he was one of our own. He was born in Québec; when he finished his career as strong man, he came back to Québec. And that's where he's buried. His marker in the cemetery at St-Jean-de-Matha near Montréal says:

ICI REPOSE LOUIS CYR
CHAMPION DES HOMMES FORTS
DÉC LE 10 NOV 1912
AGÉ DE 49 ANS ET 1 MOIS

The Family in the Cellar

Judy, my travelling companion and navigator, was quite willing to go everywhere my graveyard research took me, everywhere, that is, except down into the damp, dark cellar beneath the Papineau Chapel in Montebello. At that, she drew the line.

It was a bit bizarre, I have to admit, but Louis-Joseph Papineau is a big name in Québec. I was determined to see his last resting place, his and about ten others of the Papineau family who are buried in white concrete bunkers beneath the little chapel in the woods near the Papineau manor. You get a guide first, of course, and your guide explains the various generations of the Papineau family, explains how Louis-Joseph became a symbol of French Canadian independence, explains how he ended up with a big house and this small private chapel in which we stand. Then and only then does she pull out a flashlight and open the trapdoor leading to the dark cellar below.

That's when Judy decided to take a walk in the park, and I have to admit

Louis-Joseph Papineau is buried beneath a chapel on the grounds of the Papineau manor, near Montebello.

it was a bit creepy especially when the guide shone the flashlight on one of the ghostly bumps and said, "That one blew up once."

However, everything has been secured since then.

The first Papineau in Canada was a seigneur, which means he was sort of a feudal lord complete with land and tenants. His son Louis-Joseph took over the seigneury in his time, which made him sort of a feudal lord too, but for some reason or other, he became the champion of the little guy. It was Papineau who went to London to argue against the union of Upper and Lower Canada. It was Papineau who said Québeckers should have a say in how their tax money was spent. It was Papineau and other Patriotes who drafted the famous Ninety-two Resolutions and presented them to the government.

And it was Papineau who hightailed it to the US when some of his fellow Patriotes actually fought for what they believed. Their insurrection was easily contained, but it's never been forgotten. For one thing, there's a huge monument in Notre-Dame-des-Neiges cemetery in Québec City called Monument Des Patriotes, and "Les Victimes Politiques, 1837 and 1838," are listed on six sides of the huge column.

Why Papineau was still a big hero when he returned from exile in France in 1845, I can't quite understand. After all, he had run away when the going got tough. But my guide, a sensible older woman like me, said, "Me, I just love Louis-Joseph. He is here," and she pointed to her heart.

So, I guess that answers my question. He spoke for Québec. He was Québec. And you can't understand that unless you are also Québec.

There's no marker on his underground bunker, but there is a sign in the chapel above, which, when translated, says in part:

MEMBER OF THE LEGISLATIVE ASSEMBLY FOR 38 YEARS
PRESIDENT OF THE ASSEMBLY OF LOWER CANADA FOR 23 YEARS
LEADER OF THE LIBERAL PARTY FOR 14 YEARS
EXILED IN 1837, RETURNED IN 1845
AN ELOQUENT ORATOR, A STATESMAN
OF PRINCIPLE AND PROGRESSIVE IDEAS.

A Royal Walkabout

Papineau is Québec's real royalty, but there are a few other title-holders in their midst.

For instance, Queen Victoria's half-brother is buried in Québec City's oldest Protestant cemetery, St. Matthew's, or so the story goes. Edward, Duke of Kent, fourth son of King George III of England, governed Halifax for a while at the end of the 1700s. While there, he enjoyed the company of Julie de Montgenet and had a son by her. When Papa, the king, ordered Edward back home and into a proper royal marriage, the child was left behind with a foster father. Where Julie went, I'm not sure, but the child became Robert Wood and grew up in Canada, eventually becoming a lumber merchant in Québec City.

In the meantime, his half-sister, born within the proper marriage, became the Queen of England and all the other pink parts of the world. Did Robert Wood know what he was missing, I wonder?

None of this interesting stuff is mentioned on his gravemarker, but the government has erected historical panels throughout the cemetery, making it one of the best history lessons around. I hope that schoolkids are regularly trailed through it to read and wonder about the people who came before them.

For instance, there's Thomas Scott, younger brother of Sir Walter Scott, whose gravemarker tells us that he was "late paymaster of the 70th Regt., died 1823," but whose historical panel tells us he may have written some of Sir Walter's stuff. For heaven's sake.

There's Lieut. Col. B.J. Frobisher, whose name sounds awfully familiar, and it is, as it turns out. His father was Joseph Frobisher, fur trader and explorer. Canada was a small world in the first few hundred years. The same names kept turning up all over the place.

The same awful tragedies do as well. Cholera hit Québec City just as it did every other major centre. James McLean died of Asiatic cholera, July 31, 1832, his gravemarker tells us. The historical sign adds that thirty-five other cholera victims were buried the same day as McLean. And there are always the same sad tales about young lives.

SACRED TO THE MEMORY OF JANE,
WIFE OF GEORGE RABY,
SERGT. 24TH BATTALION OF COLDSTREAM GUARDS
WHO DEPARTED THIS LIFE 12 OCT., 1810
AGED 28 YEARS
ALSO OF HER INFANT TWINS THOMAS AND JANE
WHO DIED A FEW DAYS BEFORE HER.

From One Extreme to Another

Minta Coates, 1862-1924, was, I hope, a no-nonsense person because her epitaph in the Eaton Cemetery in the Eastern Townships certainly is:

SHE HATH DONE WHAT SHE COULD

Sounds like faint praise to me but it's not, I am told. Indeed, it's supposed to be one of the highest accolades a Christian could expect on his or her grave. The funny thing is it is usually found on women's graves.

Men are more likely to have their accomplishments spelled out, like this inscription in the Mount Hermon cemetery in Québec City, a cemetery that pays a lot of attention to commerce:

SACRED TO THE MEMORY OF WILLIAM GUNN, ESQ.
BORN AT LANARK IN SCOTLAND, 1802
DIED IN QUÉBEC 16 DEC. 1856.
FOR TWENTY YEARS A FAITHFUL AND EFFICIENT SERVANT
OF THE BANK OF MONTREAL HE WAS IN 1848
APPOINTED MANAGER OF THE BRANCH IN THIS CITY
WHICH RESPONSIBLE OFFICE HE RULED TILL HIS DEATH.
OF STRONG DOMESTIC AFFECTIONS AND UNIMPEACHABLE
INTEGRITY IN BUSINESS TRANSACTIONS, HE WAS WARM
IN HIS FRIENDSHIPS AND ZEALOUS IN THE DISCHARGE
OF CHRISTIAN DUTIES.
IN TOKEN OF THE ESTEEM AND RESPECT
IN WHICH HE WAS HELD, THIS MONUMENT IS ERECTED
BY THE MERCHANTS AND CITIZENS OF QUÉBEC,
AND BY FRIENDS IN DIFFERENT PARTS OF THE PROVINCE.

Obviously, Mr. Gunn hath done what he could, I thought as I wrote down the long inscription. But what about Mrs. Gunn? What hath she done?

She lived and died, that's all, if I am to believe the other side of the huge stone. Mind you, I don't believe it. Women have always done what they could, and more. They just don't get the same press.

The Graveyard Most Likely to Be in the Headlines

To get to Oka, you do not take a bridge. You take a ferry. And when you get to Oka, you do not see angry citizens scowling at the world. You see a lovely, small town nestling in green trees alongside Lac des Deux Montagnes.

In other words, it's not what the headlines would have us expect. But Oka is the site of the Indian graveyard that started a confrontation we're not likely to forget—Indian warriors barricading a bridge, police officers and soldiers nearby, guns on the ready on both sides. It was awful.

Oka itself is about the most peaceful place you can imagine. The confrontation did not take place there, however. It was staged on a bridge on the Caughnawaga Reserve about thirty-two kilometres away, a bridge that carried thousands of commuters each day. Because Montréal is an island, closing any bridge is a major inconvenience, so it's no wonder the action got so much attention.

The trouble started when there was talk of expanding the golf course next to the Oka Pine Hill cemetery. Apparently, developers cast envious eyes on the neighbouring graveyard. I don't know why—the graveyard is small, barely big enough to hold a good-sized green let alone additional holes. Perhaps there is more land involved in the controversy; perhaps I can never understand all the underlying passions that go along with this story. But I do know that the graveyard is located on a small corner of land near the entrance to the golf course, almost invisible in a large stand of pines. Ironically, we had to get directions from a golfer who was unloading his clubs in the nearby parking lot. "Right through those trees," he said cheerfully. And there it was, gravemarkers scattered here and there, many bearing the last name Oke. One wooden headstone, for example, remembered Susan Oke, died December 12, 1929, aged eighty-five years. Another more modern one recalled Chief Louis Simon, 1913-1974.

It wasn't terribly beautiful. It didn't contain nationally recognized names. But it was a graveyard, and that, I think, is the point.

Graves That Stand Alone

James McGill and Simon McTavish lived within shouting distance of one another when they were both successful fur traders and members of

Montréal's monied establishment. They're still within shouting distance of one another although with all the racket that goes on around McGill University, I don't suppose shouting would do the trick any more. Maybe that's why McTavish haunts his old neighbourhood, or so they tell me, because he can't make himself heard any other way.

McTavish was an original. Born in Scotland, he made money in Canada with the Northwest Company and decided to show it off. What's the good of having money if you can't flaunt it? So he commissioned a huge mansion on the height of Mount Royal where he would be the king of the castle. But before the castle was finished, he caught cold and died, which is why the only building he ever inhabited on that lonely hillside was the mausoleum.

Through the years, the unfinished mansion was badly vandalized and had to be torn down. The mausoleum had to be covered with rocks and dirt to prevent a similar fate. It's there still, I am told, at the top of McTavish Street where Pine Avenue bends, but I couldn't find it. For one thing, there's so much traffic on Pine that I didn't dare slow down, let alone stop. I did see the jog in the road, however. I got that close.

It's much easier to get to McGill's grave since it is located on a "spot of ground" in front of the Arts building on the campus of McGill University. It wasn't always so fortunately located, however.

When McGill died in 1813, he was buried in a Protestant cemetery on Dorchester Street, now René Lévesque Blvd. His wife, being Catholic, would not be buried in a Protestant cemetery so when she died a few years later, she was laid to rest in the crypt of Notre Dame.

Somehow, McGill was forgotten over the years, and the old cemetery deteriorated so badly that the city decided to close it and reinter the bodies elsewhere. That's when McGill University finally woke up and decided they should bring their founder back home and give him a monument worthy of the name.

There was some question as to whether they had the right bones in place, and then they had to get the Anglican bishop into the act to properly consecrate "the spot of land" for his reinterment. But finally all details were complete and James McGill got a place of honour—just down the hill from his old neighbour.

The monument says:

> TO THE MEMORY OF THE HONBLE. JAMES MCGILL
> A NATIVE OF GLASGOW, NORTH BRITAIN
> AND DURING SEVERAL YEARS A REPRESENTATIVE

OF THE CITY OF MONTREAL IN THE LEGISLATIVE ASSEMBLY,
AND COLONEL OF THE BATTALION OF MONTREAL MILITIA
WHO DEPARTED THIS LIFE ON THE 19TH DAY OF DECEMBER,
1813 IN HIS 69TH YEAR.
IN HIS LOYALTY TO HIS SOVEREIGN AND HIS ABILITY,
INTEGRITY, INDUSTRY AND ZEAL AS A MAGISTRATE
AND IN THE OTHER RELATIONS OF PUBLIC AND PRIVATE LIFE
HE WAS CONSPICUOUS.
HIS LOSS IS ACCORDINGLY SINCERELY FELT
AND GREATLY REGRETTED.

The Artists among Us

I'm asking for trouble, I know, when I rank artists, but here goes anyway. As far as I can tell from reading about the artists of Québec, Émile Nelligan seems to come out on top. He was a poet who wrote like mad for five short years, then went mad for sure and for certain and never wrote another line.

But the poetry he produced in those five intense years between the ages of fifteen and twenty is said to be brilliant. He is buried at Notre-Dame-des-Neiges in Montréal beneath a handsome pedestal that says:

EMILE NELLIGAN, POÈTE
1879-1941
"SES MATS
TOUCHAIENT L'AZUR,
SUR DES MERS
INCONNUES."
("His mast touched
the heavens over
unknown seas.")

One of the largest markers in Notre-Dame-des-Neiges cemetery belongs to the poet Émile Nelligan.

D'Arcy McGee was also a poet, but not in the same league as Nelligan. Nobody was in his league, I gather. McGee would have been moderately famous as a poetic politician, but he went and got himself murdered, forever ensuring his fame in Canadian history.

He's buried at Notre-Dame-des-Neiges in Montréal as well, in a handsome stone mausoleum with shamrocks and maple leaves decorating a plaque that says:

IN MEMORY OF THOMAS D'ARCY MCGEE
THE MOST ELOQUENT VOICE
OF THE FATHERS OF CONFEDERATION
BORN IN CARLINGFORD, COUNTY LOUTH, IRELAND
MAY 13, 1825
ASSASSINATED IN OTTAWA APRIL 7, 1868

It was those shamrocks that got him into trouble. The Irish community in the US hoped that D'Arcy McGee would support their plans to attack Canada in order to attack Britain. It's all too complicated for modern Canadians to contemplate, but in those days the Irish fought the English wherever they went, including Canada. When D'Arcy McGee turned into a Canadian nationalist and began charming the birds out of the trees on behalf of Canada, the Irish Fenian militants turned against him; shot him in the back of the head one night in Ottawa as he bent over to unlock the door of his boarding house. Or so the theory goes. The murder was never solved.

We sing "I'm Dreaming of a White Christmas" once a year and can rhyme off the name of its composer, Irving Berlin, without hesitation. But we sing "O Canada" all the time and couldn't for the life of us name the composer.

Well, I'm here to tell you that Calixa Lavallée wrote the music. He was a Québec musician who couldn't make a living as a musician in Canada, so he moved to the States. Where have you heard that before? There, he gained a reputation as an all-round musician, and at one concert played successively the piano, violin, and cornet. He died in 1891 and was buried in Notre-Dame-des-Neiges in Montréal.

When I first found his grave, it was just an insignificant, little white marble marker next to a fire hydrant next to the office. When I saw it two years later, it was brand new, three times as big, and covered with words that sound suspiciously like a mini-sermon about Québec politics. "My goal," the words begin in French, "is to try to awaken our dear people once in awhile." I gather these are Lavallée's words, but it's all a bit confusing,

Calixa Lavallée wrote the music for "O Canada," though there is no mention of this on his gravemarker.

for he goes on to say that we have to learn to walk before we run.

If the new stone is courtesy the separatist Société Saint-Jean-Baptiste de Montréal, whose name appears on the base, then surely the message would be a little more direct, as in "We've walked long enough; now we must run. Let us get on with separation and get on with our lives as a nation."

See—you can find it all in a graveyard—political messages, religious messages, even mystery now and then.

Napoleon, Here I Come

Camillien Houde was "colourful," or at least that is the word most often applied to him. He was the mayor of Montréal for years. He was elected to the House of Commons but refused to go. He was enormously fat. He had a huge nose. He got into trouble all the time. He went to jail for a while because he opposed conscription. And always and forever, he was a huge hero. When he died, he was buried in a tomb modelled on Napoleon's in Paris. He wanted it that way. It stands in a front row in Notre-Dame-des-Neiges.

The information on the tomb is of the official sort—dates and political service. But he once said, "As long as we keep a good balance between prayer and sinning, I know my city is not going to sink into wickedness."

Lavallée's new gravestone re-flects current Canadian politics.

That should have been on the tomb that Houde built.

But Where Is the Mrs?

I've always admired David Thompson, not just because he was such a remarkable explorer and adventurer but because he stayed loyal to his Native wife, Charlotte. A lot of the early explorers and fur traders took Native wives, used them until they were finished with the hard work in the wilds, and then left them. That's what Hudson's Bay Company Governor George Simpson did. He left his Native woman and his "bits of brown," his tacky way of referring to the mixed-blood children that he left in his wake, and married a so-called "proper" wife from England.

But Thompson didn't do that. He brought Charlotte and some of their thirteen children to Montréal when he retired. They weren't welcomed into high society, of course, but then Thompson didn't have enough money for high society anyway. This was the bravest and best man. He had found a passage through the impassable Rockies to the Pacific but did he have enough to live on in his old age? No. He died nearly blind and penniless.

There's a handsome grey column erected by the Canadian Historical Society in his memory in Mount Royal cemetery:

DAVID THOMPSON, 1770–1857
TO THE MEMORY OF THE GREATEST

OF CANADIAN GEOGRAPHERS
WHO FOR 34 YEARS EXPLORED AND MAPPED
THE MAIN TRAVEL ROUTES
BETWEEN THE ST. LAWRENCE AND THE PACIFIC.

But there's no sign of his wife. I wrote to the Canadian Historical Society and they could not help me. Where is Charlotte?

For That Matter, Where Are the Mothers?

Wherever you go in Montréal, you hear about Marguerite Bourgeoys, Jeanne Mance, and Marguerite d'Youville—noble ladies all three who gave their lives to good works and good causes. But where are they buried?

Particularly did I ask that question when I was in the remarkable cathedral in Montréal known as St. Mary Queen of the World. Bishop Bourget is there in a magnificent room in a magnificent tomb surrounded by other magnificent names and tombs. Cardinal Paul-Émile Leger, 1904-1991, for instance, is also there.

In other sections of this incredible church are huge pictures, room-sized pictures of the three women, but no mention of their last resting places.

Camillien Houde is buried in Notre-Dame-des-Neiges beneath a tomb styled after Napoleon's in Paris.

I still haven't figured it out. Maybe it's obvious: they are buried in the institutions that they helped found. Maybe it's not so obvious. Maybe it has something to do with being a woman in a man's world—which the world of the church in the 1600s and 1700s certainly was.

However, to get off my soap box for a moment, I have since learned that Jeanne Mance, who was the first of the trio to arrive in this god-forsaken country—in 1641—is buried under the chapel of l'Hôtel Dieu, the hospital she founded so many years ago.

Marguerite Bourgeoys, who arrived in Montréal about ten years later, kept up the good work. She started schools and just generally looked after the homeless and helpless, among them the King's Girls who came out from France to marry the King's Boys. Canonized in 1982, she is buried in the chapel of the Congregation of Notre Dame in Westmount.

And finally, the other Marguerite—Marguerite d'Youville—founded the Grey Nuns in Montréal in 1737, and is therefore buried in the chapel of the Grey Nuns on rue Saint Matthieu.

Silent Stories That Need to Speak Up

In 1807, Ezekial Hart was the first Jew elected to a Canadian legislature, but he never got to actually sit in the Québec National Assembly, even though he was elected three times. How come? He was a Jew. Therefore, he wouldn't swear an oath on the Bible. He would swear on the Old Testament only. But the other members wouldn't allow that, saying it was anti-Christian, so Hart had to work for equal rights from outside government. He got it too. In 1831, the Bill of Equal Rights gave Jews the right to accept and hold public office without compromising Jewish law. But it was too late for Hart. He died in 1843 and was buried in the Hart cemetery in Trois Rivières.

That cemetery was closed in 1909 and all the bodies and headstones brought to Mount Royal in Montréal. Ezekial is there, but his gravestone says nothing about his challenges to the biases of Canadian society in the 1800s. Too bad.

The story of Pierre Laporte is such a black hole in Canadian history for two reasons. First, Laporte died at the hands of the FLQ terrorists who kidnapped him, and second, the War Measures Act was invoked. This meant that hundreds of Canadian citizens were rounded up, without due process of law, and imprisoned just because they were known separatists.

I hoped that Laporte's grave in Notre-Dame-des-Neiges might at least hint at the history he represents, but it doesn't. Only the date gives it away—1970. The only story I can uncover from the family gravemarker is that his mother was alive throughout that terrible time. She didn't die until two years later, aged seventy-nine. What a terrible ending to her life.

And finally, René Lévesque, the premier who preached Québec separatism while dripping cigarette ashes all over himself. Speak of politically incorrect! Speak of politically interesting! He is buried, the officials told me several times, in St. Michel in Sillery on rue René Lévesque in Québec City. No sweat, they said. You can't miss it.

I should have known.

The first time I went, it was raining. My feet were wet. I was tired. I was rushed. I checked the big monuments first—no luck. Then I did a quick tour—no luck. So I decided to come back the next day with reinforcements.

The next day, three of us fanned out, did a systematic search. No René Lévesque. Nowhere. Back at the hotel, I phoned another office and got the same information—he's at St. Michel in Sillery. I did one more check, couldn't find him. It bugged me. How could I miss someone so important?

Two months later, I checked again. Still no René Lévesque, and this is where my halting French did me in. I couldn't determine whether he was buried there but not yet marked? It takes some skill to ask delicate questions of this sort.

I still don't know. It is my biggest aggravation. How could I miss him?

The Last Word

If this warning on a gravemarker in the Gisla cemetery in the Eastern Townships doesn't stiffen your spine and send you down the road to redemption, I don't know what will. It's on Angus D. Campbell's marker. He drowned in 1891, aged thirty-six years, five months, and four days:

> FEW ARE THY DAYS AND FULL OF WOE,
> OH MAN OF WOMAN BORN,
> THY DOOM IS WRITTEN, DUST THOU ART,
> AND SHALL TO DUST RETURN.
> O MAN PREPARE TO MEET THY GOD.

New Brunswick

✠

Where Silence Speaks Its Piece

IT'S FALL IN NEW BRUNSWICK.

IT'S GLORIOUS IN NEW BRUNSWICK.

A MAPLE TREE BESIDE BLISS CARMAN'S GRAVE

IN THE FOREST HILL CEMETERY IN FREDERICTON

IS SO RED I CAN'T BELIEVE IT.

WE DON'T HAVE RED TREES IN WESTERN CANADA.

WE HAVE LOTS OF OTHER BEAUTIFUL THINGS,

OF COURSE,

BUT WE DON'T HAVE RED MAPLE TREES IN AUTUMN.

At last I understand the poem we all had to memorize so many years ago in Alberta schools, a Bliss Carman poem that includes the lines: "The scarlet of the maples can shake me like a cry/ Of bugles going by."

Bliss Carman's grave includes, as it should, a poem:

HAVE LITTLE CARE THAT LIFE IS BRIEF,

AND LESS THAT ART IS LONG,

SUCCESS IS IN THE SILENCE,

THOUGH FAME IS IN THE SONG.

Bliss Carman is buried beneath a scarlet maple in the Forest Hill cemetery in Fredericton.

As I read it, I wonder if he's taking one last poke at Canada? At the fact that the literary world always sniffed a bit at his work, using words like "undistinguished" even while school kids all across the country were reciting and trying to imagine the scarlet of the maples.

Mind you, I also wonder as I stand there if it's true that long-term respect is better than short-lived song. It's a good question, and even though the graveyard is a completely suitable setting to think these deep thoughts, it's the first time that poetry has demanded philosophy in a graveyard. Score one for poetry, I decide.

Near Bliss Carman is his cousin Charles G.D. Roberts, another Canadian poet, with another poem on his marker:

UP, SOUL, AND OUT
INTO THE DEEPS ALONE
TO THE LONG PEAL
AND THE SHOUT
OF THOSE TRUMPETS
BLOWN AND BLOWN.

I'm not sure what Roberts is telling us: that there is life after death and it will be fine and trumpets will blow? Maybe, but I just like the words. Wonderfully large words they are—the long peal and the shout—how can you beat that? Score another for poetry.

Alden Nowlan, 1933–1983, is also buried nearby, marigolds fighting for space among the maple leaves in front of his grave, his words asking:

> REST LIGHTLY ON HIM, O EARTH
> HE LOVED YOU SO.

Which makes Forest Hill the most poetic graveyard in Canada. It has poets, it has poetry, it has red leaves drifting silently out of crimson trees, it has marigolds. But does it have bliss without the capital letter?

For that, I went to Blissville. Actually, Blissville came to me. We were driving along a highway taking turns saying, "Isn't that gorgeous? Have you ever seen anything more beautiful?" when the name Blissville appeared on a sign. Then a church appeared, and a graveyard. I braked.

Who could resist? Just as I couldn't drive past Livelong, Saskatchewan, so did I have to stop at Blissville. Would Blissville graves be any different from, say, Livelong? Would they reveal the secret to a happy life?

Maybe I wouldn't know bliss if I fell over it, but the gravemarkers in Blissville told the same stories as most others gravemarkers do—lives that ended sooner or later, better or worse, richer or poorer. Araminta Nason died in 1877, for example, aged thirty-four years. A good woman, I gather, since the last line of her inscription says:

> AND SINNERS MAY HOPE
> SINCE THE SINLESS HAS DIED.

I'm not sure that the literary world would call that poetry, but I do. It may even be bliss, come to think of it.

Come with me then through New Brunswick. I'll try not to mention the beautiful trees more than is absolutely necessary.

The Silence of the Acadians

We drove into New Brunswick via the northwest corner, also known as the Republic of Madawaska. The area was first settled in large part by Acadians, who were an independent bunch. That, and being far away from British authority, meant people got into the habit of running their own show, thus the title of Republic.

Acadians descended from the first French settlers in Maritime Canada. If France and England hadn't loved war so much, the Acadians would have had an easier time of it. As it was, every time France won a battle or two, the Acadians were secure in their homes and property. Every time Britain won, they were in danger of losing everything.

Thus the Treaty of Utrecht, 1713, by which England took possession of New France, was bad news for the Acadians. They tried to keep their heads down and remain "neutral," but it didn't work. In 1755, the governor of Nova Scotia, Col. Charles Lawrence, decided that Acadians were a threat to British security; they would have to swear allegiance to the British throne or else.

They wouldn't, so he expelled them, just like that. Put some ten thousand men, women, and children on boats and sent them away—some to France, others to the United States, others to the bottom of the sea because a number of boats were lost enroute. It was a terrible thing, but do you think I could find any evidence of the story in graveyards? Not a word. I had hoped there would be the occasional marker that said something like, "Descendant of an Acadian who was cruelly deported by the dastardly British," but I didn't.

Some Acadians came back to Canada when the coast was clear; others melted into isolated areas such as Madawaska and stayed clear of authorities. Likely, they were buried as quietly as they lived. Thus, I can't find specific mention of the expulsion on a gravemarker. However, in Ste. Basile, in the midst of the Republic, I did find a plaque on an old chapel beside the graveyard that paid homage to the pioneers who came in 1785: Pierre Duperre, Paul Potier, Joseph Daigle, Baptiste Fournier, Jacques Cyr, Firmin Cyr, Alexandre Ayotte, Antoine Cyr, Baptiste Thibodeau, Louis & Michel Mercure, Olivier & Pierre Cyr.

In Buctouche, on the other side of the province, I found another memorial to "Les Fondateurs, arrives en 1785: Leblanc, Breau, Girouard, Bastarache."

And in Newcastle when I asked about Acadian graves, I was sent to "The Enclosure," a park outside the town with a few gravemarkers concealed deep inside its bush and trees. It seems as if Acadians should be here, the place is so hidden and silent, but a sign says it was the site of the first Presbyterian church in Northumberland County. Acadians were by and large Roman Catholic; they would not have been buried with the Presbyterians, so either the Presbyterian church came later or the Acadians are not here after all, which brings me right back to where I started—no graves that tell the story, conspicuous only by their absence.

Conspicuous by Their Presence

Fredericton's story, by contrast, tells itself at every opportunity.

We got there in the evening and found, in the gloaming alongside the

Saint John River Park, the Loyalist Provincials' Burial Ground. Get used to that word, Loyalist. That's the story told in Fredericton.

It's not told very well at the old burial ground in spite of its name. There wasn't much there that night—a pair of lovers smooching under a tree, if you must know—but a plaque on a worn grey cross began the explanation:

> ERECTED 1934 TO THE MEMORY
> OF UE LOYALISTS
> WHO DIED AND WERE BURIED HERE
> DURING THE WINTER OF 1783-84 AD.
> (ALSO) ALL OTHERS WHO MAY HAVE BEEN
> BURIED HERE ON EARLIER OR LATER DATES.

In other words, the very first British loyalists to migrate from the United States to Canada had a rough beginning. Here's what happened next according to gravemarkers in the Old Burying Ground, the second graveyard established by the Loyalists in what is now downtown Fredericton:

> EDWARD WINSLOW, 1746-1815
> FOURTH IN DESCENT
> FROM GOVERNOR EDWARD WINSLOW
> OF PLYMOUTH COLONY.
> HE SERVED AS MUSTER MASTER GENERAL
> OF THE LOYALIST FORCES IN THE REVOLUTIONARY WAR.
> IN 1783, HE SUPERVISED THE SETTLEMENT
> OF THE DISBANDED REGIMENTS
> IN THE VALLEY OF THE SAINT JOHN.
> A FOUNDER OF THE PROVINCE AND OF FREDERICTON.
> HE BECAME A MEMBER OF HIS MAJESTY'S COUNCIL IN 1784.
> APPOINTED TO FIRST COUNCIL
> OF THE COLLEGE OF NEW BRUNSWICK IN 1800,
> AND TO THE SUPREME COURT IN 1807.
> HE SERVED IN 1808 AS PRESIDENT
> OF THE GOVERNMENT OF NEW BRUNSWICK.

The revolutionary war referred to on Winslow's stone is the American War of Independence. This took place when the United States got sick and tired of King George III and his everlasting taxes, so they declared themselves a republic. Goodbye, king, except that some American citizens did not want to say goodbye to the king. They were British to the core; they wanted to stay that way. So they fought against American independence and when they lost the war had to get out of town. For most Loyalists, that meant Canada.

In death, as in life, Edward Winslow was loyal to king and country. His monument is in the Old Burying Ground in Fredericton.

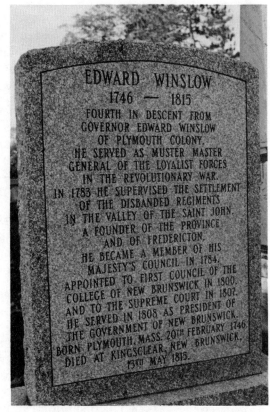

Once here, they were rewarded for their loyalty by grants of land, but that led to other complications, like who got what and how do you measure land where there are no roads, no survey lines? It was one big can of worms, and men like Edward Winslow spent years untangling the mess.

Samuel Denny Street, another of Fredericton's early movers and shakers, went so far as to fight a duel over who had a right to rule and hold land in New Brunswick, emotions were that high among Loyalists who expected certain rewards for their sacrifices. However, when I found his gravemarker in the downtown cemetery, I was disappointed to see that the duel was not mentioned. I have yet to find the word "duel" on a gravemarker, as a matter of fact. However, all was not lost. The message on the Street marker did mention "independence of mind," and it did illustrate the kind of extravagant praise that used to go on gravemarkers if you had the words and the money. And many of those original Loyalists did have money because they got such generous land grants. Do I sound like a jealous westerner or what?

This is the loving message on the tombstone for Mr. and Mrs. Street from their sons:

THIS MONUMENT IS ERECTED BY THEIR SONS
AS AN HUMBLE TRIBUTE OF RESPECT AND FILIAL AFFECTION
TO THE BEST OF PARENTS AND FIRMEST OF FRIENDS,

WHOSE LIVES WERE DISTINGUISHED BY STRICT INTEGRITY
AND INDEPENDENCE OF MIND
ACCOMPANIED BY A TRUE SENSE
OF RELIGION AND VIRTUE.

The Best Graveyard in New Brunswick

The Old Burying Ground in downtown Fredericton is the best—lots of old old stones, lots of words, lots of stories and secrets, lots of young kids and moms walking through the graveyard as if it were the most natural thing in the world to do, which it is.

To be sure we don't forget the Loyalists, however, there's a monument at the graveyard entrance that says:

COMPELLED TO LEAVE THEIR HOMES
IN THE THIRTEEN COLONIES
FOR THEIR LOYALTY TO THE CROWN,
THEY FOUNDED THE PROVINCE OF NEW BRUNSWICK IN 1784
TO SECURE BRITISH INSTITUTIONS FOR THEMSELVES
AND THEIR POSTERITY.

And then just to make sure we don't forget that it was a tough job keeping Fredericton and area safe for Loyalists and others, there's a grey granite cross to the memory of officers and men of the British army who served the Fredericton Garrison between 1784 and 1869:

ACROSS THIS FLAT LYETH BRITISH SOLDIERS
WHO DIED IN FREDERICTON

We're walking across "this flat" as we read the message. It's a funny feeling, being inches away from soldiers who died for King and Country and New Brunswick and Other Capital Letters two hundred years ago while we complain about the soggy sandwiches that we got from a deli across the street.

I've already mentioned Edward Winslow, who is remembered on his gravemarker for soaring great deeds and important accomplishments. This is what his wife is remembered for on her gravemarker in the Old Burying Ground:

TO THE MEMORY OF MRS. HANNAH WINSLOW
WIDOW OF EDWARD WINFLOW, EFQ.
FORMERLY OF PLYMOUTH
IN THE PROVINCE OF MAFFACHUFETTS BAY;
WHO DIED ON THE 23RD DAY OF MAY 1796

WHOFE UNAFFECTED PIETY, PECULIAR DIGNITY,
FERENITY OF TEMPER AND BENEVOLENCE OF HEART,
RENDERED HER JUFTLY AND UNIVERFALLY BELOVED
AND REFPECTED TO HER LATEFT HOUR.
THIS TRIBUTE OF AFFECTION ERECTED BY HER CHILDREN.

John Saunders was another influential Loyalist who became part of the governing group, trying to sort out who owned what and who did what. His gravemarker in the Old Burying Ground is a huge thing with words covering four substantial side panels. At the base of one of the panels is a hand that points to the next side of the marker, just so you understand there's more about Mr. Saunders on the next page, as it were. However, his daughter gets one panel all to herself:

THIS MONUMENT IS ALSO INTENDED TO COMMEMORATE
THE MANY VIRTUES OF ELIZA CHALMERS FLOOD
WHO WAS BORN MAY 25, 1794, AT FREDERICTON
AND DIED JAN. 8, 1821.
SHE WAS THE DAUGHTER OF JOHN SAUNDERS, ESQ.
LATE CHIEF JUSTICE OF THIS COLONY AND PRESIDENT
OF HIS MAJESTY'S LEGISLATIVE COUNCIL OF NEW BRUNSWICK,
AND WIFE OF R. FLOOD, ESQ. LIEUT. AND ADJUTANT
OF THE 74TH REGT. OF BRITISH INFANTRY.
SHE WAS DURING HER YOUTH AN OBEDIENT AND DUTIFUL
DAUGHTER, AND DURING HER MORE MATURE YEARS
A KIND AND AFFECTIONATE WIFE,
AND HER CONDUCT WHILE IN THIS DREARY ABODE
OF MORTALITY SHEWED HER TO HAVE BEEN POSESSED
OF ALL THAT CAN RENDER HUMAN LIFE TRULY HAPPY
BY CHRISTIAN PIETY AND GENUINE VIRTUE.

The words don't tell us why Eliza died—childbirth is a logical guess—but they do demonstrate that women were defined by the men in their lives.

As for childbirth, I've found it mentioned specifically only three times in graveyards across Canada. One of the three is in the Old Burying Ground:

IN MEMORY OF FRANCES SARAH BLAIR
WHO DEPARTED THIS LIFE MAY 7, 1832 AGED 38 YEARS
ALSO IN THE SAME GRAVE ARE DEPOSITED THE REMAINS
OF HER TWIN DAUGHTERS WHO WERE BORN MAY 5, 1832,
AND DIED ON THE 3RD AND 5TH OF JUNE FOLLOWING.

As you know, unhappy stories about children abound in old grave-yards. Near the Blair marker is a tall black slate tablet that lists six children, three of whom died as babies, three others in their youth, the children of Robert and Margaret Chestnut. The epitaph explains with Christian forbearance:

> THREE BROTHERS AND THREE SISTERS
> SLEEP CALMLY IN THE DUST
> TO AWAIT THE ARCHANGELS TRUMP
> AWAKE YE JUST.
> YOUR SOULS HAVE LONG BEEN WITH ME
> IN THE REALMS ABOVE
> COME FORTH WITH JOY TO CELEBRATE
> YOUR NUPTIAL LOVE.
> GLORY TO JESUS, AMEN.

And William, son of Jedediah and Ann Slason, died in 1823 at the age of sixteen years and eleven months:

> THIS PROMISING YOUTH CAUGHT
> THE SMALL-POX AT THE CITY OF ST. JOHN
> WHICH PROVED FATAL TO HIM IN A FEW DAYS.
> HIS LOSS IS MUCH LAMENTED
> BY HIS RELATIVES AND FRIENDS.

It was noon hour when I visited the Old Burying Ground. School was out, and dozens of promising youths had opted to eat their lunches in the graveyard. Good for them. That much alone gave them a chance to learn the lessons around them, but I wanted more. I wanted a soapbox to stand on and say, "Count your blessings, darlings. Look around you. Not one of you has to worry about smallpox any more. You girls will have modern medicine on your side when you give birth, and your babies will more than likely live their three score years and ten." Fortunately for everyone, there was no soapbox handy. I ate my soggy sandwich instead and shut up.

Saint John's Claim to Fame

We got to Saint John in the late afternoon and went immediately to the Reversing Falls. That's how they are referred to in every tourist magazine and on every billboard—with capital letters—the Reversing Falls. Why, I don't know, because first of all, there are no falls. There's sort of a muddle of water that doesn't know if it's coming or going, but it's not falling. It reverses, I guess, but I'm not sure it deserves all those capital letters.

That's not quite the last discouraging word I'm going to say about Saint John because from the falls, we went to the Old Burying Ground downtown. Every Maritime city has varying degrees of graveyards: old, fairly old, somewhat old, hardly old at all. Anyway, Saint John's is old; there's no getting around it. It's also something of a mess, although we could see signs of a cleanup in progress. This is the graveyard where the family of the terribly successful industrialist K.C. Irving, proposed to erect a statue of their famous father, but such a storm of negative public opinion followed upon the announcement that they quietly decided to put him somewhere else.

The furore arose over the fact that the statue might cover some unmarked graves in what used to be a potter's field, an area in years gone by reserved for the burial of paupers. Not kind, not cool, public opinion seemed to say, so the Irvings abandoned the idea and gave money instead for the upgrading of the place. *Noblesse oblige.*

Most of the remaining gravestones are darkened beyond recognition, or toppled over, or covered with grass, but here and there, a story reached out. Polly Stevens, for instance, died at age thirty-two on October 26, 1803. Her children Lemuel, Eliza, and Charles died at various times in the year preceding her death. They lie together beneath this message:

> BENEATH THIS STONE INTERRED DOTH LIE
> THE SUBJECT OF DEATH'S TYRANNY
> THE MOTHER IN THIS SILENT TOMB
> SLEEPS WITH THE OFFSPRING OF HER WOMB.
> BUT ALL THIS MALICE SHALL PROVE VAIN
> FOR TREE AND FRUIT SHALL RISE AGAIN.

It's meant as a Christian message of resurrection and everlasting life, but it seemed appropriate for an old graveyard that's going through some renewing of its own.

Like Fredericton No More

Saint John's history paralleled Fredericton's for some years as Loyalists streamed into their part of the country as well. Here's what it says on Nehemiah Merritt's grave in the Old Anglican cemetery:

> NEHEMIAH MERRITT, ESQUIRE
> WHO DEPARTED THIS LIFE MAY 25, 1842
> IN THE 72 YEAR OF HIS LIFE.
> A NATIVE OF NEW YORK, HE AT AN EARLY AGE,
> LEFT THAT COUNTRY TO RETAIN UNSULLIED

HIS ALLEGIANCE TO HIS SOVEREIGN
AND ACCOMPANIED THE LOYALISTS WHO IN 1783
LANDED IN THIS PROVINCE WHERE BY A LONG
AND UNWEARIED COURSE OF INDUSTRY, PRUDENCE
AND INTEGRITY, HE ACQUIRED THE RESPECT AND ESTEEM
OF THIS COMMUNITY AND WAS FOR SEVERAL YEARS
ONE OF HER MAJESTY'S JUSTICES OF THE PEACE
FOR THE CITY AND COUNTY OF SAINT JOHN.

There it is in a nutshell—why I came to Canada and what I did when I got here. Same story as Fredericton, but then the Irish arrived in Saint John in the 1840s and 1850s and changed everything.

It was rotten potatoes and rotten landlords that led to the exodus of the Irish, the potatoes suffering from a terrible blight and the landlords ditto when they decided to throw their tenant farmers off their land in order to make room for sheep. So thousands of immigrants got on overcrowded, disease-ridden boats and came to the New World.

And thousands died, some enroute, some after they got here. Causes varied, but generally, the deaths were due to disease—cholera, smallpox, and typhus. For a while, a "pest" house was established on Partridge Island in Saint John harbour. All incoming passengers had to submit to a medical examination. If healthy, they could enter the country. If not, they stayed on the island and either got better or died.

A big black marble marker in St. Mary's Catholic cemetery in Saint John explains:

WE REMEMBER AND WE CELEBRATE THE 15,000
WHO LIE BURIED HERE, MANY OF THEM NAMELESS
AND FORGOTTEN, MANY OF THEM ONCE PROMINENT CITIZENS,
BUT FOR THE MOST PART, ORDINARY MEN AND WOMEN
WITH NO PARTICULAR CLAIM TO FAME,
BUT WHOSE OFFSPRING STILL COMPRISE A MAJOR PORTION
OF THE POPULATION OF MODERN DAY SAINT JOHN.

The graveyard gives away its Irish roots in subtle ways. The Tagney/Quinn stone has the words "God Save Ireland" carved into the curved top. Many stones mention the old country: "Natives of Tralee, Co. Kerry, Ireland, May they rest in Peace," or "Born in Co. Waterford, Ireland." There's one with a shamrock design worked into the border, and several with versions of the Celtic cross. But the gravemarkers represent, as the sign indicates, a mere sampling of those buried here, a reminder of the terrible price that the first Irish immigrants had to pay.

The Tagney/Quinn stone in St. Mary's cemetery in Saint John displays the Irish roots of those who rest beneath it. Note the shamrock border and the words "God Save Ireland" across the top.

We Hardly Knew Ye

Usually I have to talk very fast and look very normal when I meet someone new and explain to them what I am doing in graveyards, which is why it was such a pleasure to connect with Mary McDevitt in Saint John. She's a graveyard explorer as well, looks perfectly normal, and talks faster than I do. Maybe it's an occupational hazard. Anyway, she has written a book about St. Mary's called *We Hardly Knew Ye,* but she's full of information about other graveyards as well. For instance, she told me to check out the Wesleyan cemetery across from the Old Anglican cemetery across from Canadian Tire. I love unlikely juxtapositions like that.

The Wesleyan would be quite different from the Catholic St. Mary's, she said, because people from the Puritan religious tradition are great on written words but stick with no-nonsense, rather stark markers. Anglicans also like lots of words, but they'll add a fancy tombstone, if they can afford it. Catholics, on the other hand, aren't much for saying things on their gravestones, they don't like fancy markers all that much either, but they do like beautiful churches where beautiful words are said and familiar ritual is observed.

Her explanation went a long way in helping me understand the silence in Roman Catholic cemeteries, and she was also right about the Wesleyan graveyard. On a big black no-nonsense marker for Mrs. Mary Chapman, who died in 1847, aged seventy-five, and her husband, Robert Chapman, who died in 1848, aged seventy-eight, were the words:

> THEY WERE BOTH NATIVES OF ENGLAND
> AND EMIGRATED TO THIS COUNTRY FROM DEVONPORT
> IN DEVONSHIRE. THEY WERE BOTH MEMBERS
> OF THE WESLEYAN METHODIST CHURCH
> FOR UPWARDS OF HALF A CENTURY,
> AND HAVING FINISHED THEIR COURSE WITH JOY,
> THEY FELL ASLEEP IN JESUS.

Across the street in the Old Anglican cemetery were lots of words and big markers, just as Mary had said, one of which told the sad tale of someone who did not get to finish his course with joy:

> ERECTED BY THE MEMBERS
> OF PORTLAND DIV. #7 SONS OF TEMPERANCE
> IN MEMORY OF THEIR MUCH RESPECTED AND LAMENTED
> BROTHER JAMES BRIGGS JR. R.S., AGED 31 YEARS,
> WHO WAS SHOT BY SOME RUTHLESS ASSASSIN
> AS HE WAS PASSING THE LONG WHARF, PORTLAND,
> ON HIS WAY HOME FROM THE DIVISION ROOM
> ON THE NIGHT OF SEPT. 6, 1847.

Saint John historians are divided on this story. Some think that James was simply in the wrong place at the wrong time, that his murder was a case of mistaken identity. Others say it was clearly the Catholic Irish fighting Protestant Irish. Or it might have been robbery. The murder did accomplish one thing: Saint John got itself a police force.

Here a Hazen, There a Chipman

It was in the Fernhill cemetery in Saint John that we found the Hazens and Chipmans. At first, I tried to keep track of the generations and the family connections, but without a family tree to explain it all, I was hopelessly lost. Suffice it to say, they were two large, important families in Saint John. I'll start with Sarah:

> SACRED TO THE MEMORY OF SARAH HAZEN
> WIDOW OF THE HONOURABLE WILLIAM HAZEN, ESQUIRE
> WHO WAS BORN IN THE PROVINCE OF MASSACHUSETTS BAY
> ON THE 22 FEBRUARY 1719

AND DIED IN THIS CITY APRIL 3, 1823.
EXEMPLARY FOR CHRISTIAN PIETY AND BENEVOLENCE
AND THE EXERCISE OF EVERY FEMALE VIRTUE
SHE BEARS TO HER GRAVE THE FOND RECOLLECTIONS
OF A NUMEROUS HOST OF DESCENDANTS
AND THE ESTEEM AND RESPECT OF THE COMMUNITY.

If I've got this right, Sarah lived to be 104 years old!
Near Sarah is a table monument for Ward Chipman, Jr.:

SACRED TO THE MEMORY
OF THE HONOURABLE WARD CHIPMAN
FOR MANY YEARS A MEMBER OF THE PROVINCIAL LEGISLATURE
H.M. ADVOCATE AND SOLICITOR GENERAL
AND SOMETIME RECORDER OF THE CITY OF SAINT JOHN.
AFTERWARDS ONE OF THE JUDGES OF THE SUPREME COURT.
AND FROM 1834-1850 CHIEF JUSTICE OF NEW BRUNSWICK
AND THE ONLY CHILD
OF THE LATE JUSTICE CHIPMAN DIED AGED 64.

As you can tell, the Chipman and Hazen men were in the thick of New Brunswick political and business affairs. One became treasurer of the

The Odell graves in the Old Burying Ground in Fredericton are interesting examples of "table" or "bench" monuments.

province back before it was a province. Another became a senator when New Brunswick became a province in a brand new country. Yet another became the premier in 1908, and one became a casualty of World War I. James Murray Hazen was killed April 19, 1916, and buried in a military cemetery in Belgium.

That's a story I often found in graveyards—families that turned out famous members generation after generation, and then, boom, along comes a war and there's a pause, a break in the lines, as young men have to go to war and die.

After the Empire, Go for Dominion

Even as New Brunswick tried to figure out how to be a province, it had to deal with the matter of union with other Maritime and/or Canadian provinces. Some politicians jumped on the Confederation bandwagon, arguing that New Brunswick would get itself a much-needed railway if it joined Canada. Then, as if the railway were a sure thing, factions began fighting over where it should go. Elections were held, reputations won and lost. But when the dust settled, New Brunswick was one of the original four to form the Dominion of Canada in 1867.

I found two of New Brunswick's Fathers of Confederation: Charles Fisher, 1808-1880, buried at Forest Hill cemetery in Fredericton, and Samuel Leonard Tilley, 1819-1896, buried at Fernhill in Saint John. Both have government plaques in front of their graves. Otherwise, you'd never know they were part of our beginnings.

Around the World in Eighty Days

Another famous name in Saint John is the *Marco Polo*, a sailing ship that surprised everyone, especially its Saint John builders. On its launch, it fell off the slip and got mired in the mud. It took weeks to get it up and running again but when they did, it turned out to be the fastest thing on sails. By 1854, its owners boasted that it could do "Hell or Australia in Sixty Days." I don't know about hell, but Liverpool to Australia generally took eighty days or more, but not for the *Marco Polo*. It was the "Fastest Ship in the World."

This was all very exciting for the Saint John ship-building industry: they had the *Marco Polo*, they had the timber from New Brunswick forests, they had the builders, they had the water. Their future, the city's future, was secured . . . except that on one hot summer day in 1877, most of Saint John burned down. And if that wasn't setback enough, somebody in the United States invented steam, and there went the neighbourhood.

Those two stories are not mentioned prominently in Saint John graveyards. I had hoped to find a word or two about the *Marco Polo* or the terrible fire, but I didn't. They may be there; I just didn't find them.

I did find the Mackay family and a mention of the lumbering industry, which continued in New Brunswick even after the shipbuilding glory days were over:

COLIN MACKAY M.C.
SECOND SON OF W. MALCOLM AND SUSAN MCMILLAN MACKAY
BORN IN SAINT JOHN, SEPT. 6, 1889
EDUCATED AT ROTHESAY COLLEGIATE SCHOOL,
HE SAW SERVICE IN BOTH WORLD WARS
AND CARRIED ON THE LUMBER BUSINESS
ESTABLISHED BY HIS FATHER UNTIL HIS DEATH IN 1963.
BE VALIANT TO THE END.
BE TRUE.

All the Mackay graves ended with this injunction: Be valiant to the end; be true. Another example of New Brunswick's willingness to speak noble words on its gravemarkers.

Rags to Riches and Timbits

After Saint John, we travelled up the eastern side of New Brunswick, which brought us back into bilingual territory. At Tim Horton's one morning, a rumpled gentleman ordered his breakfast in very fast French and then added as an afterthought, "Ah, oui, les Timbits, s'il vous plait."

In Buctouche, we found a statue of K.C. Irving, not his grave, however. The gentleman working in the park near the cemetery said he thought K.C. was buried in Bermuda "or some rich place like that there." Irving's story sounds like rags to riches, although I'm not sure it was ever quite at the rag level, but the plaque beneath the statue explained that K.C. Irving, whose name is on most service stations in the Maritime provinces, started as the Ford dealer in Buctouche and went on from there. Not bad for a homegrown boy. "He spoke often of the practical small town lessons and work ethics he learned here as a boy," the plaque continued.

Also, there's mention of Irving's interest in reforestation, which explained to Judy and me why we had found a huge rock alongside the road between Saint John and Moncton that looked like a gravemarker but turned out to be a memorial to the two-hundred-millionth tree planted in Irving's reforestation program. Two hundred million trees. Not a bad memorial.

The other name that we found all the time in New Brunswick was that of Lord Beaverbrook, otherwise known as William Maxwell Aitken, who grew up in Newcastle. His name turned up on the art gallery, playhouse, and university in Fredericton, and then as we drove along the northeastern coast of the province, there it was on a statue near Escuminac. The statue is a haunting thing, a modern sculpture of three sailors with their backs to the sea, a fitting statement, since the memorial marks fishermen who lost their lives in the Escuminac storm June 20, 1959. According to the plaque, Beaverbrook was the first to pledge money toward the memorial.

Even though he spent most of his life in England, he came home to be buried, which is why there's a big black bust of him in Newcastle's Town Square guarding the ashes beneath.

Sorrow, Sorrow, My Sorrow

Newcastle has a full and interesting town square including flowers, benches, a commemorative plaque for another Father of Confederation, Peter Mitchell, and a beautiful monument that consists of a sailing ship mounted atop a tall column. It wasn't the monument that got me, however. It was the words on it referring to the early settlers of the area:

> THEY SPREAD THEIR POVERTY
> OVER THE RICH ACRES
> THEY SOWED THEIR CHILDREN
> BROADCAST UPON THE UNTESTED SOIL.

We did that all over Canada, I thought, as I read the lines, especially the one, "They sowed their children." Everywhere I've been, I've found so many little lambs and doves and angels marking children who, for one reason or other, were victims of settlement in a new land. Then I went down the road to St. Paul's Anglican cemetery in nearby Chatham and read more of the same:

> SACRED TO THE MEMORY OF ANN
> WIFE OF JOHN JACKSON
> AND SIX OF THEIR CHILDREN
> THE MOTHER AGED 41 YEARS WITH THREE OF HER CHILDREN
> JOHN, AGED 15 YEARS MARGARET AGED 6 YEARS
> AND ANTHONY AGED 10 MOS.
> PERISHED TOGETHER IN THE FLAMES

ON THE MEMORABLE NIGHT OF 7 OCT. 1825.
THE OTHERS DIED IN CONSEQUENCE OF THE INJURIES
THEY SUSTAINED BY THE FIRE
ROBERT DIED ON THE 11 OCT. AGED 12
WILLIAM DIED ON THE 14 OCT. AGED 13
JOSEPH DIED ON THE 25 OCT. AGED 9
FORESTS WERE SET ON FIRE—BUT HOUR BY HOUR
THEY FELL AND FADED AND THE CRACKLING TRUNKS
EXTINGUISHED WITH A CRASH AND ALL WAS BLACK
ALL EARTH WAS BUT ONE THOUGHT—
AND THAT WAS DEATH.

The Miramichi fire of 1825 killed hundreds of people, destroyed farms and towns in its wake, and burned up 15,500 km of forest. Just say the word "Miramichi" and longtime New Brunswickers will finish the phrase with "fire." It was incredibly awful.

But so many things were incredibly awful in those days. Down the road from the Anglican cemetery in Chatham is Middle Island, a piece of land that pokes out into the Miramichi River. On the farthest end of the little island is a Celtic cross with the information:

THIS CELTIC CROSS
ERECTED IN MEMORY
OF THE IRISH IMMIGRANTS
WHO DIED OF TYPHUS
FEVER CONTRACTED
DURING THEIR VOYAGE
FROM IRELAND

On Middle Island near Chatham is a Celtic cross in memory of Irish immigrants who never made it to the New World.

ON THE LOOSTOCK IN 1847 AND ARE BURIED HERE.
THIS CROSS ALSO COMMEMORATES THE DEVOTION
OF DR. VONDY WHO WHILE MINISTERING TO THE VICTIMS
HIMSELF CONTRACTED THE DISEASE
AND DIED AT THE AGE OF 28 YEARS.

The words on the front of the cross say simply, "Sorrow, Sorrow, My Sorrow."

The Last Word

It's an epitaph to keep a body humble and a mind troubled. It's on the tombstone of Agustin Glynick in Forest Hill cemetery in Fredericton:

BOAST NOT THYSELF OF TOMORROW
FOR THOU KNOWEST NOT
WHAT A DAY MAY BRING FORTH.

Nova Scotia

✝

Where Graveyards
Are Taken Seriously

THE ONLY CANADIAN GRAVEYARD TO BE DESIGNATED
A NATIONAL HISTORIC SITE IS IN NOVA SCOTIA.
TELLS YOU SOMETHING, DOESN'T IT—
THAT NOVA SCOTIANS TREASURE THEIR GRAVEYARDS
AND LOOK AFTER THEM. WHICH IS A DARNED GOOD THING
BECAUSE THEY HAVE A LOT OF THEM.
IN FACT, AS I RECALL, I DIDN'T NOTICE MUCH
IN THE LINE OF SCENERY IN NOVA SCOTIA.

In Alberta, I had to see a lot of scenery because there was so much distance between graveyards, but in Nova Scotia, the next graveyard was always just over the railway tracks or just around the corner or just beyond the church. Before I could adjust my eyes unto the hills around, I had to adjust them unto the ground around.

I'm not complaining, mind you. Why else was I in Nova Scotia but to see graveyards?

I could cavil just a bit about rain, however. How does one enjoy the scenery when one doesn't know if there's scenery out there? But I got the sense that one should not carry on about the wet stuff. I said to a waitress at noon one day, "Is it always like this?"

"Like what?" she said.

So I shut up.

Among other things, Nova Scotia has Canada's oldest known gravemarker. It's in the cemetery next to the old fort at Annapolis Royal, and it's dated 1720. That's some 270 years ago. Western Canada wasn't even explored yet. Peter Fidler hadn't seen the Rocky Mountains yet. The Indians knew they were there, but who knew the Indians were there?

Canada didn't even have a name. It was simply a hunk of territory for France and England to fight over, and that's why Annapolis Royal had a fort there and that, I guess, is why Bathiah Douglass lived and died there:

> HERE LYES Y BODY OF BATHIAH DUGLASS,
> WIFE TO SAMUEL DUGLASS
> WHO DEPARTED THIS LIFE
> OCTO THE 1ST, 1720,
> IN THE 37 YEAR OF HER AGE

It's an amazing stone. Deborah Trask at the Nova Scotia Museum guesses that it was made in Boston and shipped somehow to Annapolis Royal. The words are still clear—the "O" in Douglass carved above the "U" to save space, and the death's head as lovely as it ever was.

That's how the churches advertised in the eighteenth century. Carve a terrible-looking skull on top of a gravemarker, make the teeth grin horribly and the eyes look out of empty, staring sockets, and you've got a very compelling reason to get to church next Sunday and make your peace with God. It was kind of a visual sermonette, and quite a common image on gravemarkers throughout the 1700s. By the 1800s, the image had softened somewhat to angels and gates of heaven and such. By the 1900s, images gave way to words, and by the late 1900s neither one found much favour on gravemarkers, but that's another story for another time.

Suffice it to say that Nova Scotia has it all as far as Canadian graveyard history is concerned, and my happy problem there was when to quit, not where to start.

In the Beginning Was Port Royale

In 1605, Champlain sailed up the Bay of Fundy into the Annapolis Basin. Here he found a sheltered harbour, lots of fish in the water, lots of wood

This is the oldest extant gravemarker in Canada, dated 1720. It is in the cemetery next to the old fort at Annapolis Royal.

on land, and lots of reasons to stay for a while. So they did, and established the first permanent European settlement in what was to become Canada.

At first it was called Port-Royale, but after England and France fought over it for the next one hundred years or so, it emerged as Annapolis Royal, named for the British queen of the day. In other words, the British won the final round. Canada wasn't really a player in the battles; we were more like the prize in the Cracker Jack box.

Throughout the various battles, Annapolis Royal hung in there, and by the early 1700s became the capital of Nova Scotia. Its population was an interesting mix: the Micmac, who had been there all along; the Acadians, descended from the first French immigrants; and the British, who came along to run the place. Rev. Thomas Wood apparently tried to cover all the bases:

REV. THOMAS WOOD BORN IN NEW JERSEY
PHYSICIAN AND SURGEON
ORDAINED 1749 FROM 1752
AS MISSIONARY OF THE SPG IN NS
MINISTERED IN ENGLISH, FRENCH, GERMAN AND MICMAC
FIRST VISITED THIS TOWN 1753
LIVED HERE LAYING THE FOUNDATION OF THE PRESENT PARISHES
FROM 1764 TO HIS DEATH DEC. 14, 1778

That was the first time I found the letters SPG on a gravemarker, which, it turns out, stand for the missionary society known as the Society for the Propagation of the Gospel in Foreign Parts. That's what Canada was—foreign parts, and that's what Christianity was—an organization with the God-given responsibility to take the Christian religion to all corners of the earth. Canada was one such corner.

Annapolis Royal lost its title as capital of Nova Scotia in 1749 when Halifax came along, but it carried on as the centre of commercial activity on the north shore of Nova Scotia, trading in lumber, fish, ships, and apples.

Fiction Stronger than Fact

What's the good of being the conqueror if you can't conquer? That must have been the thinking behind the British governor's decision to expel some ten thousand Maritime Acadians between 1755 and 1763. If they wouldn't swear allegiance to the British crown—and they wouldn't—then they'd have to go.

I still can't believe we did that, and I can't believe we don't know more about the story. I, for one, heard nothing about the real live Acadians at school. I did hear about Evangéline, but I thought she was strictly a figment of the poet Longfellow's imagination. Poets dramatize things, I thought. This sort of thing would never have happened.

But it did.

In the poem, two lovers, Evangéline and Gabriel, are forced onto separate boats during the expulsion, never to find one another again until both are near death. He dies, she dies, they are buried together. It's a three-hankie story and critics scoff at its sentimentality, but the point is, it's based on fact. Shame on us.

At the national historic site at Grand-Pré, it's the statue of Evangéline that tourists come to see. She's become more real to us than the true-to-life Acadians, but at least once we're there we can learn something of the actual story via the site's interpretive panels and the paintings in the nearby church.

As we left the church, the guide suggested we might like to see something even sadder. Go down that dirt road about a mile, he said. There's a cross beside the railway tracks. That's where they got onto the ships.

I thought the statue and church were about sad enough, but he was right. The cross is on dry land now but back in the mid 1700s, that's where the sea started, and that's where the Acadians boarded their ships for somewhere.

213

Eventually, some came back, and that's why the sea isn't where it used to be. The Acadians knew how to drain land and make it grow productive crops, which is what they did at Grand Pré, but lest we forget, some of the descendants put up the cross in the 1920s.

The Acadians were barely out of sight before the governor sent an invitation to New Englanders. Come and settle on our newly vacated lands, he said, and many did. They were known as the Planters, and just as I looked for the word "Acadian" on a gravemarker and couldn't find it, neither could I find the word "Planter." I'm sure it's out there somewhere, but I didn't see it. Somebody told me to check out the old Horton-Wolfville Burying Ground, but all I found there were some words that might apply to some of the nastier parts of our history:

DEATH IS A DEBT THAT MUST BE PAID.

The Grave-Looking Historic Site

No wonder the Old Burying Ground in Halifax has been designated a national historic site. It's got everything, except perhaps a snappy name. Mind you, in 1749 when the graveyard was established, people were not naming their graveyards Golden Glades or Sunset Slopes or any of those other titles that deny death. They called a spade a spade and used them in the Old Burying Ground. Period. No nonsense.

It's still pretty straightforward—mostly graves and grass, hardly a petunia in the bunch, but what it lacks in pretty, it makes up in interesting.

When Halifax became administrative headquarters for Nova Scotia, Edward Cornwallis arrived from England to govern the place. Along with him came his aide-de-camp, Richard Bulkeley, and it is because of Richard that the Old Burying Ground got its most remarkable gravemarker. Richard is buried in the crypt of St. Paul's Church in Halifax—it was still the custom to bury important people near or under the church—but his wife Mary, died 1775, and son Freke, died 1796, ended up nearby in the Old Burying Ground under the Adam and Eve stone.

It's known as the Adam and Eve stone because the carving on one end of the marker shows two people, male and female, standing awkwardly beside a fruit-laden tree. As they stand there, wondering what to do next, a snake winds its way up the trunk of the tree, and you know that pretty soon they will take the fatal bite out of the fatal apple. Humankind is about to be doomed, to be expelled from the Garden of Eden.

But wait, on the other end of the tomb is another message. A skeleton

This unusual representation of Adam and Eve about to fall from grace appears on a gravemarker in Halifax's Old Burying Ground.

reclines across the bottom of the panel, its bony ribs and knock-knees telling us all too graphically about death. But lo and behold, above the skeleton is a winged figure with a trumpet. This figure wears strange-looking underwear, sort of a tasselled loin cloth, a cut above, I must say, the baggy pants that Adam and Eve are wearing. Anyway, the message is that after death comes resurrection for those who obey God, and don't eat apples.

It's a treasure, both for the folk art it represents and the Christian message it conveys. I wonder if Marshall McLuhan had seen something like this when he wrote that the medium is the message.

Here's another Christian sermon presented with words and pictures on a gravemarker. This one marks two children, James Cook, died December 15, 1806, aged three years and six months, and his brother Robert Cook, died December 16, 1806, aged one year and three months. The words first:

> THE DEAREST OBJECTS OF OUR CARE
> ARE IN A MOMENT GONE
> AND JAH DECLARES THAT NONE SHOULD SHARE
> OUR HEARTS BUT HE ALONE.
> THESE BABES WHO PRATTLED ON THE KNEE
> ARE GONE TO REALMS ABOVE

TO SHOUT THROUGH ALL ETERNITY
A SAVIOUR'S DYING LOVE.
THEIR LITTLE TALES DID OFT AMUSE
THE TIME AS IT DID GLIDE
BUT NOW THEY REST IN CALM REPOSE
WHILE LYING SIDE BY SIDE.

Thus do the Cooks reassure us, and themselves, that their beloved children have gone to a better place, and just to make doubly sure, they have added two winged heads to the top of the shared gravemarker. Called soul effigies, these are quite unusual. I haven't seen any others like them.

These unique "soul effigies," images of everlasting life, are found in Halifax's Old Burying Ground above the graves of the Cook children.

It's feast or famine in this graveyard; the inscriptions are either completely worn away by age, or they're long and legible but so sad you can barely stand to read them, like this one for the two eldest sons of James and Elizabeth Wilkie:

THE FORMER OF WHOM
IS SUPPOSED TO HAVE PERISHED AT SEA
ON A VOYAGE FROM HENCE TO BOSTON

DURING THE WINTER OF 1839
IN THE 25TH YEAR OF HIS AGE.
THE LATTER DIED IN HIS PARENTS ARMS
ON THE 19TH DAY OF APRIL, 1847
AGED 22 YEARS AND 4 DAYS.
"ONE LIES IN OCEAN'S BED
HERE SLEEPS THE OTHER'S DUST
BUT WHEN THE SEA YIELDS UP HER DEAD
AND THE COLD GRAVE ITS TRUST
LORD MAY WE BRING THE CHILDREN THOU HAST GIVEN
AND SHARE WITH THEM
THE CEASELESS JOYS OF HEAVEN."

Not all the Old Burying Ground gravemarkers are imbued with Christian acceptance. Some of them deal with the realities of life for Maritimers:

SACRED TO THE MEMORY
OF MR. WM. B. DECOURCY VOLR. 1ST CLASS
WHO DIED ON THE 2ND JULY, 1842,
AT SEA OF YELLOW FEVER, AGED 17 YEARS.
THIS STONE IS ERECTED AS A TRIBUTE
OF RESPECT AND IN TESTIMONY OF HIS WORTH
AND HIGH QUALITIES BY THE OFFICERS
OF HER MAJESTY'S SHIP VOLAGE.

Beneath William's details are the names of ten more men who died on the same ship, whether of yellow fever or some disaster at sea, it doesn't say.

Capt. Ellinwood built the ships that men went down to the sea in, but just because he stayed on dry land, doesn't mean he escaped trouble:

HERE LIES THE REMAINS
OF CAPT. BENJAMIN ELLINWOOD
LATE OF LIVERPOOL, NS,
WHO WAS FOUND CRUELLY MURDERED
JAN. 31, AD, 1815 IN THE 32 YEAR OF HIS AGE.
HE HAS LEFT A WIDOW AND FOUR CHILDREN
TO LAMENT HIS LOSS.

It seems that Ellinwood got into a fight with his partner in the shipbuilding business and the next day was found dead. The partner was tried, convicted, and executed, but as I stood in front of the old black slate marker so many years later, I was also interested in his wife and her four children. The widow, I learned later from reading newspaper accounts of the trial, was called Epiphany. Did her name help her? Did she have a sudden revelation that helped her get on with her life? I hope so.

Not many in this graveyard lived their three score years and ten. The women died young in childbirth, the men went to sea and died there, and if they didn't do that, they went to war. Same difference. It was the exception rather than the rule to find stones like this:

SACRED TO THE MEMORY
OF THOMAS MATTHEWS
GATE PORTER OF HER MAJESTY'S
NAVAL YARD AT HALIFAX
WHO DEPARTED THIS LIFE
17 SEPT. 1840, AGED 73 YEARS.

And just in case you think Nova Scotia had run out of wars, think again. Here's the story, written on a huge table tombstone, of a British soldier who changed the history of the United States and then came to Canada to be buried:

HERE ON THE 29TH OF SEPTEMBER 1814
WAS COMMITTED TO THE EARTH
THE BODY OF MAJOR GENERAL ROBERT ROSS,
WHO AFTER HAVING DISTINGUISHED HIMSELF
IN ALL RANKS AS AN OFFICER IN EGYPT, ITALY,
PORTUGAL, SPAIN, FRANCE AND AMERICA WAS KILLED
AT THE COMMENCEMENT OF AN ACTION
WHICH TERMINATED IN THE DEFEAT AND ROUT
OF THE TROOPS OF THE UNITED STATES NEAR BALTIMORE
ON THE 12TH OF SEPTEMBER, 1814

That's what it says—the defeat and rout of the US forces near Baltimore—but as far as I can figure, it was a standoff. Canadian/British forces said they had won, and left for home without bothering to burn and destroy the city; American forces claimed victory because the enemy had taken off. So there you are, take your pick. The War of 1812 was like that—a bunch of skirmishes on the Canadian/US border with few clear winners but many clear losers, the losers being the dead on both sides of the war; men such as Robert Ross, who died on the first night of the Baltimore battle.

The next night, British warships got close enough to the city to lob in the newest artillery—the Congreve rocket. A Baltimore lawyer, Francis Scott Key, was so moved by the sight of the Stars and Stripes flying in the face of the enemy attack that he composed the American national anthem. "The rocket's red glare" was ours. While there's a certain secret pleasure in

This stone arch at the entrance to the Old Burying Ground in Halifax is a memorial to two young men who died in the Crimean War.

knowing there's Canadian content in the American national anthem, one could wish for a nicer entry.

Robert Ross and his fighting men affected American politics in one other important way—they changed the colour of the president's residence. Just three weeks before the Baltimore stand-off, Ross and his troops marched into Washington and set many of the government buildings on fire, including the president's residence. It didn't burn to the ground, but the exterior was so smoke stained that it had to be whitewashed. Thus, the White House was born.

Another dubious accomplishment for Canada.

Ross was brought back to Canada for burial, and the war more or less petered out.

The Old Burying Ground petered out too. Actually, it ran out of room and closed in 1844, but it had one more story to tell. In 1860, a huge red stone arch with an imposing-looking lion stalking across the top was erected to commemorate two Haligonians, A.F. Welsford and W.B.C.A. Parker, who had died at Sebastopol in the Crimean War. It stands at the entrance to the graveyard and is a noble thing indeed.

As I paused beneath the arch to wipe my glasses—I'm not saying it was raining that day, I'm just saying I had to clean my glasses a lot—I thought I'd seen it all. It's such an amazing collection of words, deeds, and images. But as it turned out, I had only just begun.

Camp Hill and the Caretaker

I explored the next graveyard, Camp Hill cemetery, rather quickly because my glasses needed cleaning so often. However, when I dared to murmur something to a caretaker about all the rain, I got another lesson in keeping my mouth shut. "I can't even fall back on the old bromide about farmers needing the rain," I said to him.

"Why not?" he said. "We've got farmers."

Point taken. Not the right time, I decided, to get into a discussion about what constitutes a "real" farm, at least from the point of view of a biased westerner who likes her wheat in big fields.

And he was right. When I got into the centre of the Camp Hill cemetery, one of the first markers I found said this:

IN MEMORY OF JOHN YOUNG
FOR MANY YEARS A PROMINENT MEMBER
OF THE PROVINCIAL PARLIAMENT
AUTHOR OF THE CELEBRATED "LETTERS OF AGRICOLA"
PUBLISHED AD 1818.
HIS THEORIES OF HUSBANDRY WERE CARRIED INTO PRACTICE
ON HIS MODEL FARM AT WILLOW PARK, HALIFAX
BORN IN SCOTLAND AD 1774
DIED AT HALIFAX OCTOBER AD 1837
HIS BELOVED WIFE AGNES RENNY
AND THREE SONS SURVIVED HIM.
SHE DIED JULY, 1863, AGED 84 YEARS.
BOTH HUSBAND AND WIFE DEPARTED THIS LIFE
FIRMLY TRUSTING IN CHRIST.

The gravemarker pretty well tells the tale. Under the pseudonym of "Agricola," John Young wrote a series of columns about farming: how to do it scientifically and how to organize agricultural societies for the mutual benefit of members. And he did all of this before Alberta had even been named, let alone farmed. I was glad I hadn't explained "real" farms to the caretaker.

Agricola eventually came out from behind his disguise and went into politics. Why not? Everybody else was. The wars between the British and French may have ended, but Nova Scotians picked right up where they left off and started fighting one another: those who were loyal to Britain, come what may, *versus* those who thought Nova Scotia might be able to run its own affairs. The leader of the second group was Joseph Howe, said by some to be the greatest Nova Scotian ever. He had a way with words, both written and spoken, and I hoped his gravemarker might reflect that. But his marker at Camp Hill says simply:

IN MEMORY OF THE HON. JOSEPH HOWE
LIEUT. GOVERNOR OF NOVA SCOTIA
13TH DECEMBER 1804 DIED 1ST JUNE, 1873.

I wouldn't even have found the simple marker but for the now-friendly caretaker, who decided I wasn't hopeless after all since I wanted to find Howe. On the other side of the unassuming marker was the information:

IN REMEMBRANCE OF THE CHILDREN
OF JOSEPH AND SUSANNA HOWE
MARY, DIED 1829, 1 MONTH OLD,
SOPHIA, DIED 1837, 1 YEAR OLD
JAMES, DIED 1830, 4 MONTHS OLD
MARY, DIED 1853, 21 YEARS OLD
JOHN, DIED 1856, 10 YEARS OLD.

We hear lots about Howe's opposition to Confederation, an idea that he termed a "botheration scheme," but not a thing about those five children who died before their time. What happened to them, and why aren't they ever mentioned in accounts of the day? Surely their deaths must have affected their father and his politics.

When Confederation happened in 1867, much to Howe's disgust, Nova Scotia was one of the original four. Then for the next twenty years or so it tried to get out of the arrangement. See what I mean about the fighting Nova Scotians?

In the midst of all this turmoil, Abraham Gesner quietly went ahead and invented kerosene:

ABRAHAM GESNER, M.D., F.G.S. GEOLOGIST
BORN AT CORNWALLIS, N.S. 1797 DIED AT HALIFAX 1864
HIS TREATISE ON THE GEOLOGY AND MINERALOGY
OF NOVA SCOTIA 1836 WAS ONE OF THE EARLIEST WORKS
DEALING WITH THOSE SUBJECTS IN THIS PROVINCE
AND ABOUT 1852 HE WAS THE AMERICAN INVENTOR
OF THE PROCESS OF KEROSENE OIL.

Blow me down. I had no idea a Canadian had a hand in kerosene, as it were, even though he is mistakenly referred to as an "American." The marker was put up by Imperial Oil many years later, a token that was "too little, too late," according to one Haligonian who thought he deserved better. Still, it's there. It tells us more than we knew before.

And just in case we might be tempted to forget that Nova Scotians go down to the sea in boats, here is stark evidence of the fact:

IN LOVING MEMORY
OF JOHN IVES DOULL
SON OF JOHN AND HELEN DOULL
DIED ON BOARD THE SHIP "SOBRAON" FEB. 28TH. 1882
DURING A VOYAGE FROM MELBOURNE TO LONDON
AND WAS BURIED AT SEA AGED 27 YEARS.

Don't Go to London to See the Queen

Halifax produced two Canadian prime ministers: Charles Tupper, whose grave in the Anglican cemetery is so worn you can barely read it, and John Thompson, who speaks up loud and clear from the Holy Cross cemetery:

THE RIGHT HONOURABLE SIR JOHN S.D. THOMPSON
PRIME MINISTER OF THE DOMINION OF CANADA
WHO DIED SUDDENLY AT WINDSOR CASTLE DEC. 12, 1894
SHORTLY AFTER BEING SWORN IN
AS A MEMBER OF HER MAJESTY'S PRIVY COUNCIL
HIS REMAINS WERE
BY COMMAND OF HER MAJESTY QUEEN VICTORIA
BORNE TO CANADA BY THE BRITISH MAN-OF-WAR BLENHEIM
BURIED JAN. 3, 1895, AGED 50 YEARS

Apparently, John Thompson was in London to see the Queen, and at the special luncheon that she laid on for him, he choked on a piece of food and died on the spot. Queen Victoria was so upset by this chain of events that she ordered an all-out military funeral in London, and then sent the body back on one of her own ships for another elaborate funeral.

Same kind of bad luck with Charles Tupper. He too died while on official business in England, but he didn't do it right in front of the Queen. Nevertheless, she sent him home on another of her ships and ordered up another state funeral.

Speaking of the Queen, a Foster Sister

Even before I got to Halifax, someone told me about Queen Victoria's foster sister. She's in the graveyard at the Little Dutch Church, they said, and you'll want to find her, of course.

Of course. We Canadians do like any connection we can make to royalty so off I went to the Little Dutch Church. This is what I found:

Prime Minister John Thompson died in the presence of Queen Victoria. He is buried in the Holy Cross cemetery in Halifax.

- St. George's Church, otherwise known as the Little Dutch Church, locked tight. Not a soul in sight. A sign on the outside wall, however, told me it was erected in the years 1754 and 1755 by German settlers. So how come it's called the Dutch church, I asked the wall. No answer.
- A graveyard, sure enough, around the church. Not only was it locked, but the stone fence around it was topped by sharp stone bits. No way I could unobtrusively climb over it without involving an ambulance. So, I took a picture. One white stone on the far side that stood apart from the others. Must be it, I decided.
- It wasn't. Sent the picture to Deborah Trask at the Nova Scotia Museum later. It's on the other side of the church, she said. You've missed it entirely, but here's what it says:

> IN MEMORY OF RESTELLAR JANE A. RATSEY
> FOSTER SISTER TO HER ROYAL HIGHNESS
> THE PRINCESS ROYAL OF ENGLAND
> AND DAUGHTER OF MR. R. RATSEY
> OF H.M. ROYAL NAVAL YARD
> DIED OF MALIGNANT SCARLET FEVER MARCH 1, 1844
> AGED 3 YEARS, 4 MONTHS, 15 DAYS.

• Nice of her to send the words, I said to the walls back at home, and then finally asked the essential question, "What the heck is a foster sister and why do we care?"

Queen Victoria was never in Canada. Her father Edward was when he was Commander-in-Chief of Most Everything in Halifax and built the Citadel and the Round Church and Government House and whatever else he could talk his father, King George III, into supporting. It is said that Edward had a son while he was in Canada by his friend and constant companion Julie St. Laurent, and said son is said to have lived and died in Québec City. (See Robert Wood in the Québec chapter.)

But Edward eventually went back to England, married a proper princess, and had Victoria in 1819. She became queen in 1837. Where does a foster sister fit into this picture? You tell me. The walls haven't been much help.

Reminders of the Titanic

It took me a while to find the Fairview cemetery in Halifax, so by the time I got there, it was nearly five o'clock. "I'm sorry to be so late," I said to the growly man at the office, "but I really want to see the Titanic graves. Can you show me where they are?"

He looked at me as if I were mad. "It's raining," he said as if I wasn't already dripping all over his floor. "I know," I said, "but I thought I wasn't supposed to mention it."

He rolled his eyes as if to say, "It's been a long day and now I have her." However, he unbent long enough to point vaguely toward a distant part of the graveyard. "They're over there," he said.

Maybe it was the right way to see those long rows of small grey box markers, each one with the same date: April 15, 1912. Some fifteen hundred people died that awful night when the unsinkable Titanic did the unthinkable and sank. Halifax was the nearest major port. Many of the bodies were brought there in the next few days; some stayed there:

IN MEMORIAM
ERNEST EDWARD SAMUEL FREEMAN
LAST SURVIVING SON OF CAPT. S.W. KEARNEY FREEMAN, RN
HUSBAND OF LAURA MARY JANE FREEMAN
LOST IN THE TITANIC DISASTER APRIL 15, 1912
"HE REMAINED AT HIS POST OF DUTY
SEEKING TO SAVE OTHERS REGARDLESS OF HIS OWN LIFE
AND WENT DOWN WITH THE SHIP."

SACRED TO THE MEMORY
OF EVERETT EDWARD ELLIOTT
OF THE HEROIC CREW S.S. TITANIC
DIED ON DUTY APRIL 15, 1912 AGED 24 YEARS
"EACH MAN STOOD AT HIS POST
WHILE ALL THE WEAKER ONES WENT BY
AND SHOWED ONCE MORE TO ALL THE WORLD
HOW ENGLISHMEN SHOULD DIE."

Long, solemn lines of small markers identify victims of the Titanic in Halifax's Fairview cemetery.

Among the markers for the crew members are also markers for passengers, and because I am always moved by the death of children, this one stood out:

ALMA PAULSON AGED 29 YEARS
WIFE OF NILS PAULSON
LOST WITH FOUR CHILDREN APRIL 15, 1912
IN THE TITANIC
TORBURG, AGED 8
PAUL, AGED 6
STINA, AGED 4
COSTA LEONARD, AGED 2

Imagine being on a ship that suddenly sinks, and you have four young children to look after, and there's no time, no lifeboats, no nothing. That's when the rain seemed right that day—cold, drizzly, sad.

The World Missed a Beat

Fairview cemetery revealed even more stories of unexpected and terrible tragedy. In another corner is a big black, flat marker that says:

> TO THE MEMORY OF THE UNIDENTIFIED DEAD
> VICTIMS OF THE GREAT DISASTER
> DEC. 6, 1917

On that day, two ships collided in the Halifax harbour. One of them caught fire. Then it blew up. The trouble was it was a munitions ship, full to the gunnels with bombs and ammunition for the war in Europe. When it blew in the Halifax harbour, it literally bombed Halifax.

A survivor said later that it seemed as if the world missed a beat. Time stood still. Then everything blew up, everything went black, and everything began to burn. Some 2.5 km² (1.7 mi²) on both sides of the harbour were levelled—homes, churches, schools, businesses—all gone. People too. More than sixteen hundred died instantly, nine thousand more were injured.

One of the other graves in Fairview says:

> IN LOVING MEMORY OF LIZZIE LOUISE
> WIFE OF REV. W.J.W. SWETNAM
> AGED 38 YEARS
> ALSO THEIR ONLY SON
> CARMAN ALLISON AGED 7 YRS. 10 MOS.
> BOTH OF WHOM DIED DEC. 6, 1917
> GONE TO BE GOD'S GUESTS

On that terrible morning, Mrs. Swetnam was seated at the piano, accompanying Carman, who was practising his solo for the upcoming Christmas concert. Rev. Swetnam stood in the doorway of the living room and six-year-old Dorothy sat in the rocking chair across the room. One moment, they were fine. The next moment, they weren't.

Mrs. Swetnam and Carman were crushed and killed beneath the piano. Dorothy found herself pinned under beams and a part of the wall. "Where are you, Daddy?" she cried and miracle of miracles, he was there and able to get her out before fire consumed the house. It was double jeopardy: if you weren't killed by the terrible explosion, you were caught by fire.

Dorothy, now Mrs. Clayton Hare of Calgary, remembers that some time later her father heard a fellow minister claim that the explosion and the ensuing deaths were "God's will." Not so, her father reacted angrily. "If this were the work of God, I would tear off this clerical collar," he said.

The grisly job of finding and identifying bodies went on for weeks. Finally, just before Christmas, ninety-five were buried in mass graves in the Protestant and Catholic cemeteries and marked simply, "Unidentified."

The next spring, one man found in the rubble beneath his house what he presumed were the bones of four family members burned beyond recognition. He put the bones in a shoe box and buried that. It was unspeakably awful, all of it, made more so by the knowledge that the ships need not have collided if only they had obeyed the rules of harbour traffic.

The Search for Richard Preston

When I finally got to our B and B later that evening, W and C (Wet and Cold), I mentioned to our hostess that I had not found any evidence of the black population of Halifax—not in the graveyards, at least. Oh, she said, read this. It was a book called *Africville* and, indeed, it told me a great deal about the black communities in Nova Scotia. Because I can now spot the word "cemetery" from a mile away, I noticed that it mentioned that Richard Preston is buried in the Crane Hill cemetery in East Preston.

That's not very far away, the B and B lady said, so the next morning, we headed for East Preston. We could have been in East Podunk, for all I know, because fog had entered the picture.

Another weather lesson: It's okay, apparently, to talk about the fog. I stopped at two service stations enroute to Preston to get directions to Crane Hill. Both times, the attendants started the conversation with, "Terrible fog, eh?" Then when I found the Crane Hill road, I stopped three more times to ask directions to the cemetery. "Terrible fog this morning," they all told me. And I never did find the graveyard. One guy said it was near the golf course. Another said it was beside the bridge where the road turns. Another said he'd never seen a graveyard in this area. But it could be the fog, he said.

It wasn't. I learned later from my desk in Calgary that there's nothing much left of the graveyard. And Richard Preston, they said, was never properly marked. Too bad. He sounds as if he made a huge difference to the black population of the Halifax area. As a minister, he founded eleven black Baptist churches between 1832 and 1853, and as a community activist, he organized schools and medical care and cooperative associations.

But none of that is on his grave because there is no grave.

When I complained about that to the Black Cultural Centre, they told me to check the grave of James R. Johnston, the first black lawyer in Halifax. He was really well known, I was told, especially after he was murdered in 1919 because of his colour. This time, I found the grave, thanks to his great nephew Noel Johnston in Halifax, but it says nothing about the man other than he lived and died. Dalhousie University has a chair named for him, but there's no hint of any of that on his gravemarker. Another blank.

I finally succeeded in finding a piece of black history when I lucked onto the story of William Hall, 1829-1904. He's buried on the grounds of Hantsport Baptist Church, beneath a handsome cairn that says:

THE FIRST NOVA SCOTIAN
AND THE FIRST MAN OF COLOUR
TO WIN THE EMPIRE'S HIGHEST AWARD "FOR VALOUR."
ON NOV. 16, 1857, WHEN SERVING IN HMS SHANNON,
HALL WAS PART OF A CREW UNDER COMMAND
OF A LIEUT. WHICH PLACED A 24 POUNDER GUN
NEAR THE ANGLE OF THE SHAH NUJJIFF AT LUCKNOW,
WHEN ALL BUT THE LIEUT. AND HALL
WERE EITHER KILLED OR WOUNDED,
HALL WITH UTTER DISREGARD FOR LIFE
KEPT LOADING AND FIRING THE GUN
UNTIL THE WALL HAD BEEN BREACHED
AND THE RELIEF OF LUCKNOW HAD BEEN ASSURED.

He stayed in the navy for another twenty years and then quietly retired to a farm in Nova Scotia. Nobody knew of his achievement until one day in 1901 when British veterans held a parade in honour of visiting royalty, the future King George V. The king-to-be noticed Hall's Victoria Cross medal, stopped to talk to him about it, and the cat was out of the bag. Even so, Hall was buried in an unmarked grave for many years until the Canadian Legion got into the act, moved Hall's body to its present location, and erected the monument.

The Pride of the Hector

It's not nearly so hard to find words about Scottish settlement in Nova Scotia. At the gate of the Pioneer cemetery in New Glasgow is a sign:

THIS FENCE WAS ERECTED IN 1992
BY DIRECT DESCENDANTS OF COLIN MACKAY
A HECTOR PASSENGER
1730-1804
DUINE GASDA

I don't know what that last line means—it's in Gaelic—but I have learned about the *Hector*. It was a leaky old trap of a boat that brought Scottish immigrants to Nova Scotia in 1773. In spite of a terrible crossing, what with storms and bad food and sick children, 178 passengers survived and eventually thrived in the Pictou area of Nova Scotia. As the years passed, the *Hector* took on mythic qualities and is mentioned with great pride then and now:

> HERE LIES THE BODY
> OF COLIN MCKAY
> WHO DEPARTED THIS LIFE
> JAN. 30, 1804, IN HIS 74TH YEAR,
> AND HIS SON COLIN, 1772-1850,
> BOTH ARRIVED PICTOU 1773
> ON FIRST TRIP OF THE BRIG HECTOR.

The Pioneer graveyard is full of McKays or Mackays. Both spellings appear. This is one of the more dramatic stories about the numerous clan:

> IN MEMORY OF ALEX'R MCKAY
> SON OF ANGUS MCKAY
> HE WAS STRUCK DOWN
> IN THE FULL VIGOUR OF HEALTH AND HOPE
> BY THE BLOW OF A HORSE:
> AND AFTER LINGERING FIVE DAYS, IN GREAT AGONY,
> HE DIED, WE TRUST A CHRISTIAN.
> 24TH NOVEMBER, 1849,
> AGED 19 YEARS AND 7 MONTHS.

The Men of the Deeps

When coal was discovered in the Pictou area, the Scots did what they always did—they became coalminers. So did other newcomers from the British Isles. Graveyards in the area soon reflected that occupational choice. The following are both in the Duff Pioneer cemetery in New Glasgow:

> IN MEMORY OF JOHN DAVIES
> SON OF JOHN AND RUTH CAREY
> WHO WAS KILLED BY FALLING
> DOWN THE BYE PIT SHAFT JULY 8, 1862
> AGED 19 YEARS.

> IN MEMORY OF EDWARD BURNS
> WHO WAS KILLED

AT THE DRUMMOND COLLIERY EXPLOSION
MAY 13, 1873
WHILE HEROICALLY ATTEMPTING
TO SAVE THE LIVES
OF HIS FELLOW WORKMEN.
AGED 33 YEARS.

There are other reminders of the terrible toll the mines took. One is a statue called The Highlander that lists name after name of those killed. Another is a monument at Westville called simply The Miners Monument. I liked it because it mentioned the families of the men killed in an explosion at the Drummond Colliery, May 13, 1873:

OH, WHAT A SUDDEN SHOCK THEY IN A MOMENT FEEL
NO TIME ALLOWED TO BID THEIR FAMILIES FAREWELL.
WEEP NOT FOR THEM, NOR SORROW TAKE,
BUT LOVE THEIR FAMILIES FOR THEIR SAKE.

And in case you forgot to be serious for a moment, there's another line:

BE YE ALSO READY

I'm sure that was good advice, the only advice, for families of men who went down into the deeps, but how could you live that way, I wondered. How could a mother sleep at night when her boy was in the mines in the dark? Do you get used to it?

In Springhill, we learned even more about the dangers of mining. Beside the Miners Hall in the town, for instance, are five big monuments covered with hundreds of names of miners lost between the years 1876 to 1969 in underground explosions, accidents, and cave-ins. Once again, I wondered how the moms could do it, could see their sons go underground. I wondered how the sons could do it, for that matter.

There were a couple of men talking over the day's events on the steps of the Miners Hall, and when I asked them for directions to the local graveyard, one of them said, "Just follow me."

There's a miners' hill in the graveyard, he pointed out. There's no special cairn or anything, but he knows the men there, can tell by the dates just which "bump" or fire or explosion caused their death. No wonder the town has a cairn honouring the Provincial Workman's Association, the first legalized trade union in Canada. Its plaque explains: "Organized Sept. 1, 1879, in the woods by lantern light at Springhill, NS, by Robert Drummond and William Madden during a strike for wages and conditions. These two great leaders laid the foundation for the Nova Scotia Coal Miners Act."

In the Garden of Eden

I loved the Garden of Eden lady in her wedding dress. I knew it was her wedding dress because everyone in Pictou county told me so. Be sure to see the Wedding Dress monument, they said wherever I went, and while you're there, get a load of her hands.

So I went to the Garden of Eden cemetery near Moose River, and there she was, a life-sized figure of a woman standing high above other gravemarkers in the cemetery. Her dress with its bustle and exact folds could easily have been a wedding dress, and I was ready to accept hook, line, and sinker the popular story that her husband arranged this loving memorial to his wife because she had loved her dress so.

IN LOVING MEMORY OF MARY SUTHERLAND
DAUGHTER OF GEORGE AND ELIZABETH SUTHERLAND
OF THE GARDEN OF EDEN, NS
AND WIFE OF RODERICK MORRISON
OF ROXBOROUGH, ONT.
DIED JULY 26, 1882 AGED 34

However, when I looked around there was no husband near her. Her folks were there, but no Roderick. How come? I asked some more Pictou folks.

Well, they weren't too sure, but there was some talk that he hadn't paid the bill for the monument so probably moved away to avoid bill collectors. Others said he soon remarried and relocated. One would-be art critic said he wouldn't pay for that monument either. Look at the size of her hands, he said.

A Small Marker for a Large Man

In Englishtown, we found the Nova Scotia giant. We wouldn't have known it was a giant's marker—it was no bigger than anyone else's—but the words told us so:

IN LOVING MEMORY OF ANGUS MCASKILL
THE NOVA SCOTIA GIANT
WHO DIED AT HIS HOME IN ST. ANNS
AUGUST 6, 1863 AGED 38 YEARS
HEIGHT 7 FT. 9 IN. GIRTH 80 IN. WEIGHT 425 LBS.
"A DUTIFUL SON, A LOVING BROTHER,
A TRUE FRIEND AND LOYAL SUBJECT
A HUMBLE CHRISTIAN"

Angus just grew, that's all. Nobody else in the family was unusually tall, but by the time Angus was a teenager, he was over two metres tall. His dad had to raise the ceilings in their house and lengthen Angus's bed by half a metre. When pressed for a reason for his size, Angus used to admit that he liked a bowl of oatmeal and cream after every meal.

He was a gentle giant most of the time, just now and then riled enough to pitch a noisy tormentor over a nearby woodpile or flatten a smart aleck who "accidentally" stepped on his feet once too often. Just because his bare feet stuck out onto the dance floor was no reason to step on them, he figured, so he hit the guy with his huge hands. Nobody much messed around with McAskill after that.

When a touring company approached him to join their show as the Cape Breton Giant, he agreed reluctantly—the money was too good to turn down in hard times—but as soon as he could, he came back home and set himself up with a store and a grist mill.

And that should have been the end of the story, that the Gentle Giant lived happily ever after. Except that he didn't. He died suddenly at the age of thirty-eight. The doctor at the time said it was brain fever, but the guess now is that it was some form of meningitis. So an extra-long coffin was built, and they buried the giant beneath a small marker in the small cemetery near his home.

Flying on Cape Breton Island

We were on the famous Cape Breton Island by this time, a feast in every way. I may have grumbled about the unmentionable (rain) at the beginning of our travels in Nova Scotia, but by the time we got to Cape Breton, everything shone—the sun, the sea, the lakes, the flaming trees. It was incredible.

In Baddeck, we stopped to eat at the Yellow Cello Cafe and Pizzeria. Who could resist such a name? I said to Judy, however, that it wasn't very maritime after all. We should have picked a place called The Anchor Inn or Tide's Up Pub or something. Just then, the world's longest boat, yacht, cruiser, whatever, drove past the window, going on forever. In the West, we have RVs that long. In Cape Breton, it's boats.

There's your maritime, Judy said.

Facing page: The "wedding dress" monument stands in the Garden of Eden cemetery in Pictou county.

After lunch, we went in search of air ace John McCurdy and famous inventor Alexander Graham Bell. One was right out in the open for all to see; the other was not:

HONORARY AIR COMMODORE THE HONOURABLE
JOHN ALEXANDER DOUGLAS MCCURDY
M.B.E., K.G.ST.J., D.ENG, L.L.D., D.C.L., M.E.
FIRST BRITISH SUBJECT TO FLY IN THE BRITISH EMPIRE
FEBRUARY 23, 1909
LIEUTENANT GOVERNOR OF NOVA SCOTIA 1947-1952
BORN BADDECK AUGUST 2, 1886
DIED JUNE 25, 1961
BELOVED HUSBAND OF MARGARET BALL
NOV. 8, 1898–DEC. 4, 1977

The gravemarker in the Baddeck cemetery pretty well tells the tale. In 1909 McCurdy flew the plane he designed and built, the *Silver Dart*, for

a kilometre or so over the nearby Bras d'Or Lake when it was frozen, a sensible precaution in those crazy first days of flight. The flight represented a whole lot of firsts, but that wasn't enough for McCurdy. He built planes, risked his neck and his money over and over again, and didn't really come down to earth until he became lieutenant governor.

One of the men who worked with him through those crazy first days of flight was Alexander Graham Bell, who, in between

A story of firsts and flying is found on John McCurdy's gravemarker in the Baddeck cemetery.

inventing the telephone and other technological marvels of the day, also founded the Aerial Experiment Association. Bell had land near Baddeck, a property he called Beinn Bhreagh, and it was there that McCurdy and Bell and others worked on their flying machines. When Bell died, he was buried at Beinn Bhreagh, but his is the grave I couldn't see. The Bell estate is closed to the public, but the Alexander Graham Bell Museum in Baddeck gave me a picture and information about the grave. For instance, it is situated directly beneath the apex of the tetrahedral tower that he used in many of his scientific studies. Don't ask me what a tetrahedral tower is, but the museum people used the word as if we should all know, and I guess we should if we're to understand Bell's work. (It's a solid figure with four faces, like a pyramid. I looked it up later.) Anyway, the grave is there, hewn out of solid rock, with his name, dates, vocation (inventor), and this rather surprising last line on a plaque:

DIED A CITIZEN OF THE UNITED STATES.

He wanted that, apparently. He was born in Scotland, came to Canada with his folks when he was young, but did most of his work and teaching in the United States. So he divided himself up at death—buried in Canada but bespoken to the US.

The Eyes Have It

Nova Scotia graveyards are so rich in symbolism that it's scary. Literally.

There I was one sweet autumn morning in the Truro cemetery, red and yellow leaves drifting down onto the grass, music drifting across the road from Wacky Wheatley's and Dutchy's Like Nu Clothing. A benign bucolic scene, I think the movie makers would say, although I wonder what a Wacky Wheatley's is by any other name.

Anyway, I was drifting along when suddenly I came face to face with the most horrifying death heads, all too clearly carved into side-by-side gravestones for John McKeen, Efq., and his wife, Martha, both of whom died on December 30, 1767. Now, I had met death heads before, but they're usually grey on grey, shapes and lines drawn into grey slate. You have to look hard to find the grinning teeth and empty eye sockets but not with these. In very clear grey on black, they grinned out of their bony heads like bad Hallowe'en costumes. Good grief.

When I regained consciousness, as they say in bad comedy routines, I gave a thought to the McKeens. What happened that they both died on December 30, 1767? And did the combination of the

In Truro cemetery are two fierce-looking "death heads" that warn us to behave or else.

death-head imagery and the last line on the markers make a difference to church attendance in Truro?

THE RIGHTEOUS FHALL BE HAD IN EVERLAFTING REMEMBRANCE

The same thing happened in the Stewartdale cemetery in Whycocomagh. I was wandering around, reading stories of Scottish immigration like this one:

IN MEMORY OF ANGUS CAMPBELL
WHO WAS BORN IN THE ISLE OF SKYE, SCOTLAND.
HE EMIGRATED TO THIS COUNTRY IN 1833
AND SETTLED IN SKYE GLEN IN THIS PARISH
WHERE HE DIED ON OCT. 15, 1856.

when what should appear but a big bulbous eye looking right at me. It was carved into an arch on the marker for Roderick McQuien, 1847-1878, and it managed to look everywhere at once, which is the general idea, I guess, since it is the Masonic symbol that means the all-seeing eye of God. In the arch above the eye are the words, "In God is our trust; Be just and fear not," advice that I would gladly have taken if that eye hadn't followed me so closely.

Masons love symbols. Besides the eye, they put compasses, the sun and moon and stars, ladders, candlesticks, anchors, and other symbols that are meaningful to them on their gravemarkers.

But What about the Hands?

Hands are another favourite on gravemarkers. At first, they were strictly a religious symbol: a hand with one finger pointing upwards meant a reunion with God, a trip to heaven. When I found a hand with the finger pointing downward, I thought maybe the opposite direction was indicated, but I was told that it simply meant that God was looking after the soul of the deceased below.

John F. Walker's obelisk in the New Glasgow Pioneer cemetery makes doubly sure that God and man get the message. The forefinger on his hand points upward to the words, "Yonder is my home."

Two hands meeting in what looks like a handshake can also have religious overtones—the hand of God accepting the hand of the deceased. It also symbolizes a human farewell—goodbye cruel world, as it were. Whichever meaning is intended, the image is usually carved into the surface of the stone, but in the Windsor graveyard is a pair of very lifelike hands

that look as if they were cut off at the wrist and just nailed on. Takes a minute to get used to, believe me.

They're on the grave-marker of William and Sarah Davis.

But the weirdest hands of all belong to Michael Muir in the Duff Pioneer cemetery in New Glasgow. The carver must have been new at his craft, I think. He has carved two hands. Both have spindly, long, creepy-looking fingers. One set might belong to a man;

Carved hands are a favourite religious symbol, but they are usually less realistic than these in the Windsor cemetery.

An old marker in the Duff Pioneer cemetery in New Glaslow features hands that seem better suited to Hallowe'en.

there's sort of a no-nonsense cuff on it. The other might belong to a woman; it has scallops on the cuff. Between them, the two hands hold bunches of Scottish thistle. Maybe the stone mason had seen more thistles than hands in his artistic endeavours because the thistle isn't bad. It's the hands that leave such an indelible impression.

The message is one of immigration and integration, I think.

A Mystery Unfolds

When I first found Petter D. Brodair's grave in St. James Anglican churchyard in Pictou, I thought the message was an original way of referring to a heavenly home. This is what it says:

IN HIS LAST AND BEST BEDROOM

But to my great delight, I found out later that there's another explanation for the epitaph. I was speaking to a group in Calgary. There in a meeting room halfway around the world from Pictou, a man put up his hand and asked if I had ever been in Pictou, and if so, had I seen a certain gravemarker about a bedroom?

Well, yes, I had.

Did I know, he said, that the words referred to the fact that Mr. Brodair had moved from boarding house to boarding house in the Pictou area, never satisfied with his accommodation? Always complained about his bedroom?

No, I didn't know that, I said, but I'm delighted to know it now.

That's been the fun of so much of this graveyard work. Little by little, the mysteries are revealed, the stories are told.

I went home from that meeting feeling as if I had struck gold.

The Last Word

Nobody has ever figured out who "J.W." was, but he's got gravemarkers scattered all through central Nova Scotia, especially in Hants county. He's the sculptor, and he puts his initials front and centre. Then he gets down to business and warns the reader to pay attention with openers like this, "Stand. All hear. Read this!" Once he's got your attention, he socks it to you. This is his favourite verse:

LIFE IS UNCERTAIN
TYRANT DEATH APPROACHES
THE JUDGE IS AT THE DOOR
PREPARE TO MEET YOUR GOD
LAST REPENTANCE BEING SELDOM SOUND.

Prince Edward Island

✝

Where a Red-Haired Girl
Makes All the Difference

PRINCE EDWARD ISLAND IS SO POLITE,
SO PROPER, SO CONTAINED.
THE STREETS ARE CLEAN, THE ROADS WELL MARKED,
THE YARDS AND FARMS TIDY AND MANICURED,
THE COWS ON THEIR BEST BEHAVIOUR.
IT DOESN'T PUT A FOOT WRONG, DOES PEI.
AT LEAST, THAT'S WHAT ONE COULD ASSUME
IF ONE LOOKS ONLY AT THE SURFACE,
THE RED-SOILED, RED-HAIRED ANNE SURFACE.
ANNE WITH AN "E."

"Don't you get sick of Anne, with or without an 'e'"? I asked a PEI citizen who shall remain nameless for fear she is run off the lovely island because she answered "Yes."

Anne is everywhere. I knew she'd be big, but I didn't know how big. It was only when I saw a sign in a store window that I understood. The sign said, "Nostalgic treasures from Anne's Island." That's what it is—Anne's Island. No wonder my anonymous friend sighed.

Mind you, we didn't cotton onto this Anne thing at first. At first, PEI seemed like any other part of Canada. We got off the ferry in the evening, part of a long string of cars going hell-bent for leather somewhere, so we stayed with them. I think that's what you do when you get off the ferry unless you know exactly where to turn and you do it quickly. Otherwise, the long string of cars runs over you, as far as I can tell.

We would have stayed at Betty's B 'n B, or Cranberry Cove Farm Vacation Hideaway, or Y Not Rest Cottages, but invariably we were past the signs before we could turn. So we ended up in Charlottetown, which looked and acted like any other city at that time of night—street signs that we couldn't read, motels that were full, fast-food places.

However, the next morning was bright and sunny. It would have caused Anne with an "e" to wax poetic about shining waters and golden glades and God's red earth. It really is red, by the way, although we had to wait until we got to a cemetery to confirm that because Charlottetown doesn't leave a lot of it lying around. See "neat" above. But the paths and flower beds in the Peoples cemetery revealed red earth as advertised. It didn't reveal much else, however, being fairly new and fairly quiet about itself. It wasn't until we found the Elm Avenue cemetery that I was able to wax poetic. Nancy with a "y."

The Best Graveyard in PEI

After raving about the tiny perfect island that PEI seems to be on the surface, I have to admit that the Elm Avenue cemetery in Charlottetown isn't much to look at. A bit run down, a little careless in the corners as if the caretakers had forgotten to dust lately, and for sure, no red earth peeking through the grass and weeds. It nevertheless manages to maintain a stiff-upper-lip politeness. Like the old lady who's seen better days but still wears gloves. This is what it says, for example, on the stone for Joseph Hopkins, a native of England who died in 1841, aged twenty-six years:

> THIS STONE IS ERECTED
> BY HIS YOUTHFUL FRIENDS IN P.E. ISLAND
> AS AN HUMBLE TESTIMONY OF THEIR ESTEEM
> FOR THE AMIABLE AND GENTLEMANLY DEPORTMENT
> WHICH MARKED HIS CHARACTER
> DURING HIS FIVE YEARS RESIDENCE
> AMONGST THEM.

Imagine putting such extravagant praise right out where people can see it. We would never do such a thing in western Canada. But it typifies PEI for me, where things seem to be nice, always. Like Anne.

Guess what. They weren't.

SACRED TO THE MEMORY
OF PHILLIPS CALLBECK
HIS MAJESTY'S ATTORNEY GENERAL,
LIEUTENANT COLONEL OF THE MILITIA,
AND LATE SPEAKER OF THE HOUSE OF ASSEMBLY
OF THIS PROVINCE, BY WHOSE ORDER THIS MONUMENT
IS ERECTED AS A TESTIMONY OF THEIR ESTEEM
AND A GRATEFUL TRIBUTE TO A GENERAL BENEFACTOR
OF THIS ISLAND WHO DEPARTED THIS LIFE
THE 28TH DAY OF JANUARY, AD 1790,
AGED 46 YEARS

These are the exact words that were supposed to go on Callbeck's grave back in 1790, to be paid for by the government. But they didn't make it until recently when a family member bought a marker and had the words inscribed thereon. It doesn't seem fair. Callbeck went through a lot, both for PEI and jolly old England, but for years he lay beneath a small white marble marker with only the initials P.C. to identify him.

This is when you begin to realize that PEI is not all Anne with an "e." Its history is just as hair-raising as anybody else's, even if that hair is likely red.

In the late 1700s, PEI was ruled by British governors who dropped in now and then to check on things and then rode off into the sunset. In the absence of one such governor, Phillips Callbeck was in charge. One morning, he woke up to find two American ships in the Charlottetown harbour, their guns pointing right at the innocent little town. Since fight wasn't feasible and flight a bit late, Callbeck walked out on the jetty, alone, armed only with moral indignation.

It didn't work. The American privateers took Callbeck prisoner, looted the government offices and private homes, and rode off into the sunset, Callbeck still in the hold. His moral indignation worked better when they landed in the US and Callbeck was able to make an official protest to General George Washington. Washington apologized, reprimanded the men, but Callbeck never did get his stuff back.

Not surprisingly, he laboured mightily for the next few years to get an army, a fort, a frigate, a gun or two, anything to protect Charlottetown from similar attacks from the outside world. But as it turned out, he should have been watching for long knives from within. He was disgraced and forced out of office by opponents of his land-reform schemes, schemes that sound perfectly sensible now. But we have to remember that PEI was a British colony. The absentee British landowners weren't about to sell their lands to those who actually worked them and lived there. That's what Callbeck proposed, and that's what led to his political demise.

In the meantime, as politicians lived and died fighting battles that seemed so vital then, others just lived and died. Here's the story of another Anne, this one on a worn black slate marker in the Elm Avenue cemetery:

IN MEMORY OF ANNE,
DAUGHTER OF THOMAS AND HANNAH TREMLETT
OF DARTMOUTH, COUNTY OF DEVON, ENGLAND
SHE DEPARTED THIS LIFE ON HER BIRTHDAY,
APRIL 12, 1822, AFTER A LONG AND PAINFUL ILLNESS
WHICH SHE BORE WITH UNCOMMON FORTITUDE
AND RESIGNATION LEAVING, OF A NUMEROUS FAMILY,
BUT ONE SURVIVING BROTHER THE CHIEF JUSTICE
OF THIS PROVINCE TO LAMENT
HER IRREPARABLE LOSS
AGED 43.

And here is one of the few times I actually found words on a gravemarker about a mother who died in childbirth. Generally, I have to figure it out from dates and surrounding markers, but this one comes right out and says so:

TO THE BELOVED MEMORY
OF LOUISA AUGUSTA, WIFE OF JOHN PIPPY
SHE DEPARTED THIS LIFE ON 13 MAY, 1824
AGED 23 YEARS
AFTER BEING MARRIED 17 MOS. AND ONLY 16 DAYS
AFTER SHE HAD GIVEN BIRTH TO A LOVELY BOY
WHO HAS SURVIVED HER.
NO MAN ON EARTH HAS POWER TO SAVE
FROM THE RELENTLESS YAWNING GRAVE.
THE TENDER MOTHER FROM HER BABE IS TORN
THE CHILD IS MOTHERLESS AS SOON AS BORN.
THE LOVING HUSBAND LOOKS TO HEAVEN AND SIGHS,
SPARE WIFE AND CHILD BOTH UNTOMBED, HE CRIES.
YET NOT MY WILL BUT THINE, O LORD, BE DONE.

If not childbirth, then fire, an ever-present, ever-awful possibility in the bad old days when houses were usually built of wood, and fire equipment wasn't built at all:

TO THE MEMORY OF EDWIN JOHN
WHO DIED JUNE 14, 1824 AGED 8 MONTHS
ALSO OF PETER HAMILTON
WHO WAS UNFORTUNATELY BURNED TO DEATH
ON FEBRUARY 4, 1827 AGED 5 YEARS.
CHILDREN OF WATSON AND SARAH DUCHEMIN
BENEATH THIS STONE TWO INFANTS SLEEP
ONE DIED AN AGONIZING DEATH
THE OTHER IN HIS MOTHER'S ARMS
GENTLY RESIGNED HIS FLEETING BREATH.

In 1830, three years after Peter's untimely death, Charlottetown council passed a resolution that every chimney in town had to be swept every two months in the summer and every month in the winter. As well, householders were required to hang in the front hall of their dwelling place a leathern bucket "to contain not less than two gallons" that could be used to carry water for fire-fighting.

All the leathern buckets in PEI could not have stopped the worst fire of all, however—the 1866 fire that destroyed two hundred buildings in what is now downtown Charlottetown. That year, city council went one step further and bought a fire engine.

The Cradle of Confederation

The second-most important thing about PEI, Anne being first, is the Charlottetown Conference of 1864, when Sir John A. Macdonald and others in high hats came to town to make themselves a country, a confederation of provinces. After reading about the social events dished up by Charlottetown, I can't figure out how they ever found time to write a constitution. But somehow they did, and three years later we had ourselves the Dominion of Canada.

George Coles was one of the PEI men who attended that first conference, which means he has a plaque in front of his grave at St. Peter's Anglican cemetery in Charlottetown identifying him as a "Father of Confederation." Fair enough, but give a thought to Mercy, who lies beside him. Mercy was Coles's wife. She had twelve children in twenty-five years, which means she had a baby every two years. Mercy is right. I keep getting sidetracked by facts like that. Incidentally, Mercy lived to be seventy-six years old.

In the same graveyard are the tombstones of the Harris brothers. I knew in advance that the markers had been especially designed by the architect brother, William, so I hoped to find something unusual, different at least. Gravemarkers tend to look pretty much the same year after year. These were a bit different but nothing radical—both of them grey, rounded boxes with Latin crosses worked into the design on top of the markers. Sort of like hot cross buns.

William C. Harris is well known as the designer of many of Charlottetown's older homes. But his brother Robert just happened to be at the right place at the right time and walked off with a prize place in Canadian history. It was he who painted those blessed Fathers of Confederation, standing and sitting around the conference table at Province House during the pre-Confederation talks. The original painting burned years later but by then enough copies had been made that none of us needed the original to remember it. It was etched into our minds. This is what it says on Robert Harris's grave:

IN LOVING MEMORY OF ROBERT HARRIS,
C.M.G., R.C.A. 1849-1919
HE LIVED THAT DEEP IDEAL LIFE
AND HIS RAPT SPIRIT KNEW
THE MIGHTINESS OF THINGS UNSEEN
AND LOOKED THESE SHADOWS THROUGH.

The Last Public Hanging, Thank Goodness

Just because we were drawing up a country and setting up rules whereby provinces might coexist in spite of our differences doesn't mean we had our personal lives in order. For instance, the year after Confederation, a seaman called George Dowie killed a fellow seaman in a brawl in downtown Charlottetown. After a long nasty trial, he was sentenced to hang.

On the designated day, quite a crowd showed up to see justice done, which is one way of explaining why you'd want to attend a public hanging. Anyway, Dowie made the most of his audience. He sat in an armchair arranged over the trapdoor on the platform and read a poem he had composed while in jail. For some twenty-five minutes, he went on and on until those who had perhaps been on his side through the trial began to think differently. If only he could have written a few more verses, he might have had a smaller audience at least.

But finally he was done, the noose was put around his neck, the trapdoor opened.

Robert Harris painted The Fathers of Confederation, *thereby assuring himself a place in history and a unique gravemarker in St. Peter's Anglican cemetery in Charlottetown.*

Maybe the rope didn't like poetry either because it broke. Dowie fell about five metres to the ground. Unfortunately, he survived the fall and they started all over again. This time, the rope was too long. Dowie's toes touched the ground. The crowd had had enough, both of the delays and the indignities heaped upon the hapless criminal. Some of them grabbed the rope and held Dowie aloft for the dirty deed to be done.

This was, not surprisingly, PEI's last public hanging. Dowie's body lies in the Elm Avenue graveyard, right alongside the movers and shakers of the town. He is not marked. Of course.

The Silent Acadians Again

In Mont Carmel on a simply stunning day—sunshine sparkling on the waters of Northumberland Strait, blue sky, blue water, white clouds—we found the last resting place of Father Pierre P. Arsenault, 1866-1927. The graveyard is next to the church, both right on the water, and with the sunshine and water behind them, it was a photo op if ever there was one. But for some reason or other, I took my pictures into the sun so that they all came out with little rainbows across them, almost like the old pictures I remember from Sunday School days. Christ with rays of light shining forth, that sort of thing. In fact, there may be a lesson here—did you see it coming?

Fr. Arsenault accomplished miracles in his own way. He got the huge red brick Mont Carmel church and presbytery built, for one thing, with the help of volunteer labour and various fund-raising efforts that we think we invented but which Fr. Arsenault was using at the turn of the century. He sold each of the bricks that went into the church for five cents, for example, and then organized a huge lottery.

The lottery idea worked so well that he used it again to set up scholarship funds so that young Acadians from the area could go out to university. In between all of this, he encouraged local agricultural cooperatives—an egg-marketing system, for example, and a model farm.

But it's the Acadian part of his story I wanted to hear about. In PEI, as in neighbouring New Brunswick and Nova Scotia, the descendants of the first French settlers, the Acadians, were sent packing after the Brits beat the French in one of those wars that they seemed to enjoy so much in the 1700s. Thus, some two thousand Acadians from PEI were loaded onto boats and shipped off to France or the US. Of that number, some seven hundred died when two of the boats went down crossing the Atlantic. How to make a terrible story worse.

Only thirty families or so managed to elude capture by taking to the bush—literally—which is why the same surnames occur again and again in

The names in the Mont Carmel cemetery hint at the story behind the Acadian expulsion.

Father Pierre Arsenault is buried in this mausoleum next to the Mont Carmel church that he and his ideas helped build.

graveyards like the one at Mont Carmel—Gallant, Arsenault, Doiron, Blanchard, Bourque. That's how you find the Acadian story in the Maritimes. The words "Acadian" or "Dastardly Expulsion" never appear.

Fr. Arsenault, however, tried to break down the silence a bit. He collected Acadian folk songs, encouraged the inclusion of Acadian history in school curriculums, started a collection of artifacts that eventually went to the Acadian Museum. Honestly, even as I write these facts, I can't believe that one man could do so much. Probably he darned his own socks too, just like Fr. Lacombe out in Alberta.

The words over his mausoleum in the centre of the Mont Carmel cemetery don't say any of that, of course. They say, in French, that the monument was erected in memory of L'Abbé Pierre P. Arsenault, curé at Mont Carmel for thirty-one years, and in memory of their ancestors.

Who shall not be named.

Anne of Green Gables with Two "G"s

From Acadian country, we travelled north to Cavendish and Anne country. How did we know it was Anne country? Well, we saw signs for the Anne Shirley Motel and Cabins, the Silverwood Motel, the Green Gables Golf Course, the Shining Waters Motel, the Cavendish Wax Museum, which features, wouldn't you know, a wax version of Anne of Green Gables. In stores, we could have bought Anne dolls, an Anne of Green Gables pop-up dollhouse, Anne's island seeds, and at the Green Gables Postal Outlet and Museum, we could have mailed a letter that would have been stamped with the famous Green Gables address. How our loved ones would have cherished that. Mind you, we were there in October. Some of these pleasures were closed to us. Anne is a summer thing, I gather.

It's overwhelming actually to realize just how this one fictional character has become so important. Even the graveyard is no longer called the Cavendish cemetery, which is what you might expect of the only graveyard in town. Instead, there's a huge arch over the entrance that says, "Resting Place of Lucy Maud Montgomery." Don't the other people in the graveyard count? Do the good folks who actually live in Cavendish put up a different sign through the winter months when once again they can claim their own town?

To be fair, the author Lucy Maud Montgomery did not draw attention to herself in her lifetime and doesn't on her gravemarker either. The gravemarker she shares with her husband Rev. Ewen Macdonald just lists their names and dates. No mention of Anne. There's a small subdued sign

Anne of Green Gables is everywhere on Prince Edward Island except where one would expect to find her—on the gravemarker of her creator, Lucy Maud Montgomery, in the Cavendish cemetery.

near the grave that says "Grave of L.M. Montgomery." Similar signs point out the graves of her mother and grandparents. Other than that, no bells and whistles, no neon lights. Thank goodness for small mercies.

When Lucy Maud Montgomery's mother died, her father left her with her maternal grandparents and went west. From then on, he saw very little of his daughter, but even he is brushed by the Anne thing. When I was in Prince Albert, Saskatchewan, several oldtimers told me I should look for Mr. Montgomery's grave. They weren't sure which graveyard he was in, but they knew he was there somewhere and that he was Lucy Maud Montgomery's dad. "She wrote *Anne of Green Gables*," one of them explained.

I knew that then, but I didn't know how important it was.

The Darker Shores of Cavendish

Cavendish is on the north shore of PEI, and like others who know the area through Anne's eyes only, I thought it was one lovely sun-dappled, blossom-laden, green-boughed, red-earthed scene after another. No muss, no fuss, just beauty forever, amen. Well, it is that on its good days, but it is also subject to terrible storms, which have led through the years to terrible shipwrecks all along the north shore. One of the worst was the Yankee Gale in 1851, a freak storm that came out of nowhere and wrecked some seventy vessels. Bodies washed up on shore for weeks afterwards and in most cases were simply buried in local cemeteries, unmarked, unknown. The town of New London contains one of the few official monuments marking that terrible time—a cairn in memory of American sailors lost during the storm.

There's another story about PEI's North Shore that's not at all Annelike. During prohibition in the 1920s and 1930s, certain shipowners saw a way to make a little extra money by smuggling liquor from the US or the Caribbean. Lots of ships tried it, but none were as successful as the *Nellie J. Banks,* a schooner that flouted the law so long and so successfully that poems and folk songs were composed about it. (One of them is called simply the "Nellie J. Banks," and it's sung by the popular Lenny Gallant. See Acadian names above.)

One day the authorities pulled a dirty trick on the crew of the *Nellie J. Banks.* They extended provincial control from the accepted three miles (4.8 km) to twelve miles (19.3 km)—for one day only. In the space of that day, they swooped down on the *Nellie J. Banks* and closed her down.

None of this interesting stuff is mentioned on a gravemarker, of course. All I could find was a passing mention on a cairn in the Allendale shipbuilding yard. And when I took the ferry back to the mainland, I found in the gift shop a book called *The Nellie J. Banks* by Geoff and Dorothy Robinson. "That's the last one," the clerk said. "Everyone seems to be interested in rum running."

The sweet Anne and the rum-running *Nellie J. Banks.* Go figure such a combination.

The First Selkirk Settlement

We who live in western Canada think we have exclusive rights to Lord Douglas Selkirk, he and his slightly crazy idea of bringing Scottish settlers to Canada and leaving them here to figure out how to survive in an entirely different and sometimes hostile environment. That's what happened to the poor souls who came to Manitoba in 1812. First they had to walk hundreds of kilometres from northern Manitoba to the Red River settlement, then they had to fight a few fights, then they had to survive Canadian winters. That they stayed the course is remarkable.

But PEI, I discovered while I was there, had Lord Selkirk first. He brought three shiploads of settlers to the south shore in 1803, a relocation venture that went much more smoothly than the western one. Had

Manitoba been Selkirk's first experience with good deeds, he probably would have called it a bad job and quit there. But the Scots who arrived in PEI did just fine, by and large. In the town of Belfast is a monument to their achievements:

> IN MEMORY OF THE ARRIVAL
> OF THE SCOTTISH IMMIGRANTS
> WHO CAME TO THIS ISLAND
> BY LORD SELKIRK'S SHIPS,
> THE POLLY, THE DYKES AND THE OUGHTEN,
> AND MADE HOMES FOR THEMSELVES AND THEIR FAMILIES
> IN THE WOODS OF BELFAST.

In the nearby Polly cemetery are the graves of many of the original settlers, including one for Mary Halliday, said to be the illegitimate daughter of Lord Selkirk. That's another first for a westerner. In our history lessons, Lord Selkirk was always held up as a paragon of altruism, a model of good intentions and noble deeds, someone who wouldn't say boo if his mouth was full of it. To think that he left behind the results of unsanctioned relationships is interesting indeed.

Come to think of it, Selkirk and PEI share more than just a bit of history.

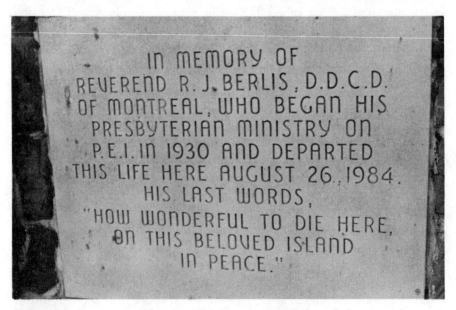

Reverend Berlis was as much a fan of PEI as was Anne with an "e."

They are both perceived as squeaky clean, on the dull side, just too good to be believed. But it ain't necessarily so.

The Last Word

The Reverend Berlis must be a fan of Anne with an "e," but like Anne, he is a wonderful treat in a world that generally sees the bad in everything. His words are on a plaque at the Cavendish cemetery:

> IN MEMORY OF REV. R.J. BERLIS,
> D.D.C.D. OF MONTREAL,
> WHO BEGAN HIS PRESBYTERIAN MINISTRY
> ON PEI IN 1930 AND DEPARTED THIS LIFE
> HERE AUG. 26, 1984,
> HIS LAST WORDS,
> "HOW WONDERFUL TO DIE HERE,
> ON THIS BELOVED ISLAND IN PEACE."

Newfoundland

✝

Where Even the Moose Visit Graveyards

WE'RE FROM THE PRAIRIES, REMEMBER?
WHAT DO WE KNOW OF WATER AND FERRIES
OTHER THAN THE BC FERRIES THAT TAKE US
FROM THE BC MAINLAND TO VANCOUVER ISLAND,
AND THEY'RE SUCH PUSSY-CATS, THEY BARELY RIPPLE
AS THEY CROSS THE WATER.
SO WE DROVE ONTO THE FERRY AT SYDNEY, NOVA SCOTIA,
EXPECTING A NICE QUIET TWELVE- TO FOURTEEN-HOUR PASSAGE
ACROSS THE GULF OF ST. LAWRENCE TO ARGENTIA,
NEWFOUNDLAND.
NO SWEAT.
WE EVEN THOUGHT WE MIGHT SEE WHALES.

And for sure, we were going to see "The Rock." A friend back in Alberta had told me again and again that I had to get up at 6 A.M. and go out on deck to see The Rock as we arrived. "You'll never forget it," she said.

I'll never forget it all right, not one thing about that trip will I forget. First of all about an hour out of port, the ferry began to rock, then rock and roll, then line dance, then move every which way at once. I couldn't believe it, but because I'm a grownup, of course, I couldn't lie down on the floor and cry. But real Atlantic Canadians did just that—they didn't cry, but they spread out their sleeping bags and pillows and blankets and went to sleep on chairs, benches, and the floor, as if this were the most normal thing in the world.

How could anyone sleep when this bark on the vast ocean was bobbing around like this? "Is it always this rough?" I asked the clerk in the gift shop. "Oh, this is nothing," he said. "You can still stand up tonight." Thanks a lot.

Lesson #1 about Newfoundland: It is an island. You always have to cross water to get there. You always have to cross water to get out. It's something like the northern part of Alberta where I grew up. We always used to refer to "going out" to Edmonton, then and only then would our trip begin.

Lesson #2: There's no use complaining. I remember how I hated to hear newcomers to our part of the country carry on about "vast distances to the frontier" and how it took them forever to get here. What could I do about it? Same thing with this boat to Newfoundland. I shut up and went to bed.

Now, "bed" might be exaggerating the truth a bit. When you buy a berth on the overnight ferry, you get a plastic shelf. That's really the only way I can describe the sleeping arrangements down in the hold. There are four shelves in a cubicle, a flat plastic mattress on each, a grey blanket, and a small pillow. There are no unnecessary frills like a curtain or a drawer in which to store your valuables. You sleep on your valuables in more ways than one.

And people did sleep. I heard them all around me, snoring, snorting, turning over and hitting the plastic wall next to them, which sent reverberations all down the line, then getting up to go to the bathroom and actually going to sleep again. How they did it, I couldn't figure, but the next morning, I heard a lot of talk about Gravol and little white pills.

Lesson #3: Come prepared, and don't worry about your valuables. Somehow, the people who go back and forth to The Rock are a trustworthy lot.

And, yes, I did get up at 6 A.M. to see The Rock, just as my friend had urged, but there was nothing to see except fog and total darkness. I could have been on the dark side of the moon, for all I knew. So I went back to my cosy little plastic shelf and slept.

The Graveyards of St. John's

The fog barely lifted that first day, which is why St. John's began as a bit of a mystery to me. We drove to Signal Hill, of course, which is supposed to offer a view all the way to Ireland, but Ireland could have been right beneath our noses, for all I knew. Signal Hill was socked in. All we could see were the cannons and the various fortifications over which England and France fought for about three hundred years. I wondered how they ever found one another long enough to fight, but I was just being grumpy. See sleep, above.

There were so many battles fought between England and France over the centuries that over time, they begin to blur, especially as they relate to central and Atlantic Canada. You'd think our eastern coasts were one big war trophy, and I guess they were in many ways. For a while, Newfoundland belonged to whoever got there first in the spring, then France got it, then they lost it in 1713 under the Treaty of Utrecht, then they got some back in the Seven Years' War, then they lost that too, and Britain was once again in control via The Treaty of Paris, 1763.

It was all very confusing—still is—but eventually a few hardy souls hung in there and settled Newfoundland. Then a few more hardy souls wrested a bit of independence for the island. One of the wrestlers was William Carson. He is buried in the graveyard next to the Anglican Cathedral in St. John's.

IN MEMORY OF HON. WM. CARSON, M.D.
WHO DIED FEB. 26, 1843, AGED 73 YEARS.
SON OF SAMUEL AND MARGARET (MACGLACHERTY) CARSON
OF THE BILLIES, KIRKCUDBRIGHT, SCOTLAND
WHO FOR 35 YEARS STROVE
FOR THE WELFARE OF NEWFOUNDLAND.

Carson believed that Newfoundlanders ought to have a say in their own government. How could the governors sent out from London know what would work best for Newfoundland? It didn't make sense. So he petitioned, he wrote letters, he organized, and by golly, in 1832, Newfoundland got its own elected legislature. It was still a British colony, still a piece of the pink on the world map, but at least it could make its own laws concerning property, roads, schools, hospitals, fisheries, and the like.

While the newcomers to Newfoundland fought wars at home and

Many of St. John's first citizens, such as the indefatigable William Carson, are buried around the Anglican cathedral of St. John the Baptist.

overseas, the people who had been in Newfoundland all along, the Beothuk, were totally ignored—or worse. This is what it says on a cairn alongside a main road in St. John's:

> THIS MONUMENT MARKS THE SITE
> OF THE PARISH CHURCH OF ST. MARY THE VIRGIN
> DURING THE PERIOD 1859-1963.
> FISHERMEN AND SAILORS FROM MANY PORTS
> FOUND A SPIRITUAL HAVEN WITHIN ITS HALLOWED WALLS.
> NEAR THIS SPOT IS THE BURYING PLACE
> OF NANCY SHANAWDITHIT
> VERY PROBABLY THE LAST OF THE BEOTHICS
> WHO DIED ON JUNE 6, 1829

Nancy was the "last" of her kind for a whole lot of reasons, but the ugliest of all is that some early European settlers of Newfoundland "hunted" the Natives. It was considered sport.

It started as a terrible mistake. In 1612, when Newfoundland was just a big fishing ground as far as Europe was concerned, John Guy of England sailed into Trinity Bay one spring day and met the Natives. No problem. They were friendly; the British crews were friendly. Arrangements were made to meet again, but it wasn't John Guy who first sailed into Trinity Bay the next spring. It was another British ship whose sailors were somewhat alarmed by all the dancing and hoopla awaiting them on shore, so they diplomatically shot everyone. When in doubt, shoot. Naturally, the rest of the Beothuks headed for the hills, and that's where they stayed for the next two hundred years or so. There were never very many of them, maybe one thousand or so when the settlers first arrived, but through the years those numbers decreased even further, mostly due to disease and starvation, somewhat due to the settlers' guns. Eventually, Newfoundland found its conscience, but it was too late. There weren't any Beothuks left. Nancy, her mother, and her sister were captured in 1823 and brought to St. John's. The mother and sister died soon after of tuberculosis, but Nancy lived another six years, part of that time with William Epps Cormack, the man who first explored the interior of Newfoundland. It was he who reported there were no Beothuks left, and it was he who took a special interest in Nancy.

She turned out to have a talent for drawing, and her pencil sketches remain as the only first-hand record of her people.

When she died, she was buried in the Anglican churchyard. But the exact location of her grave was lost in the shuffle when a new road was built through the area. Thus Nancy disappeared, just like all the rest of her people.

Nancy's last resting place is the Old Old Old Anglican cemetery; Wm. Carson's is the Old Old Anglican cemetery; these differentiations tripped us up time and time again in Atlantic Canada. When we found the Old (just one Old) Anglican cemetery, we found the kind of history we had expected to find, the kind of history we don't find on the prairies:

THOMAS C. ROBINSON
LOST AT SEA
AUGUST 19, 1882
AGED 13 YEARS.

GEORGE ROWLES
KILLED BY FALLING FROM THE CLIFF
AT BACCULIEU ISLAND
JULY 24, 1869 AGED 18 YEARS

IN MEMORY OF EDWARD WALLBRIDGE
ABLE SEAMAN AGED 30 YEARS AND 10 MO'S
WHO WAS DROWNED AT ST. JOHN'S, N.F.
30 MARCH 1909
ERECTED BY THE OFFICERS, SHIPS COMPANY
AND ROYAL NAVAL RESERVEMEN OF H.M.S. CALYPSO
OH GOD OUR HELP IN AGES PAST.

We also found the first Newfoundland mention of the SPG, the British missionary society with the arrogant-sounding name, the Society for the Propagation of the Gospel in Foreign Parts:

IN AFFECTIONATE REMEMBRANCE
OF REV. THOMAS WOOD
MISSIONARY OF THE SPG
RECTOR OF ST. THOMAS IN THIS CITY
AND FOR SEVERAL YEARS BISHOP'S COMMISSARY
AND RURAL DEAN OF AVALON
WHO DEPARTED THIS LIFE AUG. 16, 1881
IN THE 74TH YEAR OF HIS AGE
AND 50TH OF HIS MINISTRY IN THE DIOCESE.

And it was in the Old Anglican cemetery that we found the one and only mention of Guglielmo Marconi's achievement in 1901 when he received the first transatlantic wireless message on Signal Hill in St. John's. It was just a faint "S" in Morse code that bounced its way from a telegrapher in England to a receiving set in Canada, but it was the start of something much bigger—radio and other modern methods of communication.

OF YOUR LOVE
PRAY FOR THE SOUL
OF HENRY WM. GANDEY
WHO WAS ACCIDENTALLY KILLED
AT THE ST. JOHN'S WIRELESS
TELEGRAPH STATION
SEPT. 14, 1917 AGED 21 YEARS.
"JESU MERCY."

Also, much to our surprise, we found a Father of Confederation in the Old Anglican cemetery, one of the men who had been present at the negotiations leading up to the Confederation that did *not* include New-foundland in 1867. He was Sir Frederick Bowker Terrington Carter, 1819-1900, a premier of Newfoundland who supported Confederation when it was first discussed in 1864 but never could get Newfoundlanders behind the idea. For one thing, Newfoundland couldn't stop fighting over Catholic *versus* Protestant issues, some of which arguments spilled over into Confederation, and so it went for another eighty years or so.

It took Joey Smallwood to finally pull the thing off: Newfoundland joined the rest of Canada in 1949. He's buried in the Mount Pleasant cemetery on the other side of the city beneath a big black marker that says simply:

Joey Smallwood, the last Father of Confederation, is buried in St. John's Mount Pleasant cemetery.

JOSEPH ROBERTS SMALLWOOD
1900-1991
FATHER OF CONFEDERATION

The Most Beautiful War Memorial in Canada

The next day, the fog had lifted, thank goodness, because I wanted to see the caribou statue in Bowring Park in St. John's. It's the most beautiful war memorial in Canada for my money. So many war memorials show warlike things—young men running into battle with guns firing, old soldiers standing at attention, generals saluting. But the caribou doesn't say war at all. It's a caribou. It symbolizes Newfoundland more than it symbolizes war, and because the Royal Newfoundland Regiment did itself so proud during World War I, it's a proud symbol.

When the war began in 1914, Newfoundland immediately organized to help Great Britain. No doubt about it, if the mother country needed them, they'd be there, loyal to the end. So the Newfoundland Regiment was organized and sent overseas where the men died in droves. It's an awful way to put it, but it's the truth. The regiment lost 1,305 men before the war was over, another 2,314 were wounded; the fatality rate was 20 percent.

This caribou, symbol of the famous Royal Newfoundland Regiment, stands in Bowring Park in St. John's as a reminder of lives lost in WWI.

They got the title "Royal" from the British parliament because they had both the highest rate of enlistment per capita and the highest rate of fatalities of any British Empire country. A dubious honour, perhaps, but an honour anyway. They were the only ones to get the Royal designation in World War I.

Which is why the caribou is such a powerful symbol in Newfoundland and why a huge replica stands on a bluff of rock among the trees in Bowring Park. It's not a fearsome statue, however. Young moms sat visiting on benches near the statue when I was there, and their kids climbed the rocks to read the names on the plaque: Ypres, Passchendaele, Suvla, Steenbeek.

"Get down off there," one mom hollered as her youngster tried to scale the back end of the caribou. "You don't climb statues," she said.

Well, not that one anyway. The boy went back to reading the names: Armentieres, Beaumont Hamel, Courtral. Not a bad way to learn his history after all.

The only member of the Newfoundland Regiment to receive the Victoria Cross and the youngest winner of the award in the British army was Sgt. Thomas Ricketts. He's buried in the Old Anglican cemetery in St. John's under the information:

SGT. THOMAS RICKETTS, VC
BORN MIDDLE ARM, W.B. APRIL 15, 1901
AWARDED THE VICTORIA CROSS
IN ACTION WITH ROYAL NEWFOUNDLAND REGIMENT
NEAR LEDGEHEM, BELGIUM, OCT. 14, 1918
DIED FEBRUARY 10, 1967.

Do the arithmetic and you'll see that Ricketts was seventeen when he silenced a German battery and became a hero.

Moose on the Loose

We learned two more lessons in the next few days.

Lesson #4: Newfoundland is a lot bigger than you'd think. On the map, it appears to be a fairly manageable size, just an island, after all. Forget that, folks. She's a long way across, she's a long time around, she's a far way home.

Lesson #5: Newfoundland resists rush. On the TransCanada one day as we barrelled toward Grand Falls, a lone police officer waved us over and asked about a missing front licence plate. I didn't even know it was missing, but when I explained that we'd picked up the car in Montréal, he understood. Then he took time out for a little chat. I could see cars and trucks piling up behind us—this was the TransCanada, after all—but our friendly officer was in no hurry. Where were we from? From Alberta, you say? Now, friends of his just happened to be working in Fort McMurray. We wouldn't know them, would we? And how do we like Newfoundland? And so on and so forth, for a good five minutes. It was grand.

But I'm ahead of our graveyards. After leaving St. John's, we stopped first in Carbonear and found the Anglican cemetery up on the hill. A neighbour lady came out and warned us that a moose had recently moseyed through the graveyard. Maybe we should watch out, she said. So we did.

Lesson #6: Newfoundlanders are the friendliest people in Canada. All we had to do was set foot in a graveyard and someone would be along to ask, "Can we help? Are you looking for someone in particular?" It too was grand.

In Carbonear, we found the caribou again, this time carved into the top of a gravemarker for a member of the Royal Newfoundland Regiment:

IN LOVING MEMORY OF PTE. WILLIAM ROY SAUNDERS M.M.
SECOND SON OF PHILIP AND ISABEL SAUNDERS

> WHO DIED AT CARBONEAR
> APRIL 22, 1919, AGED 24 YEARS,
> FROM WOUNDS RECEIVED
> AT PASSCHENDALE, APRIL 12, 1918.
> GREATER LOVE HATH NO MAN THAN THIS,
> THAT A MAN LAY DOWN HIS LIFE FOR HIS FRIENDS.

Next to William Roy was his sister:

> IN LOVING MEMORY OF NELLIE
> BELOVED DAUGHTER OF PHILIP AND ISABEL SAUNDERS
> WHO FELL ASLEEP
> JUNE 3RD, 1915, AGED 18 1/2 Y'RS.
> HEAVEN HAS NOW OBTAINED OUR TREASURE
> EARTH THE LONELY CASKET KEEPS
> AND THE SUNBEAMS LONG TO LINGER
> WHERE OUR NELLIE SLEEPS.

William Roy died of war-related wounds. I wonder what wounds caused Nellie to "fall asleep"?

The Pirate and His Lady

A much happier story awaited us in Bristol's Hope. I knew that Princess Sheila was supposed to be buried there, and it promised to be a great story. But we couldn't find the graveyard. We asked several people out walking around the seawall, but they didn't know. I finally decided to stop at the nearest house and ask. Judy was horrified. "You can't just go up and ask perfect strangers," she said, but I did, and they didn't even miss a beat when I told them what I was looking for. They just said, "Sure, we'll be glad to take you there."

So Cal Penney of Mount Pearl drove us to Princess Sheila's last resting place. Not a very royal setting, I must say, a patch of lawn behind the local seniors lodge. And it seems as if Sheila's actual gravemarker is no longer there. Her husband's is, but I read somewhere that hers had been removed to a museum. Still, it's where she is buried.

Hollywood could do this story, too. First of all, there's the famous pirate Peter Easton, an Englishman who looted, plundered, destroyed, and raided everything he could catch up with on the high seas. Every now and then, he ducked into Newfoundland ports to restock his supplies and recruit more men. It is said that he took the Newfoundland men by force and made them do all these terrible things, but there's always a hint that the men,

Men who served with the Royal Newfoundland Regiment, such as this soldier buried in the Carbonear cemetery, proudly display the caribou symbol on their graves.

most of whom came home richer than their wildest dreams, were not all that hard to recruit.

John Pike began his career with Easton and then went independent. On one of his raids in the British Channel, he got more than he bargained for: an Irish princess named Sheila Na Geira. Here's where Hollywood could come in. She was a dark-haired beauty apparently, and by the time the pirate ship had made its way across the Atlantic to Newfoundland, Pike and the princess were in love. She talked him into giving up his nasty business, and they married and lived happily ever after in the Bristol Hope/Carbonear area. So there, and as Cal Penney said, "There's a lot of Pikes in this area." We saw the name in every graveyard after that.

Old Feuds Brought to New Lands

For every happy story, there's an equally unhappy one, like this one in Harbour Grace:

THIS MONUMENT IS ERECTED
BY THE ORANGEMEN OF NEWFOUNDLAND
FOR BROTHER THOMAS NICHOLS
WHO WAS SHOT WHILE WALKING IN PROCESSION
FROM CHURCH ON ST. STEPHEN'S DAY 1883
DIED FROM HIS WOUNDS MARCH 10, 1884
AGED 26 YEARS.

This was an old battle brought to a new country, the battle between the Catholics and the Protestants in Ireland. For a few generations at least, it continued in Canada. Thus when Thomas Nichols went marching with his fellow Protestant Orangemen through the Catholic section of town on December 16, 1883, the Catholics got riled. A fight broke out, and five people died that day.

The Most Gruesome Gravemarker

There was no signpost over the first graveyard we visited in Harbour Grace, but when I described it later to a local, she said, "Oh, that's the RC in Bennett's Lane."

That being the case, then the RC in Bennett's Lane has the most gruesome headstone around. It's all broken up now but as far as I can figure, there were five rectangular stone pieces, each the width of the grave and about sixty centimetres high. The pieces at

According to the inscription on her gravemarker in the Carbonear cemetery, Nellie Saunders "fell asleep" at the age of eighteen.

the top and bottom of the grave are still in place, the other three lie broken across the top now, but they might have been stacked at either end. I can't tell. What I can tell is that the two end pieces each have a skull and crossbones on them that would scare the wits out of the witless. They're not just carved into the surface of the stone; they stand out from the stone as if a real skull had been applied complete with empty eye sockets, grinning teeth, gaping nostrils. They are the stuff of bad horror movies, believe me.

The other three panels aren't in the same league at all. One has a cherub carved on it, the other two have lambs. Go figure. None of them has names or dates.

So what's the story? I asked Mrs. Peggy Fahey from the museum.

Well, nobody knows for sure. For a while, local legend had it that they belonged to a pirate. Otherwise, why the skull and crossbones? And Harbour Grace did have pirates in and out of its cove. Then along came the story that the grave marked a priest who had been excommunicated. The skull and crossbones indicated his fall from grace; the lambs and cherub his salvation.

What was he supposed to have done? I asked.

Oh, you didn't have to do much to get into trouble with the church in those days, Mrs. Fahey told me. So the priest story could also be true.

However, they're working on it and will let me know when they uncover more facts.

Stay tuned.

The Canadian Who Made Robert Peary Look Good

In Brigus, I went looking for the grave of Bob Bartlett, the famous Arctic navigator, and again had to ask for directions. The woman at the service station told me, "You can't miss it, my dear," but I did, and found this remarkable stone first. I don't know the story; I include it because of the social changes it signals. It's totally Christian in its acceptance of death; it's somewhat surprising in its choice of words:

LUCINDA, WIFE OF WILLIAM STENTAFORD
WHO DEPARTED THIS LIFE
MAR. 7, 1845, AGED 32 YRS, 6 MOS.
ALSO TO THE MEMORY OF ELIZABETH WILLACOTT
DAUGHTER OF WILLIAM AND LUCINDA STENTAFORD
WHO DEPARTED THIS LIFE
NOV. 4, 1844 AGED 5 YRS, 2 MOS.

"THOUGH SLEETY BLAST AND WINTER STORMS
SWEEP O'ER THESE LITTLE MOUNDS
YET FORMS IMMORTAL, HEAVENLY PURE AND BRIGHT
SHALL FROM THESE CLODS UPRISE IN LIGHT
WHEN LOUD THE ANGELS TRUMP SHALL SOUND
AND AWFUL THUNDER SHAKE THE GROUND
FOR WHAT WAS LAID IN WEAKNESS THERE
IN POWER AND GLORY SHALL APPEAR
WHEN GOD WHO MEN AND ANGELS MADE
SHALL WAKE THE SAINTED SLEEPING DEAD."

It was a decided anticlimax to find Bob Bartlett's grave, which had no words upon it except for his name and dates. It's too bad because Bob Bartlett helped Robert Peary get to the North Pole. Peary may have stepped on it first, but Bartlett showed him the way. Then he did the same thing for a whole host of people who wanted to see, feel, and touch the North. But none of that appears on his terribly modest marker.

There are Bartletts throughout this cemetery, including one Joseph Bartlett who died October 1, 1871, and left us with this no-nonsense message:

TODAY WE BLOOM
TOMORROW DIE.

The dangers that Bartlett and others faced when they tackled northern waters are illustrated on another marker at Brigus:

IN LOVING MEMORY OF GEORGE ROBERTS
WHO WAS LOST IN A STORM
AT THE ICE FIELDS 1869
AGED 26 YEARS.

I didn't find any specific mention of the worst sealing tragedy in Newfoundland's history—the one that saw sixty-five men die in March 1914 when a ship mistakenly put them down on the ice far from the sealing grounds. A terrible storm came up before they could find shelter, and more than half of the original crew died. In western Canada, we fear sudden blizzards and losing our way on the open prairie. In Newfoundland, it was a sudden blizzard, that much is the same, but the men lost themselves on ice and open water.

Another story that I'll tell more completely later in the chapter was foreshadowed in the Brigus cemetery as well:

ERECTED TO THE MEMORY
OF A LOVING HUSBAND AND FATHER

Gruesome at the ends, cherubic in the middle, this gravemarker in the Harbour Grace cemetery is a mystery.

ISRAEL BARRETT
AGED 53 YEARS
WHO LOST HIS LIFE
WHEN THE S.S. CARIBOU
WAS TORPEDOED AND SUNK
OCT. 14, 1942

The Best Graveyard in Newfoundland

Every village in Newfoundland is referred to in tourist information as a picturesque seaside village. Newfoundlanders must get thoroughly sick of it, but I must say Trinity was picturesque. It is a tiny perfect village in a tiny perfect spot, and there's a tiny perfect church up on the hill, St. Paul's Anglican. I'm not being a smart aleck. It's true.

So I pick the graveyard beside St. Paul's as the best partly because the setting is so lovely. Beyond that, however, the graveyard contains both good news and bad news, and that doesn't always happen.

The good news first:

JOHN CLINCH, 1749-1819
BORN IN ENGLAND,
THIS MEDICAL AND MISSIONARY PIONEER
CAME TO NEWFOUNDLAND IN 1775,
AND LATER SETTLED IN TRINITY (1783) WHERE HE DIED.
HE IS NOTED FOR INTRODUCING THE JENNER VACCINE
TO BRITISH NORTH AMERICA (1800)
AND FOR COMPILING A GLOSSARY
OF BEOTHUCK TERMS.

So many people in all parts of Canada had to die of smallpox in the early days, but happily for Newfoundland, Clinch went to school in England with Edward Jenner, who eventually developed the smallpox vaccine. Thus when smallpox began one of its deadly rounds in the Trinity and St. John's area, Clinch remembered his old friend's work and ordered some of the vaccine from England. Not every child was able to get the precious vaccination—some were too poor and some too far away—but it was a beginning. From Newfoundland, the knowledge of vaccination spread to other parts of North America. A first for Newfoundland.

Now, for the bad news. Disease wasn't the only danger to children in those bygone days. Listen to this story on a Trinity gravemarker:

SACRED TO THE MEMORY
OF CHARLOTTE, AE 16, ELIZABETH, AE 15,

269

AMY, AE 13, JAMES AE 9, JOSEPH, AE 7
THE CHILDREN OF JOSEPH AND MARY DAY
OF ROBIN HOOD
ALSO WILLIAM, AE 12,
THE SON OF THOMAS AND ELIZABETH RANDALL
OF THE SAME PLACE WHO ALL FELL VICTIMS TO A FIRE
THAT CONSUMED THE DWELLING HOUSE
OF THE SAID JOSEPH DAY ON THE EVE OF EASTER, AD 1855
THE REMAINS OF THE ABOVE SIX CHILDREN
HERE REST IN THE SAME COFFIN.

It seems so stark, so sad, this list of children who died in a fire, and just because deaths by fire happened all the time doesn't change anything. It's still a terrible tragedy even 140 years later. I remind myself to check our smoke detectors when I get home, and I am not being flippant or thoughtless. We are lucky to live when we do. That's the message again and again in the graveyard.

Jane Hiscock was one of the unlucky ones in her day. She died in childbirth, a fate that is actually recorded on her gravemarker in the Trinity cemetery, only the third time I found childbirth mentioned in connection with death.

SACRED TO THE MEMORY OF JANE
WIFE OF ROBERT HISCOCK
WHO DIED IN CHILD BIRTH
12TH OCTOBER, 1830, AGED 25 YEARS.
IN THE MIDST OF LIFE, WE ARE IN DEATH.

Near Jane is one of the silent gravemarkers. Mary Butler, wife of James Butler Junior, died April 26, 1852, aged twenty years. Sounds suspiciously like childbirth time, but nothing is said except some kind words of Christian resignation:

DEATH WITH ITS DART
DID PIERCE MY HEART
WHEN I WAS IN MY PRIME
MY FRIENDS, YOUR GRIEF FORBEAR
T'WAS GODS APOINTED TIME.

Tells us a lot about Mary's time. For one thing, the monument makers couldn't spell very well, but more important, was that religion had to make sense of her early death; nothing else could.

Religion is the basis of Samuel Penney's epitaph as well, although he's not quite so resigned to his fate as Mary. He died May 4, 1825, aged forty years:

DEAR FRIENDS, IT IS A SERIOUS THING TO DIE
YOU SOON WILL FIND IT SO AS WELL AS I
SET THEN YOUR HEARTS TO THOUGHTS ABOVE
DEATH SOON WILL END ALL.

I could also tell you about the cenotaph on the front lawn of the church, "To the memory of those who laid down their lives for King and country in the Great War, 1914-1918," but I've already included enough bad news. Suffice it to say that their names will always be noticed because somebody in Trinity came up with the bright idea that the church should be painted white and grey with just the occasional flash of bright red on the rose window and door frames. It's plumb lovely. Picturesque, I think, is the word.

The Biggest Bust in Newfoundland

You have to know William Coaker was big in Newfoundland when you find his last resting place in the town of Port Union. First of all, there's a hill that overlooks the town. On top of the hill is a substantial fence. Inside

The cemetery surrounding St. Paul's Anglican Church in Trinity contains good news and bad.

the fence is an equally substantial platform enclosed by another fence. On the platform is a marble sarcophagus. On the sarcophagus is a larger than lifesized bronze bust of a man.

And that, my friends, is where William Coaker lies buried. It's the biggest memorial to any one individual in the whole province.

So what did he do to deserve such grandeur?

Easy. He stuck up for the little guy. In 1908, he organized a union for fishermen, the Fishermen's Protective Union. It was unheard of, that the most independent worker of all—the fisherman—should join forces with other fishermen to influence management and governments, but that's what happened. Then Coaker took the organization one step further: he encouraged FPU members to run for election so that they could practise what they preached. They even built themselves a model town for fishery workers—Port Union.

It worked wonderfully for a while, but then along came the Great Depression. Even unions, even governments, couldn't make that better, so Coaker moved to the US, then spent his last years in Jamaica, surely a long way from home. But he was forgiven. Witness his gravemarker:

> SIR WILLIAM FORD COAKER, K.B.E. FOUNDER
> OF F.P.U.–PORT UNION–AND TRADING CO.
> BORN OCT. 19, 1871 DIED OCT. 26, 1938.

Memorials to People from Away

In Gander, we found the Commonwealth War Graves Commission cemetery, a typical veterans cemetery with everything straight and tidy and uniform. One hundred men from Canada, the United Kingdom, and Australia are buried there, mostly airmen who died while training at the base during World War II.

Flight Lieut. F.L. Robinson, DFC, RCAF, died October 2, 1943. His epitaph explains:

> HE IS NOT DEAD.
> HE FLIES AGAIN A PHANTOM PLANE.
> HIS HANGAR NOW ETERNITY GAINED.

Near him, the marker for Flight Lieut. Douglas G.C. Chown, RCAF, who died December 9, 1942, adds:

> PROUDLY HE GAVE HIS HAPPY LIFE AWAY
> FOR CANADA, FOR FREEDOM, AND HIS GOD.

He has the biggest bust in Newfoundland, a proper state of affairs for William Coaker, the man who stood up for the little guy.

Such stiff-upper-lip. I don't think I could do it, if it were me who had to go to war, and I don't think I could say it, if it were my son. But things were different then. Patriotism, Government, and God could be said in the same breath.

Not far from the Commonwealth graveyard, down a dirt road toward a small lake, is another memorial to people from other places. It's a statue called "The Silent Witnesses," and it commemorates 256 lives lost in a plane crash at that spot December 12, 1985. Whoever selected the name for the memorial did well because it was absolutely still the night we were there, still except for the sound of a plane in the background.

Life Is a Field of Honour

We looked north as we drove past the turnoff to L'Anse aux Meadows. That's as close as we could get; we had run out of time. I hated to miss it, but as far as I could tell from reading about the old Viking settlement, there were no known graves there. Certainly no markers with interesting stories writ large upon them, so it was crossed off the list. That was one of the hardest decisions we had to make, but the problem was the ferry. You make reservations on it, you be there.

By not going up north at that point, we missed the grave of Sir Wilfred Grenfell, the famous medical missionary with a floating practice. That is, he got around by boat, the only way that a lot of the really remote villages in Newfoundland and Labrador could be reached in the early days. His mission eventually included orphanages, hospitals, nursing stations, and even a co-op or two. He was a one-man social agency, willing to tackle economic and social problems right along with medical problems.

When he married an American heiress and retired to Vermont, it was expected he'd be buried there, but he came back to St. Anthony—at least his ashes did. According to friends of mine who visited Newfoundland later and found his grave, the inscription reads:

IN MEMORY OF WILFRED THOMASON GRENFELL
BORN FEBRUARY 28, 1865
DIED OCTOBER 9, 1940
"LIFE IS A FIELD OF HONOUR."

A Newfoundland Dog and All

Île aux Morts wasn't on my list of places to go, but when I read the name and realized it was just a few miles from the ferry terminal at Port aux Basques, I thought I'd just have a quick look. After all, I'm out and about looking for interesting graveyards, and here's a town with a name like a graveyard. I had to check it out.

I was glad I did. People out walking, kids and dogs ripping around on the streets, wash flapping on the clotheslines, the guy at the service station ready to show us around if we got lost. For a while, I thought the power must be off in the area; otherwise, why were people outside instead of inside watching TV? That's what happens in most places at five o'clock.

The first graveyard was near the fish plant, not that there were any fish to process, which made the graveyard symbolic of more than one kind of death. For some reason or other, I couldn't get the gate open so I stepped over the fence and sank to my ankles in water. At that moment, a woman came out of a nearby house, walked over, opened the gate, and said, "Can I help you?" In my own defence, I have to say that graveyard gates can be tricky.

Anyway, it was she, bless her, who told me the story of Ann Harvey, the seventeen-year-old girl who with her father and their Newfoundland dog—this story has it all!—rescued people from a shipwreck near the rocky shores of their town. It happened in 1828. A British ship foundered on the rocks in a terrible storm. Ann and her father secured a rope on land, then rowed out with it to the ship and, with the help of the dog, managed to attach it to that end. By means of this life-line, some 163 people were able to make it to safety.

The Harveys received medals and commendations, the dog included. "But what happened to Ann?" I asked, still standing up to my ankles in water. You don't stop a good story just because your feet are wet.

"Don't know," she said. "Ask the town manager."

He shrugged his shoulders but handed me an information sheet on the story. There, at the bottom of the page, was written, "Ann Harvey later married Charles Gilliam from Port aux Basques and is buried there."

That did it—back to Port aux Basques.

My feet got even wetter there, but no matter how hard I looked in a total of four graveyards, I couldn't find Ann Harvey Gilliam. I found this piece of good news in what was called the Old Anglican cemetery:

IN MEMORY OF MARY
THE BELOVED WIFE OF JOSEPH BRAGG
WHO DIED NOV. 7, 1858
AGED 37 YEARS, 10 MONTHS AND 14 DAYS
"THEN LET THE WORMS DEMAND THEIR PREY
THE GREEDY GRAVE MY REINS CONSUME
WITH JOY I DROP MY MOULDERING CLAY
AND REST TILL MY REDEEMER COME.
ON CHRIST MY LIFE IN DEATH RELY
SECURE THAT I CAN NEVER DIE."

But no Ann anywhere. When I found the fourth graveyard, a man who lived nearby said I'd have to have high rubber boots to get to it, let alone walk through it. "She's wet," he observed cheerfully. So I'm guessing that Ann is there, or else she has gone silently into that long night, which would be too bad. We need to know about our heroes and heroines.

The War Brought Home

It was getting on to dark by the time I gave up on Ann, but there in front of the motel was one last story I needed to know. The plaque on one side of the cairn read:

TO THE GLORIOUS MEMORY
OF THE BRAVE OFFICERS, CREW AND PASSENGERS
OF THE SS CARIBOU
WHO WERE DESTROYED BY THE ENEMY
WED. OCT. 14, 1942.

Other plaques listed the names of those who died—navy, army, RCAF, and US services personnel as well as civilians, a total of 136.

It's a horrible story that I should have known about but didn't. A Canadian ferry, the *Caribou*, enroute from North Sydney to Port aux Basques, was torpedoed by a German submarine. The war had crept into our own back yard. It was unbelievable. In the middle of the night, in the middle of pitch black darkness while most passengers slept, the ferry blew up. In just a few minutes, it sank, taking with it babies and whole families and soldiers on leave and most of the crew, including the captain and his two sons.

Some lifeboats were launched but not nearly enough to hold everyone. The water was cold; swimmers didn't last long. The warship sent to escort the ferry that night, the *Grandmère*, chose to chase the submarine. But when it became evident that the submarine was hiding underneath the scene of the disaster, thereby making it almost impossible to launch depth charges, the *Grandmère* turned instead to picking up survivors. The submarine escaped in the confusion.

Of the eleven children on board, only one survived, and that one, some say, managed to do so because his grandmother had knitted him a flannel nightie that ballooned in the water and held him up until a passing sailor saw him. That's one story anyway. I hope it's right.

The next day, when we crossed from Port aux Basques to North Sydney, we crossed on the ferry called *Caribou*. The new Caribou.

The Last Word

In the Brigus Anglican cemetery is an Atlantic farewell for Rebecca Jane Roberts, 1858-1936, and George Roberts, 1854-1942:

TWILIGHT AND EVENING BELL
AND AFTER THAT THE DARK,
MAY THERE BE NO SADNESS OF FAREWELL
WHEN I EMBARK.

The North

✝

Where Gold Fever
Is in the Bones

SIR JOHN FRANKLIN FIGURED HE COULD FIND
THE NORTHWEST PASSAGE—NO SWEAT.
WHAT COULD BE SO DIFFICULT? WATER'S WATER.
SO ONE NICE DAY IN THE SPRING OF 1821,
HE SAILED OUT OF LONDON,
BOUND FOR THE NORTHERN PASSAGES OF CANADA.
THAT TIME, HE LOST ONLY TEN MEN.
WATER, IT TURNED OUT, WAS ICE.
HE DIDN'T FIND THE NORTHWEST PASSAGE.

The next time, three years later, a little older and wiser, he got to Canada earlier and left before winter set in. He got all his men safely home but still didn't find the Northwest Passage.

By 1845, he couldn't stand it any longer. He knew there had to be a way through the Arctic waters from east to west. So away he sailed with two well-equipped boats and was never seen nor heard of again. Not in England, at any rate. There were rumours that he'd been sighted among Native peoples of northern Canada, but nothing ever came of the rumours even though Lady Franklin financed search parties for years after her husband's disappearance.

The boats were eventually found crushed and frozen into the waters near King William Island, where they had been abandoned; the bodies of some of the men were finally found, but it's still one of our biggest mysteries. One of the North's biggest mysteries, that is. The North with a capital N is its own person. It makes its own decisions. That's where Franklin went wrong. He thought he was the boss. He thought he could control the North. Wrong. Canada's North doesn't take orders. It gives orders.

Like the young man at the Whitehorse car-rental place. "Nope," he said, "there's no unlimited mileage in the North."

"Excuse me," I said, "there's nothing but unlimited mileage in the North. Haven't you noticed?"

"Could be," he said, "but we're not like those car-rental places in the south. Up here, you get the first one hundred kilometres free and after that, it's twenty-two cents a kilometre."

"I can't get anywhere in one hundred kilometres," I said.

"I know," he said cheerfully and then added that there was no windshield or tire insurance available either. "We make our own rules up here," he said. "We're the North."

I thought of him as I drove his rental car over the Top of the World highway out of Dawson City. Built on the spine of a range of mountains—or several ranges, I lost track after a while—it's the most amazing experience. Look down to the right and your stomach falls out. Look down to the left and your eyes fall out—mountains, valleys, sky all the way to Russia for all I know. Talk about unlimited mileage. The thought that I might have to pay for a new windshield on this gravel road didn't change a thing. It was still the most thrilling, scary, overwhelming experience, worth every twenty-two cents it cost.

Gold Changes Everything

I travelled to the North in the summer of 1996, exactly one hundred years after George Carmack decided to go fishing in a stream off the Klondike River and caught gold instead. He and his two companions filed August 17, 1896, on land along what is now Bonanza Creek, and the rush was on. The Gold Rush. The Crazy Years in the North. The Mad Years. Thousands of men and hundreds of women hiked, rode, sailed, rafted, cheated, charmed, and otherwise got themselves across those terrible mountain passes at the Top of the World into the gold fields around Dawson. There, some got rich, more got poor, many got dead.

The story is like the country: unlimited and amazing.

For a few years, Dawson City was the largest city west of Winnipeg and north of San Francisco. Thousands came because they heard of the gold. Men put down their ploughs, women put down their pots, and all headed north. Never mind that they knew nothing about this part of the country or about gold mining, for that matter. All that mattered was gold. It was a madness.

Most of the fortunes that were made were made by men who were already in the North when George Carmack found gold in 1896. They got the plum spots along the gold-bearing creeks; they got the nuggets that would choke a horse. Others who came in later made money with restaurants and railways and wheeling and dealing. Some made no money at all and had to return to their ploughs and their stoves. Some never returned. In Dawson City's oldest graveyard is a marker for Irol Totten, son of Joseph and Lovina Totten of Sherman, Texas, born 1871, died 1898. Above the statistics are the words, "Our Dear Boy."

At least the Tottens knew what had happened to their dear boy and where. Many other gold seekers died enroute—unknown, unmarked—leaving families waiting forever for a letter, a word.

The man who started it all, George Carmack, eventually left the North and settled in the States with a new wife, new life. The old wife, Kate, the Native woman who was living with him when he discovered gold, ended up back in the North, more or less forgotten and more or less poor. Dawson Charlie and Skookum Jim, her Tagish Indian relatives, who were also in on the original find, ended ingloriously as well, proof—as if it were needed—that gold isn't everything.

All three are buried in the Carcross cemetery, their graves no grander than many of the others there. A sign at the entrance to the cemetery explains:

> THREE OF THE ORIGINAL DISCOVERERS OF GOLD
> IN THE KLONDIKE IN 1896, KATE CARMACK,
> DAWSON CHARLIE AND SKOOKUM JIM (JAMES MASON)
> ARE BURIED HERE.

I take it that there are still treasure hunters in the North because another sign at the entrance to the graveyard says:

SACRED GROUND
THERE ARE NO CLUES, TREASURES
OR TOKEN IN THE GRAVEYARD SITE.

The Churchman, Crooked Houses, and Polly

Carcross is a small town south of Whitehorse—less than one hundred kilometres, by the way—that looks just like its pictures. Well, almost. Ted Harrison, the well-known Canadian artist, lived there for years and turned out painting after painting of village life in the North: kids and dogs playing under northern lights, igloos amid piles of snow, buildings here and there that lean and tip. It's not a put down, these tippy buildings of his, it's just the way he paints them. Anyway, I wanted to see if Carcross looked at all like the paintings.

It does. The little white church that he painted so often is actually straight as an arrow on the main street of Carcross, its corners all a neat 90°, but the shed just down the street has a wonderful lean to it. So do several other houses down by the lake. No wonder Harrison liked his houses on the wobbly side. They're more interesting that way.

The graveyard takes after the church. Mostly it's orderly—stones and fences as straight as upright citizens—but in among the standard, white-painted board fences is one made of native willow for William Bompas:

IN THE PEACE OF CHRIST
WILLIAM CARPENTER BOMPAS, D.D.
BISHOP OF SELKIRK
BORN IN LONDON, 1834
DIED IN CARCROSS, 1906

Like Franklin, Bompas left England for Canada's North, but unlike Franklin, he didn't intend to do anything grand. He just wanted to be a humble, practical missionary to the people of the North, and to that end, he walked, rode, paddled enormous distances to get to his parishioners. Unlimited mileage was his middle name. Eventually he was named first Anglican Bishop of Athabasca.

Before he died, he asked that he be buried in the North, which the Indians did with great respect and love. It was they who built the willow fence.

Carcross cemetery is also supposed to be the last resting place of Polly the Parrot, but try as I might, I couldn't find a headstone for her, er him. This is one of those northern stories that gets taller with every telling, but

Native parishioners built a willow fence around the grave of their beloved Bishop William Bompas in the Carcross cemetery.

as far as I can determine, there was a parrot who lived for a long time, some say one hundred years, in a Whitehorse hotel. When the bird died in 1972, it was buried.

It was a he, by the way. No one seemed to notice that Polly was Paul, but what did it matter? Polly was an institution. Polly was also a mean old sinner who drank whisky and swore a blue streak, which may be why I couldn't find him inside the consecrated ground.

There was a funeral of sorts at the time. According to the local paper, a friend eulogized dear Polly, said he knew there was a dog heaven for dogs so there had to be a Polly heaven for parrots. Then he sang Polly's favourite song, "I Love You Truly."

Only in the North, do you suppose?

The Dreaded Chilkoot Pass

Another one hundred kilometres or so south of Carcross is Dyea, now just a wooded, flat spot near Skagway, Alaska, but in 1897 and 1898 it was the beginning of the infamous Chilkoot Trail. It was here that thousands of people strapped hundreds of pounds on their backs and headed over the pass for gold. Nothing would stop them—not bad weather, hunger, fatigue. Gold called and they had to answer. Thus it was on April 3, 1898, that a number of would-be prospectors ignored the warnings of oldtimers who told them the snow on the pass was unstable. Don't go, they said. There's an avalanche waiting to happen.

Can't wait, they said, and some seventy people died that day when the snow pack came loose and thundered down the slope.

The Dyea Slide cemetery tells the story with markers such as this one:

E.T. HUTTON
PORTLAND, OREGON
DIED APRIL 3RD, 1898
IN A SNOWSLIDE ON THE TRAIL

Near E.T. Hutton's grave is one for Mrs. A. U. Maxon, Pumzataney [sic], Pennsylvania, and another for Ed Doran, Residence Unknown. Did Mr. Maxon ever know what happened to his wife, and did Ed Doran's mother know that her dear son had died in an avalanche? So many questions one hundred years later in a green mossy glade that's so quiet and

beautiful now it doesn't seem possible that tragedy could ever have touched it. And yet the evidence is there on weathered old wooden headstones.

Over the Pass in Petticoats

Martha Louise Black was one of the lucky ones: she climbed the Chilkoot and never looked back. She and her first husband set out from Chicago in 1898 to go see for themselves the gold

Many goldseekers began their trek over the Chilkoot Pass at Dyea; for some, the trek ended there as well.

282

lying in the streets of the mysterious North. The husband chickened out at Seattle, but Martha carried on even though she was pregnant. She climbed the Chilkoot Pass in her long skirts and petticoats, set up a business in Dawson City, did it all. By that time, she was sold on the North and ended up marrying George Black, who was variously Commissioner of the Yukon, a federal MP, and Speaker of the House. When he got too old for the political stuff, she ran—she was only seventy—and became the second woman in Canada to sit in the House of Commons. That's when she got the unofficial title of "Queen of the Yukon" and official recognition as a Fellow of the Royal Geographical Society for the books she produced on Yukon flora, the moral of her life being that if you can climb the Chilkoot Pass, you can do anything. Hers is one of those aggravating gravemarkers that say less rather than more. It's in the Whitehorse Pioneer cemetery:

BLACK, MARTHA LOUISE
O.B.E., F.R.G.S.
BORN KANSAS, U.S.A. 1865
DIED YUKON 1957
BELOVED WIFE OF GEORGE BLACK

While in Dawson City, Martha initiated an annual Commissioner's Tea held on the lawns of the official residence, which is why I got to go to a formal tea while I was there. Martha invited all and sundry to her teas—no standing on ceremony for her—so in keeping with her traditions, tourists were welcomed to this year's tea, never mind whether we had brought along a dress or not. (We had not.) The whole thing was lovely. The current commissioner, Judy Gingell, welcomed us, Brownies passed around cookies, Tom Byrne recited poetry by Robert Service, and a local teenager sang "Don't Cry For Me, Argentina."

We're in Canada's North, North with a capital N, and we're singing about Argentina. It's a small world in spite of the unlimited mileage.

Controversy in the Graveyard

Dawson City also has graveyards to recommend it. The oldest is almost invisible—just a collection of falling-down fences and scattered headstones in bush near the town. Some know it as the Epidemic Graveyard, but a local historian, John Gould, corrected that name. It was Father William Judge's first graveyard, he explained, the man who is now known as the Saint of Dawson. Father Judge came with the first rush of outsiders in 1897 and established both a church and a hospital. Not one to stand on church law, he buried the dead in the Catholic graveyard near his church, never mind their religion. When he died in 1899, another Catholic priest came to town and said that wouldn't do. There would have to be a properly segregated graveyard, so the old one fell into disrepair. Father Judge is buried near the first church, and a plaque on the present church explains:

REV. WILLIAM HENRY JUDGE, S.J.
CREDITED WITH SAVING MANY LIVES,
FATHER JUDGE WAS ONE OF THE TRUE HEROES
OF THE KLONDIKE, SERVING THE AREA
FROM MAY 1897 UNTIL HIS DEATH IN 1899.
IN THIS SHORT PERIOD, HE BUILT ST. MARY'S HOSPITAL,
A CHURCH AND RESIDENCES,
DOING MUCH OF THE WORK HIMSELF DESPITE ILL HEALTH.
DAWSON'S FIRST PRIEST BECAME KNOWN
AS "THE SAINT OF DAWSON."

There's no mistaking the denominational, fraternal, and ethnic divisions in the newer graveyards farther up the hill—Old Old Catholic, Old Catholic, RCMP, Mason, Jewish, Anglican, Community and YOOP, YOOP being the most important section of all for some proud residents of the North. YOOP stands for Yukon Order of Pioneers and to be a member you have to be two things: a resident of the Yukon for at least twenty years and male.

It was that second requirement that seemed unfair to Madeline Gould, herself a longtime resident of the North. Why should YOOP belong only to men? So she appealed all the way to the Supreme Court of Canada to have YOOP open to women as well as men. No way, the courts decided in 1996. The only concession she won was the right to be buried in a YOOP section of the graveyard, a dubious victory, one might say.

The Spell of the North

The Dawson graveyards hint at their place and past. Many there died young—men and women. The police in the NWMP and RCMP section died at ages twenty, twenty-eight, thirty-four, and forty-eight, for instance. Then there are gravemarkers the like of which are seldom seen in southern parts—huge dredge buckets and other machine parts that I can't even guess at. I once read that William Samuel McGee, known as William McGee in southern Canada, changed his name to Sam McGee in the North because it seemed as if real men had tough names. Well, the same thing shows up on gravemarkers. There's Black Mike and Big John and Hardrock Mac-Donald.

Sometimes called the Epidemic graveyard, this neglected corner of Dawson Creek speaks of unhappy endings.

And speaking of Sam McGee, he's not in the Yukon any more. He's buried in Beiseker, Alberta, under a stone that says nothing about him lending his name to Robert Service, a bank teller/poet in Dawson City who was looking for a name to rhyme with Tennessee. Robert Service isn't buried in the Yukon either, although he's there in every other way. On the outside wall of a downtown building, for instance, is written in large letters one verse of his poem called "The Spell of the Yukon."

> I WANTED THE GOLD AND I SOUGHT IT
> I SCRABBLED AND MUCKED LIKE A SLAVE.
> WAS IT FAMINE OR SCURVY, I FOUGHT IT,
> I HURLED MY YOUTH INTO A GRAVE.

The graveyards up on the hill echo that last line.

Robert Service wasn't especially proud of his two most famous northern poems: "The Cremation of Sam McGee" and "The Shooting of Dan McGrew." He thought they were doggerel and wanted to be remembered for his more serious poetry, but it was not to be. Not in Canada, at least. He's buried in France, and I often wonder what it says on his gravemarker.

His words turn up on the gravemarker of another, albeit transplanted Northerner. This is what it says on Joe Boyle's grave:

A gravemarker in the Dawson cemetery displays the prestigious but controversial YOOP title.

MAN WITH THE HEART
OF A VIKING
AND THE SIMPLE FAITH
OF A CHILD.

Though Joe Boyle came late to the Yukon he still found gold. It took huge dredging machines and fast talking, but he did it and became known as "The King of the Klondike." When he left to fight in World War I, he somehow got himself into relief work on behalf of Romania and Russia. The Queen of Romania liked him a lot, and he stayed on in her country after the war ended. It was an ethereal relationship, the textbooks tell me. I wonder what the tabloids would call it nowadays but never mind, when the King of the Klondike died in 1923, the Queen of Romania buried him in a London, England, cemetery beneath a one-thousand-year-old Romanian cross and Robert Service's words.

Later, a daughter by a less ethereal relationship had him moved home to Woodstock, Ontario, complete with the old Romanian rugged cross.

The Lost Patrol and the Mad Trapper

Dawson City was as far north as I got in the Yukon—except for a piece of the Top of the World Highway—which meant I did not get to Fort McPherson or Aklavik, both of which have important graves. At Fort McPherson, for instance, in the St. Matthew's Anglican churchyard is a marker that says:

IN MEMORY OF THE DAWSON PATROL
WHO LOST THEIR LIVES FEB. 1911
ERECTED BY THEIR COMRADES.

The Dawson Patrol went from Herschel Island—check the map, that's getting way up there—to Dawson to Fort McPherson several times a year, delivering mail enroute, checking on the people who lived in the farflung communities. The four Royal North-West Mounted police officers who left Fort McPherson in December 1910 had done the 765-kilometre trip before. Everything seemed pretty routine, but nothing is routine in the North in the middle of winter. They lost their way in storms, ran out of food, had to eat their dogs, and eventually died in the white wilderness.

The head of the search party was Corporal W.J.D. Dempster, the man for whom the famous Dempster Highway is named.

In the winter of 1931–1932, Canada was transfixed by news of the Mad Trapper, a man who would not, could not, be caught. He was a trapper, that's all anyone knew about him for sure, and he wounded a Mountie who had simply stopped to make sure he was okay. When other Mounties moved in to arrest him, the chase was on, and for the next forty-eight days, the Mad Trapper eluded Mounties, Indians, trappers, and an airplane. Yes, an airplane. Wop May, the famous bush pilot, was brought into the chase, the first time a plane was used in a manhunt in the North. Even so, the trapper killed a Mountie before the chase ended, Constable Edgar Millen, who's buried in Edmonton.

Albert Johnson, the real name, they think, of the Mad Trapper, is buried in an unmarked grave in Aklavik, although I also read that he's buried beneath a dead tree trunk on which the initials "A.J." are carved and that just a few years ago, lightning struck the tree and split it top to bottom.

How dramatic. I hope it's true.

Spirit Houses to Die For

Driving back to Whitehorse from Dawson (a mere 533 kilometres according to the map) I stopped in Carmacks to get gas (a mere 78.8 cents a litre that day) and while there inquired, naturally, about graveyards. "One's on the hill," she said, "and one's below it in the trees. You can't miss them."

For once, that line about "can't miss" was right. The graveyard presently in use is located at the top of a steep hill overlooking the town, and you have to walk up to it. No sissy stuff like cars or golf carts to take the caskets to

The police section of the Dawson City cemetery shows that many of these young men died before their time.

their last resting place. The people of Carmacks carry their friends and relations to their graves. They are involved to the end.

I was mightily impressed; the path to the graveyard is fairly steep. It would be a real test of strength and respect to carry a heavy load up there, but apparently the people of Carmacks do it. But the best was yet to come.

The other graveyard, the one in the trees, contained spirit houses, the most beautiful ones I've ever found. About 1.5 metres long and 1.2 metres high, each one looked like a tiny perfect house with a door at one end and a glass-paned window in the wall that looked down to the water. Most of the windows were just that—windows so that the spirits could see outside. That's what I was told they were, but in one case, the window was a tableau. Framed by pink lace curtains, it revealed a table set with a pink cup and saucer, a plate, and a vase that held a pink rose. It was lovely, thoughtful, personal. What was also amazing was that there were no signs of vandalism—no broken windows, no graffiti. The whole place spoke of respect and care; it had a spirit in its midst that I can't define, but it was there.

I talked later to Father John Paul Tanguay, a retired Catholic priest who married, buried, and christened all across the Yukon area. Did he have trouble with Native traditions like the spirit houses, I asked. They're not exactly part of Catholic ritual.

Not a bit, he said. The Natives also believe in life everlasting. Just because they arrange their graveyards differently doesn't mean they don't believe in God. "After all," he said with a smile, "it's a big banquet in the Bible."

He was surprised a few times, he admitted, like the time he travelled a long way to do a funeral but found it was all over when he got there. "Why did you not wait for me?" he asked. The Native people there told him that once a hole was dug for a casket, the casket must be lowered into it immediately or else the "earth will cry." If the earth cries from its open wound, it's liable to choose another person to die.

Another time, he arrived in a small settlement to hold a funeral service and discovered that a huge hole had been dug for the deceased child. "Why such a large hole?" he inquired. It turned out that everything the child had touched—his bed, his clothing, his toys—all went into the grave with him. Thus the big hole.

Meanwhile, in the Northwest Territories

The other highways that we who drive on pavement forget about are the rivers, and the steamboats that travelled on them . . . which brings me to the story of Edward Martin.

As far as anyone can figure, he came to the Northwest Territories in the 1920s and established himself as a woodcutter for the Hudson's Bay Company. Through the long cold winters, he would haul fallen timbers over the snow to the edge of the Slave River. There he would cut them into four-by-eight-foot lengths, as specified by the HBC, and leave them in a pile, the size of which also had to meet certain specifications. Because he always added a few extra logs to his pile, he became known up and down the river as the man who made honest piles.

When summer came and steamboats plied the river, Martin was nowhere to be seen. He'd stay in the back country until everything was quiet again, and then he'd come out to leave more honest piles.

One fall, however, his piles didn't appear. When authorities finally located his tiny shack, they found him dead of a self-inflicted wound. Since there didn't seem to be any family—certainly there was no will—a judge decided that the money found in his belongings should be used for a memorial to be placed on the border of Alberta and the Northwest Territories near Fort Smith. There it stands to this day bearing this message:

TO THE MEMORY OF EDWARD MARTIN
DIED JUNE 13, 1928
THE BEST WOODCUTTER OF THE NORTH
HE SUPPLIED FUEL TO STEAMBOATS
A SILENT AND LONE MAN
WHO TOOK PRIDE IN HIS WORK
AND BUILT AN HONEST PILE

Incidentally, two women came along eventually, one claiming to be a sister and one claiming to be a wife, both wanting the money that went into the memorial. I don't know how that wrinkle worked itself out, but I wonder if it doesn't give us a clue as to why Martin chose the bush in the first place.

I haven't been to the Northwest Territories where Edward Martin is buried. Nor have I been to Yellowknife. They're on the list, but in the meantime I have to rely on what I read, and I read that there's a gravemarker for Einar Broughton in Yellowknife that says:

HE DRANK OLD SAM
AND DIDN'T GIVE
A DAMN.

The Last Word, Back to Franklin

What is there about the North that encourages such independence, cussedness, strength? Could it be the cold that stabs like a driven nail? That's a Robert Service line. Could it be the silence you can almost hear? That's another Service line. Or is it isolation and loneliness? Is it hardship that makes a man or a woman? Or could it be that the White North gets into our bones? That's an Alfred Lord Tennyson line that appears on a monument in Westminster Abbey commemorating the long-lost Franklin, the man who thought he could beat the North:

NOT HERE! THE WHITE NORTH HAS THY BONES;
AND THOU HEROIC SAILOR SOUL
ART PASSING ON THINE HAPPIER VOYAGE NOW
TOWARD NO EARTHLY POLE.

Conclusion

✚

To Be Continued

IN MONTRÉAL,
WE STAYED AT A BED AND BREAKFAST
RUN BY PIERETTE.
WHEN I TOLD HER ABOUT MY PROJECT,
SHE WAS 'ASTONISHED. TO THINK THAT SOMEBODY
WAS SEEKING OUT THE GRAVES OF INTERESTING/
IMPORTANT/ORDINARY CANADIANS.
"IT IS," SHE SAID IN HER FRENCH CANADIAN WAY,
"LIKE I HAD A HOLE IN MY HEAD.
I NEVER THOUGHT ABOUT SUCH THINGS BEFORE."

Thanks, Pierette. That was the best explanation ever offered about my work—that I was filling holes in our heads about our history.

It was an amazing experience in the course of which I discovered over and over again our amazing country. I went to every province and the Yukon, but I didn't see the half of it. We are huge. We are endless.

We are lucky.

In the Millarville, Alberta, graveyard is a marker that says:

SIT WITH ME UNTIL THE SHADOWS GO,
THEN SMILE.

It was a sweet summer evening when I got there. The shadows were long on the foothills, the mountains sharp against the sunset sky. It was one of those perfect moments that come along every so often. And then to find such a thoughtful message. I was smitten. How could I not stay awhile and then smile?

There's such feeling in a graveyard. When I started, I knew I was looking for the facts of history. I didn't know I would find so much emotion.

People often ask me what epitaph I've chosen for my own—when the time comes, they add delicately.

I'm always tempted to get smart alecky and say something like:

LOVED BY ALL WHO KNEW HER
AND A FEW WHO DIDN'T

or

HER BOOKS ARE STILL AVAILABLE
AT MOST GOOD BOOKSTORES

But I generally sober up and admit I like this one that I found in the Sundre, Alberta, graveyard:

WHOM WE HAVE LOVED AND LOST AWHILE

I also like the poem that Mark Twain wrote for his daughter Susie when she died at age twenty-four in 1890:

WARM SUMMER SUN, SHINE KINDLY HERE;
WARM SOUTHERN WIND, BLOW SOFTLY HERE;
GREEN SOD ABOVE, LIE LIGHT, LIE LIGHT—
GOOD NIGHT, DEAR HEART, GOOD NIGHT.

Isn't that lovely? Poetry belongs on gravemarkers somehow.

However, I have to agree with an older woman who approached me after one of my slide shows and said, "I think I've found the best epitaph of all. It's on my husband's grave and it says:

TO BE CONTINUED

"Isn't that perfect?" she said.

"It is," I said.

Index